COMERS/ICOG Communications 1

COMERS Communications 1

ASPECTS OF GENRE AND TYPE IN PRE-MODERN LITERARY CULTURES

Edited by

Bert Roest and Herman Vanstiphout

STYX
PUBLICATIONS
GRONINGEN
1999

ISBN 90 5693 031 1

STYX Publications
Postbus 2659
9704 CR GRONINGEN
THE NETHERLANDS
Tel. # 31 (0)50–5717502
Fax. #31 (0)50–5733325
E-mail: styxnl@compuserve.com

Contents

Preface vii

Dirk Claes
Adam per Evam deceptus est, non Eva per Adam.
Biblical Repertoria in Fourteenth-Century Canon Law. 1

Geert Jan van Gelder
Some Brave Attempts at Generic Classification in
Premodern Arabic Literature. 15

Femke Kramer
Rigid Readings of Flexible Texts.
The Case of Sixteenth-Century Comic Drama. 33

Bert Roest
Medieval Historiography:
About Generic Constraints and Scholarly Constructions. 47

Monique van Rossum-Steenbeek
Boundless Papyri. 63

Anda Schippers
The Fable is Dead; Long Live the Fable!
Or, is there any life after Genre? 71

Herman Vanstiphout
"I Can Put Anything In Its Right Place".
Generic and Typological Studies as Strategies for the
Analysis and Evaluation of Mankind's Oldest Literature. 79

Niek Veldhuis
Continuity and Change in Mesopotamian Lexical Tradition. 101

Maaike Zimmerman
When Phaedra Left the Tragic Stage:
Generic Switches in Apuleius' *Metamorphoses*. 119

Bert Roest & Herman Vanstiphout
Postscriptum 129

Preface

The present volume is the result of a series of seminars held between March and June of 1996, and devoted to issues of genre and typology within the disciplinary compass of COMERS, the Groningen research centre of Classical, Oriental, Medieval and Renaissance Studies. They were attended by a mixed audience, comprising advanced students, research students and fellows, and senior researchers in all the fields represented in the centre.

In a sense, COMERS itself may be regarded as the outcome of a specific typological stratification: all those disciplines dealing with the pre-modern in language and history have been brought together, because it is assumed that within the wide disparity of scholarly interests there are some problems and issues which bind these specialisms together and set them apart from others. Many of the issues deal with the "resistance" of the source materials – which in their materiality, shape and appearance ask for special technologies, skills and typological strategies –, or with other, related characteristics of pre-modern cultures, such as e.g. a particular relationship between the oral and the written, or the importance of traditional rules governing the production of cultural artefacts.

Thus the essays collected in this volume may at first sight seem a strange and, indeed, a baroque assemblage of apparently totally unrelated topics, not unworthy, perhaps, of comparison with Borges' famous list of animals.[1] The subjects are taken from Sumerian texts (VANSTIPHOUT, VELDHUIS), Arabic literature (van GELDER), Greek Papyri (van ROSSUM-STEENBEEK), Latin novels (ZIMMERMAN), Mediaeval Canon Law (CLAES), Mediaeval historiography (ROEST), Middle Dutch comedy (KRAMER) and Middle Dutch fables (SCHIPPERS). Fortunately, the treatment is as variegated as the disciplinary location: there are descriptions of very specific genres such as Biblical repertoria in Canon Law, and Mesopotamian lexical texts (CLAES and VELDHUIS); practical and technical strategies for dealing with material that is amorphous in that it shows no obvious criteria of articulation, such as Greek papyri (van ROSSUM-STEENBEEK); discussions of the relationship between "native" terminology and classification and modern theoretical insights (van GELDER); discussions of the apparent and glaring contradictions between assumed contemporaneous labeling[2] and the articulation of the groups of texts they are referring to (KRAMER; SCHIPPERS); the intentions and effects of generic switching (ZIMMERMAN); the problems of understanding, or indeed perceiving, generic and/or typological systems in the absence of explicit generic rules or even terms (ROEST; VANSTIPHOUT). This list of methodological points of view is, of course, not exhaustive or sophisticated enough to do justice to many of the finer points treated in all contributions. We therefore suggest that the reader now turn to the essays themselves; but before doing so it might be appropriate to remark that there seems to be a double red thread running through this multi-coloured cloth: on the one hand, the

[1] See Vanstiphout's contribution.
[2] We do not want to put in doubt the existence of those labels as such; we merely question their status as eternal or immovable markers of boundaries between text groups, or their identity with modern terminology.

inapplicability of (the) Western European traditional and coercive generic system(s) to pre-modern material crops up in almost every study;[3] on the other hand there is in most contributions a strong (though not always explicit) awareness of the *dynamic* nature of genre and type as against the static, a-temporal "classicistic" view of eternal or universal generic systems.

Finally, the editors wish to thank all contributors for allowing them to incorporate their studies in this volume, and for their patience. Special words of thanks must go to the executive board of COMERS, particularly to the director, Prof. Dr. C.H.M.J. Kneepkens; to the other members of the steering group which organised the seminars (Prof. Dr. A. Harder and Prof. Dr. J. North); to Mrs. J. Renner-van Niekerk for her splendid help with the managerial, material, logistic and catering aspects of the seminars; to Dr. F. Leemhuis for his technical assistance in preparing this volume; and to the publisher for his expertise and technical advice.

Groningen, Christmas 1998
Bert Roest
Herman Vanstiphout

[3] In fact, the interpretation of genre as dependent on coercive rules is no longer accepted in modern literary theory: see e.g. the now standard statements by Culler, Fowler, Schaeffer, Todorov etc. quoted in the bibliographic references *passim*.

Adam per Evam deceptus est, non Eva per Adam. BIBLICAL REPERTORIA IN FOURTEENTH CENTURY CANON LAW

Dirk Claes

1. Since there seems to have been some discussion on the question whether Adam seduced Eve in order to make her eat the forbidden fruit, or vice versa, the fourteenth century canonist Johannes Calderinus probably added the above-mentioned Latin sentence to the keyword *Adam* in his *Tabula auctoritatum et sententiarum Biblie*.[1] Thus, he stressed Adam's presumed innocence concerning the cause of original sin. The sentence is followed by a reference to the *Decretum Gratiani*[2] and the Bible, and by several other keywords.[3] This is – in short – the main structure of the *Tabula*.

Calderinus' *Tabula* may be considered to belong to the so-called *Biblical Repertoria*, a group of mid fourteenth century texts which compile and reproduce biblical and theological textual fragments which appear in the corpus of canon law.[4] In order to gather and arrange these fragments, authors of *Biblical Repertoria* relied heavily on achievements made in the field of so-called *aids-to-study* or *consultation literature*.[5] By

---

1 Cf. Paris, *Bibliothèque Nationale de la Françe* (*BnF*), ms. lat. 3923, fol. 56ra (line 30). Other manuscripts used are: Amiens, *Bibliothèque Municipale* (*B.M.*), ms. 383, fol. 261r ff.

2 C. 33, q. 5, c. Adam (= c. 18). The chapter reads : *Adam per Evam deceptus est, non Eva per Adam. Quem vocavit ad culpam mulier, iustum est, ut eam in gubernationem assumat, ne iterum femina facilitate labatur.*

3 *Annus.a, Ebron.a, Ymago.a* (Paris, *B.n.F.*, ms. lat. 3923, folio 56r). The keywords in question refer to other locations within the *Tabula auctoritates* where more information on *Adam* can be found. See below for a description of the *Tabula*.

4 Actually a *Corpus of Canon Law* (an exclusive collection of ecclesiastical law authenticated by papal authority, i.e. commissioned by the pope) as such did not yet exist in the early fourteenth century. Several collections of law were used in canon law teaching as well as in practice; some of them were authenticated and received a status of exclusivity through papal authority, while others – in spite of their wide diffusion and great authority – never reached this status. Only in the sixteenth century did pope Pius V order an edition of the main collections of canon law, gathered in a so-called *Corpus Iuris Canonici*, corresponding to its roman law counterpart (*Corpus Iuris Civilis*). The official *editio Romana* by the *Correctores Romana* (the board of cardinals that was ordered to prepare a new edition) was published in 1582 (under pope Gregory XIII), after earlier unofficial editions by the Paris master in law Jean Chappuis (1500 and 1503). The *Corpus Iuris Canonici* (for convenience abbreviated as *CIC*) consisted of the *Decretum Gratiani* (d. 1140) and several decretal collections (new papal legislation), the *liber Extra* (Gregorius IX, 1234), the *liber Sextus* (Bonifatius VIII, 1298), the *Clementinae* (Clemens V, Johannes XXII, 1317) and the *Extravagantes Communes* (decretals from the thirteenth through fifteenth centuries, among them the *Extravagantes Ioannis* XXII). Note that this version of the *CIC* remained in use until 1917, when the *Codex Iuris Canonici* was released under authority of pope Pius X. In contrast to the *Codex*, promulgated as authentic and exclusive in its totality, only parts of the *CIC*-edition of 1582 reached this status. It never did in its entirety. In the present contribution the abbreviation *CIC* is used when referring to different parts of it. For the development of the different parts and their collection into the *CIC* see among others Von Schulte 1875; Le Bras, Lefebvre & Rambaud 1965, particularly the second part, *Formation du droit classique*, pp. 133–345; Coing 1973, particularly pp. 365–82 and 835–43 (=K.W. Nörr, *Die kanonistische Literatur* and Idem, *Die Entwicklung des Corpus Iuris Canonici*).

5 Cf. the well-known studies of R.H. and M.A. Rouse on the subject. E.g. Rouse & Rouse 1979: 3–90; Rouse & Rouse 1982: 201–25; Rouse 1981: 115–44; Rouse 1976: 115–47. See also the studies on intellectual vocabulary by Weijers 1988–1995.

doing so, these authors at the same time contributed significantly to the development of canon law, in practice as well as in teaching.

2. Before discussing whether or not these *repertoria* constitute a genre and defining the main features of this genre, it is necessary to take a closer look at some of the texts. I therefore will examine some examples, namely, Johannes Johannis' *Memoriale Decreti*, Johannes Calderinus' *Tabula auctoritatum*, and Jesselinus de Cassagnes' *Auctoritates veteris et novi testamenti*. Each of these examples will be preceded by a short biographical notice on its author, in order to gain insight in their respective contexts.

2.1.1. *Johannes Johannis*

Unfortunately not much is known about our first author Johannes Johannis.[6] He entered the Benedictine order about 1317 and became abbot of the Benedictine abbey of Joncels (diocese of Béziers) in 1328. Apparently, he seems to have studied canon law at the university of Toulouse, were he probably also took his doctor's degree.[7] From the summer of 1330 onwards, our *abbas iuncellensis* spent most of his time in Avignon, where he acted as executor of papal benefices granted mainly to cardinal Imbert Dupuis. Johannes Johannis probably was a member of the cardinal's household.[8] In 1334 Johannes received two assignments outside Avignon: he was added to a diplomatic mission to the city of Genua, and received a commission as *visitator*, in order to reform both the monastery and the order of Fontevrault.[9] Both missions failed, however, which seems to have caused an abrupt ending to Johannes' career in Avignon. He was urged to return to the Joncels monastery by the end of 1338. There Johannes started writing or perhaps collecting the *Memoriale Decreti*, which he finished in November 1339.[10] Between 1344 and 1346 he left Joncels again, this time for the university of Montpellier, to become lecturer on the *Decretum Gratiani*.[11] Johannes Johannis died in 1361, soon to be forgotten by history.

---

[6] For the scarce data, cf. Gilles 1974: 53–111 (especially 54–75); Gilles 1994: 89–93 (especially pp. 89–90); Gilles 1960: 578–602; Von Schulte 1875 II: 379.

[7] Joannes Joannis mentions the Toulouse faculty of law and its alumni in one of his sermons. Cf. Vatican City, *Biblioteca Apostolica Vaticana*, Vat. Lat. ms. 7656, fol. 176r: *Sicut rusticus, videns multos juristas Tholoze in scolis,...* as well as the fact that, once he had become a monk, his abbot sent him to Toulouse in order to recruit poor clerics for monastic life. Cf. Vatican City, *B.A.V.*, Vat. lat. ms. 7656, fol. 183v: *et tunc misit me in Tholose pro querendo et ducendo pauperes clericos...* According to H. Gilles these references might allow us to conclude that Joannes Joannis graduated in Toulouse. Gilles 1960: 579–80 & Gilles 1974: 55–56. In spite of this assumption it remains unclear whether he actually took a law degree in Toulouse or Montpellier. The only certain conclusion is that Johannes was well-acquainted with the milieu of a late mediaeval law school, since he held a doctor's degree in canon law.

[8] Gilles 1960: 582–83; Gilles 1994: 89; Gilles 1974: 58.

[9] Fontevrault was the main monastery of a mixed foundation living according to the benedictine rule. The problem urging papal intervention seemed to have been the fact that parts of the male population disagreed over the administration by the abbess, Eleanor of Brittanny. According to Gilles, Johannes made a mistake by choosing the side of the insurgent male moiety. Eleanor of Brittanny appealed against the measures taken for the reform and was finally reinstated by the *Rota*. Gilles, 1974: 62–64. For the Fontevrault order see Bienvenu 1989: cols. 627–29; Cross & Livingstone 1974: 521; Daoust 1971: cols. 961–71.

[10] Cf. Paris, *Bibliothèque Nationale*, ms. lat. 3921, fol. 469rb (line 30ff): *Completum fuit hoc opus...anno Domini millesimo CCCXXXIX mense novembris in die sancte Caecilia.* The date referred to is november 22 liturgical feast of saint Cecile.

[11] Cf. Bernkastel-Kues, *Cusanus-Stift*, ms. 227. This manuscript contains the so-called *Reportata super*

2.1.2. *The Memoriale Decreti*

The *Memoriale Decreti* is an extensive work. The Paris manuscript, for instance, contains no less than 469 folios. The work is divided into five parts, all of which are neatly introduced at the beginning of the manuscript.[12] In addition to this division, the manuscript contains further structuring devices to facilitate readers' access, namely running titles at the top of each folio indicating the part of the *Memoriale* in question, and specific searching aids placed on top of each textual column within the different sections.[13]

The first part of the *Memoriale Decreti*, the so-called *auctoritates bibliae*, enumerates biblical quotations from Genesis to Revelations. The text of this part contains different layers of information. A first layer presents biblical quotations, arranged according to the order of the biblical books. This arrangement of biblical quotations comprises in itself a second layer of information. Only about a century before, Stephen Langton had developed chapter divisions for the books of the Bible, which made it possible to use standardised references to individual chapters in biblical books.[14] Johannes Johannis used this device not only as an extra means for dividing biblical quotations, but also as a reference tool. Paragraph signs and chapter numbers were added to indicate the divisions. This structuring element was also used to create internal cross-references.[15]

Decreto, a school-type comment on the *Decretum Gratiani*. It is not quite clear why Johannes came to Montpellier. According to a marginal note in a contemporary manuscript, Johannes had taught in Avignon (cf. Cordoba, *Biblioteca de la catedral*, ms. 40, a manuscript containing *quaestiones* and *allegationes* by Oldradus de Ponte de Laude, a contemporary and fellow cleric in Avignon). Fol. 175vb reads: *Allegationes domini Iohannis Iohannis decretorum doctoris nunc Avinione ordinarie decretum legentis*. If this allegation is correct, Johannes also taught at Avignon. Most probably this would have been the introduction to other more or less unfortunate career moves. In spite of his bad luck, a certain renown as a teacher probably accompanied him, so it would have been of interest for the Montpellier university authorities to have him as one of their *ordinarii*. Another probably complementary explanation can be found in the fact that by that time the Benedictine Order had considerable influence on academic training in Montpellier. Cf. Fournier 1892: 341–562.

12 Paris, *Bibliothèque Nationale*, ms. 3921, fol. 1ra: *Primo auctoritates biblie, reducendo eas ad ordinem librorum et capitulorum biblie seriatim; secundo dicta poetarum tam metrice quam prosaice, dicta et aliquarum sanctorum; tercio aliquas auctoritates textuales magis notabiles decretorum ad ordinem alphabeti dictionaliter redactas; quarto exposiciones dictionum et quinto materias glosarum iuxta ordinem supradictum* The Paris manuscript is the only one known to give the entire *Memoriale Decreti*. Other known manuscripts (among others: Vatican City, *B.A.V.*, Vat. Lat. ms. 2679 and 2680; Borghese ms. 44; Munich, *Nationalbibliothek*, ms. 5479) only give separate sections.

13

Part of the memoriale	*Indication folio*	*Indication column*
Auctoritates Bibliae	*Biblia*	Bible book (*Genesis* etc.)
Dicta poetarum		
poetica metra	*poetica metra*	
prosayce dicta	*prosayce dicta*	letter combinations (aa,ab,etc.)
vulgaria proverbia	*vulgaria proverbia*	
cantat ecclesia	*cantat ecclesia*	letter combinations (aa,ab,etc.)
dicta sanctorum	*dicta sanctorum*	letter combinations (aa,ab,etc.)
Auctoritates textuales	*Textus*	letter combinations (aa,ab,etc.)
Expositiones dictionum	*Expo*	letter combinations (aa,ab,etc.)
Materiae glosarum	*Glo*	letter combinations (aa,ab,etc.)

14 Rouse 1976: 119.

15 E.g., Paris, *B.n.F.*, ms. 3921, fol. 2ra (line 1 ff) reads: *XIIII Melchisedech rex salem proferens panem et vinum erat enim sacerdos dei altissimi benedixit ei scilicet* ***abrahe. infra. ebre. VII.*** *de con.d.II.c.in calice.in prin.*, thus referring to textual fragments taken out of the Epistle to the Hebrews, chapter seven. Fol. 30v ff. contains excerpts from the Epistle *ad Hebreos*. Fol. 31ra (line 44 ff.) reads: *VII § Hic enim Melchisedech rex salem sacerdos dei summi qui obviavit Abrae regresso de sede regum et benedixit ei. d.XXI.c.denique*.

Each biblical quotation is followed by one or several references, usually to the *Decretum Gratiani* and/or to collections of Decretals (more sparingly); this is the third layer of information. Reference is made to those places within this corpus of canon law where the Bible quotations in question can be found either verbatim or in a more allusive way. In accordance with well established mediaeval practice, references to the corpus of canon law are abbreviated[16] and follow the order of the *Decretum* and the Decretals.

The second part, the *dicta poetarum*, contains extracts from patristic and other ecclesiastical texts, as well as from secular literature. The *dicta poetarum* are themselves divided into five smaller sections,[17] which respectively contain alphabetically arranged verses, quotations from classical authors, common sayings, quotations from saints (and saints' lives), and liturgical hymns. All of these verses and quotations are followed by abbreviated references to the *Decretum Gratiani* and subsequent Decretal collections.

In the third part – the *auctoritates textuales* – Johannes presents an alphabetically arranged list of keywords. Each of these keywords is followed by one or several extracts taken more or less randomly from the *Decretum* and/or the Decretal collections which contain the keyword concerned. Each extract is followed by one or several abbreviated references to the corpus of canon law. Two-letter combinations placed above each column (e.g. *aa. ab.*) refer to the initial letters of the keywords treated in the column in question, functioning as a searching aid for the reader. The keywords are subdivided according to their grammatical forms (e.g. *coniugium.coniugalis.coniugatus.coniunx*).

The *expositiones dictionum* make up the fourth section of the *Memoriale Decreti*. Again an alphabetically arranged list of keywords is given. But instead of extracts, now short and rather elementary explanations are given of the keyword in question.[18]

The fifth and last part of the *Memoriale*, the *materiae glosarum*, again contains an alphabetically arranged list of keywords, now followed by one or more juridical questions concerning the keyword, and by their location in the corpus of canon law which is indicated again by means of abbreviations. In most cases comments and/or contradicting opinions of several important *glossatores*[19] and contributions from Roman law are added. Johannes Johannis concludes with a *solutio aliquorum contrariorum non solutorum glosarum Decreti*,[20] a final conclusio and a colophon.[21]

---

[16] Cf. Berlioz 1994: 145–76; Ochoa & Diez 1965.

[17] Cf. footnote 13.

[18] Cf. Paris, *B.n.F.*, ms. lat. 3921, fol. 159r (line 7 ff.): *A .id est. per*. Five examples, explaining the meaning of the preposition a as per, are given: *ut.a.filio.id est.per filium.de.pe.d.I.c.sicut primi* (= *de pen., d.1, c.83*); *et.a morte domini.id est.per mortem.de.pe.d.II.c.si enim in fi.* (= *de pen., d.2, c.40*); *Et a vobis subtrahi.id est.per vos.XIII.q.I.post c.ad haec.extra.* (= *C.13, q.1, c.1*); *Et.a.iudice.id est.per iudicem.XV.q.VI.in summa. per Guid<.>* (= *C.15, q.6, c.1–5*); *Et a te.id est.per te.XXVII.q.I.c.si homo in fi. extra.* (*C.27, q.1, c.19*). The word *Guid<.>* refers to *Guido de Baysio 's* (also known as *Archidiaconus*) *Rosarium*, a most popular work commenting on the *Decretum Gratiani*. *De Baysio* (1246(?)–1313) used comparable methods to explain different meanings of words. Extra does not refer to the decretal collection carrying the same name, the *Liber Extra*, but to the fact that Johannes used a source besides the corpus in order to collect different explanations for keywords. Cf. Gilles 1974: 78–79.

[19] Referred to with the appropriate seal, e.g. *.ar.* for *Archidiaconus*, *.go.* for *Goscelinus* (or *Jesselinus de Cassagnes*), *.jo.a.* for *Johannes Andreae*.

[20] Paris, *B.n.F.*, ms. lat. 3921, fol. 436rb (line 35 ff) - 469r; in which he tried to solve some contradictions left in the *Decretum Gratiani* and in which -according to Johannes- other *glossatores* failed to do.

[21] Paris, *B.n.F.*, ms. lat. 3921, fol 469rb (line 17 ff) and (line 30 ff).

2.2.1. *Johannes Calderinus*

Born about the beginning of the fourteenth century in northern Italy, Johannes Calderinus graduated in canon law at the university of Bologna. One of his tutors was Johannes Andreae,[22] who adopted Calderinus as his son. Calderinus received his doctoral degree in canon law in 1326, to become *ordinarius* for the *Decretum Gratiani* in Bologna shortly thereafter. He would keep this position at least until 1359.[23] He died of the plague in Bologna in 1365. Calderinus was held in great esteem for his teachings as well as for his participation in Bolognese civic life.[24] Though not particularly innovative in the field of legal scholarship, his writings[25] remained influential throughout the fourteenth and fifteenth centuries.

2.2.2. *Johannes Calderinus'* ***Tabula Auctoritatum et Sententiarum Biblie***

Calderinus' *Tabula* basically consists of an alphabetically arranged list of keywords (from *Aaron* through *Zizania*). Each keyword is followed by one or more excerpts from the corpus of canon law, which in their turn are connected to corresponding biblical references (book and chapter) and to additional abbreviated references to the corpus of canon law. In addition, an ingenious system for infra-textual reference is appended. If a keyword is followed by several excerpts, their number and sequence are indicated by means of letters *in margine*. This tool is also used for infra-textual reference. Each combination of keyword and excerpt is followed by a capital R with crossed tail, as well as by a number of other keywords, most of them in their turn followed by one or more letters in alphabetical order. The capital R with crossed tail most probably is an abbreviation for the Latin verb *require*, meaning 'to search, to look for'.[26] In order to find other excerpts and – in this connection – other biblical and canonical references that contain the keyword in question, additional keywords referred to can easily be found by means of the alphabetical arrangement; the excerpts in question can then be found by means of the additional alphabetically arranged letters. Note that the reference system only works in one direction: references back to the original keyword are not given.[27]

22 For Joannes Andreae, see Schulte 1875 II: 205–29.

23 In 1360 Calderinus was added as an envoy for the city of Bologna to a mission to the papal court in Avignon. In the years preceding 1360, the papacy in Avignon had repeatedly tried to return the papal territory in Italy to its direct control. It was cardinal-legate Aegidius Albornoz who managed to do so, in spite of fierce opposition from both members of the papal curia and from the Italian territory. In 1360, the state and the city of Bologna were captured by Albornoz. Therefore a mission was sent to Avignon in order to submit the city to pope Innocent VI. Two years later Calderinus joined another mission, this time to congratulate the newly elected pope Urban V. See Schulte 1875 II: 248–249; Fasoli 1983: col. 370–374; Severino 1980: col. 310–311; Glenisson & Mollat 1964.

24 He held several positions in the government of his city during the years 1340–1360. Cf. Schulte 1875 II *l.c.* See also note 24

25 Calderinus' known writings cover a wide range of legal texts. Besides the *Tabula auctoritatum et sententiarum biblie*, he wrote several treatises on legal questions (*tractatus*), *consilia*, answers to *quaestiones* (*responsa*) and specific *casus* (*resolutiones casuum*) and a commentary on the *Clementinae* with additions (super *Clementinas* and *additiones super commentarium Clementinarum*). In the educational field he contributed *distinctiones, repetitiones* and several *arengae* (speeches held during graduation ceremonies). Besides the *Tabula auctoritatum* Calderinus also wrote another *repertorium* (*repertorium sive dictionarium iuris*), existing of an alphabetically arranged list of keywords (for the description of the *Tabula*, cf. infra), but instead of biblical and canonical textual fragments references to both canon and roman law are given. Cf. Schulte II l.c. For the *arengae*, see (a.o.) Weimar 1982: 421–43.

26 Cf. Cappelli 19906: 318, col. 2: (*R*)... *Require* (*abbr. giur.*).

27 E.g. Amiens, *Bibliothèque municipale*, ms. 383, fol. 261r: *Aaron*.

2.3.1. *Jesselin de Cassagnes*

Not much is known about Jesselin's origin or date of birth. He was born most probably in the fourth quarter of the thirteenth century, somewhere in the south of France. In 1317 Jesselin is mentioned to be *ordinarius* (in canon law) in Montpellier.[28] He moved to Avignon in 1323, where he became a member of the household (chaplain) of cardinal Arnaud de Via, and acted as papal chaplain. Thereafter he seems to make a career in the Avignon administration rather quickly. First, he becomes *executor* of papal letters, most of the time serving the interests of cardinal de Via. On April 21, 1326, he was appointed member of the *Rota*. In the meantime (between 1318 and 1333) he received at least six important benefices, all of them in the vicinity of Avignon. He died in the winter of 1334/35. In his own days Jesselin was a famous canonist, whose legal skills probably facilitated his entry in the household of cardinal de Via. He was deemed a distinguished canonist in particular because of his comments (*apparatus*) on the *Liber Sextus*, the *Clementinae* and on the *Extravagantes Johannis XXII*. As a result his works were well-known and commented upon "throughout the law schools of Europe".[29] Yet it is the fourth and less well-known work of Jesselin that is of interest here: the *Auctoritates veteris et novi testamenti*, the ascription of which was only confirmed recently.[30]

2.3.2. *Jesselin's* ***Auctoritates Veteris et Novi Testamenti***

The *Auctoritates* very much resemble the first part of Johannes Johannis' *Memoriale Decreti*, the so-called *auctoritates bibliae*. The text as such follows the order of the biblical books. Within this initial division, the *auctoritates* of each biblical book are subject to another arrangement: they are treated either *non exposite*, or *exposite*.[31] In quantity (that is, the number of references), the *non exposite* parts exceed by far the number of treatments *exposite*. The format of the *non exposite* parts consists of short sentences – excerpts from the *Decretum Gratiani* – followed first by the appropriate abbreviations used to refer to the *Decretum Gratiani*, and second by the chapter number

[*in margine*]	[excerpt]	[biblical reference]	[*CIC*-reference]
a	*Aaron post conflatum ...*	Exodus 32	di. 50, post c. *e contra*.
b	*Aaron in episcopum et...*	Exodus 22 et 29	de pen. di. 2, post c. *opponitur*. (= p.c.)
c	*Aaron datus fuit adiutor...*	Exodus 32	de pen. di. 2, post c. *opponitur*. (= p.c.)
d	*Aaron pro populo cum ...*	Numeri 16	de pen. di. 2, post c. *opponitur*. (= p.c.)

R+ *Hircus.a* / *honor.b* / *ignis.i* / *manducare.d* / *maria.a.c.g* / *moyses.a.m* / *offerre.a* / *panis.a* / *sacerdos. a* / *sacrificare.c* / *tabernaculum.a*. If we take a look at e.g. keyword hircus.a the text reads *...quam contra filios Aaron ait...*, at *Ignis.i ...filium Aaron...*, and *at manducare.d ...Aaron et omnes presbyteri de Israel manducare panem...* Each one of these excerpts is followed by biblical and canonical references.

[28] Cf. Fournier 1892: 554. For the history of law education in Montpellier, see pp. 341–562. See also: Tarrant 1979: 37–64, esp. p. 38; Fournier 1921a: 348–61, esp. p. 349; Naz 1957: col. 130–131. Unfortunately it has not been specified on which part of the corpus of canon law he was lecturing (the *Decretum Gratiani* or Decretal collections).

[29] Tarrant 1979: 37.

[30] Manuscripts: Monte Cassino, *Archivio dell'Abazia*, ms. 353 (dates the work on august 1, 1331); and Vatican City, *B.A.Vaticana*, Borghese, ms. 59. For the latter, see also Maier 1952. For a long time the fact that Jesselin composed the *Auctoritates* was only known through a note in the 1375 inventory of the papal library at Avignon (cf. Ehrle 1890: 543, no. 1370), but the manuscript was thought to be lost. This is the reason why neither von Schulte nor Fournier make mention of it (cf. Schulte 1875 II: 199–200; Fournier 1892: 348–61). Maier suspected ms. 59 in the Borghese-collection to be the lost work of Jesselin, but did not made a decisive conclusion (cf. Maier 1964: 325–56). Tarrant confirmed her hypothesis by comparing it with the manuscript she found in Monte Cassino, which shows a clear and precise attribution to Jesselin (Tarrant 1979: 62–63).

[31] Cf. Vatican City, *B.A.Vaticana*, Borghese, ms. 59, fol. 1r: *Incipiunt auctoritates veteris et novi testamenti prout sunt secundum ordinem librorum Biblie in libro decretorum inducte tam exposite quam non exposite.*

from the biblical book concerned. In the *exposite* part, the opposite order is used: after the excerpt, first the chapter number from the Bible book in question is given, followed by the appropriate abbreviation referring to the Decretum.[32]

3. *Canon law and consultation literature*

The twelfth and thirteenth centuries saw the rise of an important genre of academic literature: so called aids-to-study or consultation literature. The major incentive for producing this genre was the desire and the need to use knowledge, gathered in authoritative collections, in practice. Several important factors created this demand: the rise of universities and the nature of academic training, a renewed and more systematic attention to Aristotelian thought, and the influence of the mendicant orders, due to their preaching activities and their contribution to the academic world.

In order to use knowledge gathered in authoritative sources (e.g. the *Decretum Gratiani*, the Bible, or the collected works of Aristotle) in a practical context that differed from that in preceding centuries, a different attitude was needed towards authoritative texts. Furthermore, to facilitate the retrieval of knowledge in this practical context, it became necessary to develop additional instruments. This development has its origin in the twelfth century, when in three separate scholarly fields the first attempts were made to "put in order the authoritative source texts"[33] These attempts led to the production of the *Decretum Gratiani*, the *Sententiae* of Peter Lombard, and the *Glossa Ordinaria* on the biblical text. All three became authoritative source texts themselves in their respective scholarly fields: canon law and theology. A second step in the evolution of consultation literature was the development of the idea of searchability. This idea was

---

[32] The distinction between *exposite* vs. *non exposite* lies in the 'degree' of deriving, as far as biblical textual fragments are concerned. In the first part, the excerpts are taken out of the *Decretum Gratiani*, but they differ from the original biblical text as mentioned. In the second part, the biblical textual fragment not only corresponds with the excerpt from the *CIC*; it is also explained within the *CIC* text referred to. Some examples from the Vatican manuscript, fol.1 r.ff. In the *auctoritates libri Genesis non exposite*, we read: *Cepit Namrot esse robustus venator...coram domino idest homini oppressor et extinctor quos ad turrim hedificandam allexit.* Jesselin refers to a passage in the *Decretum Gratiani,* using the abbreviation *VI. dis. § hiis ita,* which stands for *Distinctio 6, dictum Gratiani post capitulum 3.* The text in *distinctio 6* reads: *..., unde legitur de eo: "Cepit Nemroth esse robustus venator coram Domino," id est hominum oppressor et exstinctor; quos ad turrim edificandam allexit.* Genesis 11 now tells the story of the Tower of Babel. Nemrod is mentioned in Genesis 10, 8–9: *...Chus genuit Nemrod ipse coepit esse potens in terra et erat robustus venator coram Domino.* Another example: *Ait sodomitis Loth sunt mihi due filie que nondum nover<.> viros producam illa<s> ad vos etcetera.XIIII. dis. c. quod ait. Gen. XIX.c.* The text in Gratianus (*distinctio 14, c. 1*) reads: *Quod ait Sodomitis Loth*: *"Sunt mihi duae filiae, que nondum noverunt viros; producam illas ad vos...* Genesis chapter 19, 8 however reads: *...habeo duas filias quae necdum cognoverunt virum educam eas ad vos...*

In the *auctoritates Libri Genesis exposite* both the biblical fragment and the textual excerpt from the *Decretum Gratiani* correspond to one another. An example from the Vatican manuscript, fol. 8 vo. *Abraam dixit Sarre novi quod pulcra sis mulier et cum viderint te egipcii dicturi sunt uxor illius est et interficient me... et vivet anima mea ob gratiam tua. Gen. XX (sic!).c. XXII.q.II. Ecce et c. queritur cur patriarcha.* Genesis 12, 12–13 (the reference *Gen. XX* is probably due to a scribal error) reads exactly the same text, just as the text of the *Decretum* does (*Causa 22, questio 2, c. 21*). The second reference (*C. 22, q. 2, c. 22*) gives an explanation of the biblical fragment, thus clarifying the definition *exposite* (cf. the word *expositor*, meaning 'exegete').

[33] The order of the source texts was not altered, but made more accessible by using a new technique for commenting upon text (*Glossa Ordinaria*) or by using new methods in order to arrange 'knowledge' hidden in the text, like for instance in the second part of the *Decretum Gratiani*, the *Causae*, where on the basis of *quaestiones* the appropriate legal knowledge is reproduced, without giving anythting superfluous.

connected not only with attempts to find answers to the physical limitations of the page, but also with a changing attitude towards ordering a text.[34] The new type of consultation literature embraced four basic devices: the use of arabic numerals for numbering and counting; the refinement of page lay-out, the application of alphabetical order, and the (sub)division of the text in manageable portions.[35]

Still, it took some time and the above-mentioned change in attitude before these techniques became fully accepted. Initially, thematic order, or ordering information according to the source text, was considered to be more appropriate than alphabetical order, since it stayed closer to the creational order of being,[36] or to the thematical unity of the source text. The use and combination of the principles mentioned above allowed scholars to develop complex searching aids,[37] facilitating research not only by means of indices but also by connecting different types of data. Indices made it possible to combine searching aids for several source texts and even for distinct types of source texts. The latter was achieved in Robert Kilwardby's *Tabula super originalia patrum* (about 1260), a multiple index on several independent other indices on the works of St. Augustine and other patristic sources, but also on the most important theological treatises of his day. This evolution also allowed searching aids to become interdisciplinary, which happened by the end of the thirteenth and the beginning of the fourteenth century. Now searching aids for different types of source texts became combined. Biblical repertoria clearly belong to this type.[38]

By that time, canon law was embedded firmly in university culture, by means of a separate faculty, often of major importance. Increasing practical use of canon law and the ongoing development of its authoritative text,[39] through the gathering of Decretal

---

34 Rouse & Rouse 1982: 210: *It was therefore inevitable that alternative methods of retrieving information must eventually be devised, methods that would require different notions of order, as opposed to ordering information according to the text.*

35 It has to be noticed that all of these 'principles' already existed. But now they were to be used and combined in a different way. Rouse & Rouse 1982: 202–16; Rouse 1976: 115–33.

36 In alphabetically organised commentaries or *summae* it was considered absurd to place entries like *angelus* before *Deus*. Cf. Albertus Magnus apologising for making use of non-thematical order in his *De Animalibus*. Quoted in: Rouse & Rouse 1982: 211, note 28.

37 Most known examples are collections of *distinctiones*, the (very successful) biblical concordance, developed by Parisian Dominicans, and the index on the works of Aristotle, also developed in Paris. Cf. Rouse & Rouse 1982: 221–22; Rouse 1976: 117–20.

38 For instance Johannes Johannis' *Memoriale Decreti*, which contains keyword lists connecting the Bible, classical authors, liturgy, comments by *glossatores*, and other materials to canon law.

39 Canon law became an independent academic discipline with the emergence of Gratian's *Concordia discordantium canonum* about 1140, known as the *Decretum Gratiani*. Though never sanctioned as such by ecclesiastical authorities, very soon, already in the second half of the twelfth century, the *Decretum* acquired an authoritative status in christianity. In combination with the growth of academic culture canon law began to develop in a twofold way, a decretist and a decretalist tradition. Shortly after the *Decretum Gratiani* appeared, additions were made to the original text concerning theology, roman and canon law (the so-called *paleae*). By the end of the twelfth century the first commentaries and indices were composed, and about 1220 Johannes Teutonicus composed a gloss on the *Decretum*, known as the *Glossa Ordinaria*. Of more importance was the development of new papal legislation, so-called *decretales* (papal judicial decisions in specific cases, mostly appeals made to the pope). From the late twelfth century on, jurists began to collect papal legislation for it showed to be very convenient in practice. As this led to abuses, such as the use of counterfeit decretals, papal authority began to interfere in collecting decretals. From the beginning of the thirteenth century, only exclusive collections authenticated by papal authority were to be used in practice. Furthermore this activity gave the papacy the possibility to interfere in everyday life in society even beyond the *forum internum*, for instance in jurisdiction on marriage and economic relations. The decretalist tradition culminated in three papal collections of main importance, the *Liber Extra*, *Liber Sextus* and the *Clementinae*

collections and a crust of authoritative commentaries, had as a repercussion that canon law could not escape the ongoing trend of developing consultation literature. In addition to the more education orientated genres, several specific canon law aids appeared. Starting with *Decretum* summaries, over alphabetically arranged *tabulae*, *flores* and *distinctiones*, to fully fledged concordances between roman and canon law, such as John of Erfurt's *Tabula utriusque iuris*.[40] From plain and simple indices they rapidly evolved into complex searching instruments, providing their users with multiple indices, referring to several different source texts (for example Simon Vairet's *Tabula*),[41] or giving indices for multiple source texts like the biblical *repertoria*.

4. *Biblical repertoria as a 'genre'*

In a biographical article on *Bernardo de Oliver*, the well-known legal historian from Salamanca, García y García, not only describes the *Concordanciae Decretorum cum Biblia* of this mediaeval author, but also refers to this and other *Biblical repertoria*, specifically Johannes Johannis' *Memoriale Decreti* and Johannes Calderinus' *Tabula*, as a "juridical literary genre".[42] Unfortunately, García y García restricts himself to a very concise description of the genre, treating only one of its main features, *viz.* that they are concordances between canon law (*Decretum Gratiani* and Decretal collections) and the Bible.[43] But it surely is possible to establish additional defining characteristics by looking at the application of these *Repertoria* as searching aids, for one of the constituting elements of the genre is the nature of *Biblical Repertoria* as belonging to the wider branch of consultation literature. The evolution this latter genre underwent influenced the development of *Biblical Repertoria*, concerning both contents and form.

All authors of *Repertoria* discussed in this contribution made use, to a larger or smaller extent, of the achievements made with regard to text lay-out, in order to construct a searching aid combining both canon law and theological, biblical and/or other textual fragments. Johannes Johannis, for instance, used running titles to indicate the section of the *Memoriale* in question, reference tools based on the newly standardised biblical chapter division, specific *marginalia* (such as the little pointing hands), enlarged initials and canonical abbreviations. Johannes Calderinus made use of comparable tools of lay-out: the application of alphabet letters *in margine*, referring to the number and the order of extracts, the use of biblical chapter division, canonical abbreviations and tools for cross-referencing. Jesselin de Cassagnes also used biblical chapter division, canonical

(see also note 4). Analogous to the decretist tradition all sorts of comments and *glossa* on the collections emerged. See Bellomo 1995: 65–77 and 126–48; Brundage 1995; Coing 1973: 365–82; Schulte 1875 II: 456–511.

[40] For a basic survey, see: Schulte 1875 II: 485–511. Also Coing 1973: 313–64, especially pp. 348–63. For the *Tabula*, see Schulte 1875 II: 385–91, especially pp. 387–89.

[41] Simon Vairet (d. 1347), a Parisian master in canon law, composed in his *Tabula* an index referring to at least eight other indices and/or reference books, most of them canon law treatises except for the indices on the manipulus florum (a reference book for preachers), on the *summa confessorum* and for the concordance on the Bible (*magna concordantia biblie*). Cf. Amiens, *Bibliothèque Municipale*, ms. 383, fol. 251r. See also Schulte 1875 II: 405 and Fournier 1921: 606–09.

[42] García y García 1971: 186–188, especially p. 188: "En este género literariojurídico de concordancias entre la Biblia y el Decreto y las Decretales, hay varias otras obras, entre las que merecen recordarse las de ... Juan Calderino, ... y Juan Abad Nivicellense." See also note 13 on the same page. Note that the reference *Abad Nivicellense* is based on a mistaken reading by von Schulte.

[43] García y García 1971: 188.

abbreviations and specific indications as to whether extracts had been explained in the *Decretum Gratiani* or not.[44]

All three *Repertoria* are quite easy to manage, as they make use of alphabetically arranged keyword lists and/or arrangement according to Bible book and chapter as entries for research. To clarify their procedure and to show both the quantity and the quality of the data which can be retrieved from them, one example will suffice. Let us therefore look at the extract mentioned in the title of this contribution, *Adam per Evam deceptus est.*

5. In the third part of Johannes Johannis *Memoriale Decreti*, which treats of the *auctoritates textuales*, the extract *Adam per Evam deceptus est* follows on the keyword *Adam* (together with six other extracts) and is, in its turn, followed by the abbreviation *C.XXXIII.q.V.c.adam.*[45] In Johannes Calderinus *Tabula Auctoritatum*, the extract is followed by a biblical reference, namely *Genesis III*, and by a reference to the *Decretum Gratiani* (*C.XXXIII.q.V.c.adam.*). In Jesselin's *Auctoritates* the extract is quoted in the *non-exposite* part and followed by a different reference, namely *C. XXXIX. q. V .c. mulierem.*[46] and a reference to the Bible, namely *Genesis III.*

The connection with the Bible (the reference to the book of Genesis) allows us to find further information. The first part of the *Memoriale Decreti* (the *auctoritates bibliae*) is divided following the division of the Bible in books and chapters. Extracts from the third chapter of Genesis cover the story of original sin. These are followed by various references to the *Decretum Gratiani*. This leaves us with two possibilities. First, all extracts from Genesis III can be checked for the presence of keyword *Adam*, and thus a considerable amount of references to the corpus of canon law can be found. Second, we can look for a specific extract and for the added references. Yet there is a problem, as most of the extracts in the third part of the *Memoriale Decreti* are allusions to or short abstracts of biblical text. So in the case of *Adam per Evam deceptus*, we have to look at the biblical textual fragment which approaches the extract as closely as possible. Here this is the text of Genesis chapter three, verse twelve: *Mulier quam dedisti mihi sociam dedit mihi de ligno et comedi.* Two references to the corpus of canon law are added. It should be noted that in contrast with Johannes Calderinus, Johannes Johannis did not connect the biblical authoritative textual fragments with a keyword list. In order to find the biblical locations in which the keywords from for instance the third part of the *Memoriale Decreti* are used, one has to resort to a concordance on the Bible.

Johannes Calderinus has extended this basic framework (keyword, extract, biblical reference and corpus of canon law-reference) with a cross-referencing system.[47] Calderinus added to the example-extract three keywords, followed by an alphabet-letter:

---

[44] For the description of the *Memoriale Decreti*, the *Tabula Auctoritatum* and the *Auctoritates*, cf. supra.

[45] Referring to the fifth question of *Causa* 33, the chapter beginning with the word *Adam* (= c. 18). The chapter reads: *Adam per Evam deceptus est, non Eva per Adam. Quem vocavit ad culpam mulier, iustum est, ut eam in gubernationem assumat, ne iterum femina facilitate labatur.* The fifth question deals with the relationship between man and woman. The text is borrowed from saint Ambrose's *Exameron*.

[46] Most probably this is due to a scribal error, since a *Causa* 39 does not exist. The incipit *mulierem* probably refers to the fifth question of *Causa* 33, chapter 19, reading: *Mulier debet velare caput, quia non est imago Dei*. The text is taken from the comment by saint Ambrose on the second letter to the Corinthians.

[47] Cf. the description of Calderinus *Tabula*.

annus.a, ebron. a, ymago.a. Annus.a reads: *Nongentis et coamplius annis ad Adam usque ad Abraham homines vixerunt. Genesis V. D.LXXXIIII. porro.*,[48] *Ebron.a* reads: *In Ebron Adam et Eva sepulti sunt.... Josue.XIIII....XIII.q.II.ebron. et § <ecclesie>*,[49] and *ymago.a* reads: *Creavit deus hominem, scilicet, Adam ad eternam ad similitudinem suam <...>illum. Genesis.I. de.pe. di.princeps. de homine. c.II.*[50] Each of the keywords is connected to other extracts containing the keyword referred to (in this case *annus*, *ebron* and *ymago*).

In summary we can define the genres outlines as follows. *Biblical Repertoria* contain biblical textual fragments and/or abstracts from or allusions to biblical fragments, or other kinds of textual fragments that either appear in the corpus of canon law, or are connected through searching aids with the corpus of canon law. They can be used to extract quickly certain amounts of data from different types of sources.

In spite of this enormous advantage residing in the possibility of accessing different source texts by means of one and the same reference work instead of having to search through different source texts, this feature at the same time seems to have been the Achilles heel of the genre.

6. *Conclusion*

J.F. von Schulte, the outstanding nineteenth century scholar of the history of canon law, made a telling remark describing Calderinus' *Tabula*: "für das Recht ist ihr Wert unbedeutend".[51] In discussing the historical development of law, legal historians like von Schulte have attached little importance to this type of consultation literature. In fact, consultation literature has often been considered to be the sign of a stagnation or even a decline in the onward march of the historical progress of law. Yet in contrast to this negative interpretation, and in particular from the point of view of the emergence of consultation literature, fourteenth century canonist study aids, such as *Biblical Repertoria*, represent the summit of a tradition. This tradition produced several kinds of high-quality interdisciplinary search tools and study aids, in which the scholarly development of both canon law and of consultation literature were combined.

Biblical Repertoria being study aids were closely connected to late mediaeval academic training. Changes in the academic system and renewed attention for the authoritative source text probably account for the sudden impopularity of the genre. By the end of the fifteenth century only parts of the *Memoriale Decreti* were to be re-issued in print, while others were completely forgotten. No new types of searching aids emerged, and the interest for the older tradition faded away.

But in a way, von Schultes remark is also correct. Despite the fact that *Biblical Repertoria* were excellent aids for bridging the gap between everyday practice and the authoritative source texts, they also created a new attitude towards the source texts they referred to. Gradually an almost unnoticed shift took place from the written word blessed with authority, to the authority of the reference. Authoritative *texts* were no longer read in their entirety: only extracts were taken and used. Von Schulte marked this as a sign

48 *Decretum Gratiani, di. 84, c. 6.*
49 *Decretum Gratiani, C. 13, q. 2, c. 2. and c 13, q. 2, p. c. 1.*
50 *Decretum Gratiani, de pen., di. 1*, c. 2.
51 Schulte 1875 II: 250.

of decline in canonist scholarship.[52] However, if we look at it from the point of view of consultation literature, it is clear that he underestimated the value of the genre. Whether von Schulte's evaluation is correct or not is therefore a mere matter of perspective.

[52] Schulte 1875 II: 482 says: "Sieht man auf den inneren Geist und Charakter der Werke, auf die Methode und besonders die wissenschaftliche Forschung, so tritt zusehends nach und nach ein Verfall ein".

REFERENCES

Bellomo, M.
1995 *The Common Legal Past of Europe*: 1000–1800 (Studies in Mediaeval and Early Modern Canon Law 4). Washington.

Berlioz, J.
1994 "Sources et citation," in *L'Atelier du médiéviste* 1: 145–76.

Bienvenu, M.
1989 "Fontevrault," cols. 627–629 in *Lexikon des Mittelalters* IV. Munich.

Brundage, J.A.
1995 *Mediaeval Canon Law*, The Mediaeval World. London.

Cappelli, A.
1990[6] *Dizionario di abbreviature Latine ed Italiane*. Milan.

Coing, H. (ed.)
1973 *Handbuch der Quellen und Literatur der neueren Europäischen Privatrechtsgeschichte*, I. Band, *Mittelalter (1100–1500). Die gelehrten Rechte und die Gesetzgebung*. Munich.

Cross, F.L. & Livingstone, E.A.(eds)
1974 *The Oxford Dictionary of the Christian Church*. Oxford.

Daoust, J.
1971 "Fontevrault," cols. 961–71 in *Dictionnaire d'Histoire et de Géographie Ecclésiastiques* XVII. Paris.

Ehrle, F.
1890 *Historia bibliothecae Romanorum Pontificium* I. Rome.

Fasoli. G.
1983 "Bologna," cols. 370–74 in *Lexikon des Mittelalters* II.

Fournier, M.
1892 *Histoire de la science du droit en France* III Paris.

Fournier, P.
1921 "Simon Vairet, canoniste," in *Histoire littéraire de la France* 35: 606–09.

1921a "Jesselin de Cassagnes, canoniste," in *Histoire littéraire de la France* 35: 348–61.

García y García, A.
1971 "Bernardo Oliver," pp. 186–88 in *Repertorio de historía de las ciencias eclesiastícas en España* II (Corpus Scriptorum Sacrorum Hispaniae. Estudios 2). Salamanca.

Gilles, H.
1974 "Jean de Jean, abbé de Joncels," in *Histoire littéraire de la France* 40: 53–111.

1960 "Un canoniste oublié: l'abbé de Joncels," in *Revue Historique de Droit Français et Étranger* 4e série 38: 578–602.

1994 "Les moines juristes," in *Cahiers de Fanjeaux* 29: 89–93.

Glenisson, J, & Mollat, G.
1964 *L'Administration des États de l'Église au XIVe siècle. Gil Albornoz et Androuin de la Roche (1353–1367)* (Bibliothèque des Écoles Françaises d'Athène et de Rome, 203). Paris.

Lebras, G., Lefebvre, Ch. & Rambaud, J.
1965 *L'Age classique (1140 – 1378). Sources et théorie du droit* (Histoire du Droit et des Institutions de l'Église en Occident 7). Paris.

Maier, A.
1952 *Codices Burghesiani* (Studi e testi 170). Vatican City.
1964 "Zu einigen Handschriften der päpstlichen Bibliothek von Avignon," in *Archivium Historiae Pontificium* 2: 325–56.

Naz, R.
1957 "Jesselin de Cassagnes", cols. 130–31 in *Dictionnaire de Droit Canonique* VI. Paris.

Ochoa, X. & Diez, A.
1965 *Index titulorum.* Rome.

Rouse, R.H.
1976 "La diffusion en Occident au XIIIe siècle des outils de travail facilitant l'accès aux textes autoritatifs," in *Revue des Études Islamiques* 44: 115–47.
1981 "Le développement des instruments de travail au XIIIe siècle," pp. 115–44 in *Culture et travail intellectuel dans l'Occident médiéval.* Paris.

Rouse, R.H. & Rouse, M.A.
1979 *Preachers, Florilegia and Sermons. Studies on the Manipulus florum of Thomas of Ireland* (Studies and Texts 47). Toronto.
1982 "Statim invenire. Schools, Preachers, and new Attitudes to the Page," pp. 201–25 in R.L. Benson & G. Constable (eds.), *Renaissance and Renewal in the Twelfth Century.* Oxford.

Schulte, J.F. von
1875 *Die Geschichte der Quellen und Literatur des Canonischen Rechts.* Stuttgart.

Severino, G.
1980 "Aegidius Albornoz," cols. 310–11 in *Lexikon des Mittelalters* I.

Tarrant, J.
1979 "The Life and Works of Jesselin de Cassagnes," in *Bulletin of Mediaeval Canon Law* 9: 37–64.

Weijers, O.
1988–1995 *Études sur la vocabulaire intellectuel du moyen age* (CIVICMA 1–8). Turnhout.

Weimar, P.
1982 "Zur Doktorwürde der Bologneser Legisten," pp. 421–43 in *Festgabe für H. Coing zum 70. Geburtstag* (Ius Commune, Sonderheft 17). Frankfurt-am-Main.

SOME BRAVE ATTEMPTS AT GENERIC CLASSIFICATION IN PREMODERN ARABIC LITERATURE

Geert Jan van Gelder

0. The morphology of Arabic, like that of other Semitic languages, is based on two abstractions which, when combined, render concrete words (if words can be said to be concrete): a 'root' and a 'pattern'. A root is a sequence of consonants, mostly three, in a fixed order; it is associated with a lexical set. A pattern is the configuration of vowels and consonants in which the root consonants are slotted; it is associated with syntactic and semantic sets. Thus there are patterns, for instance, for countless verbal finite forms, for participles, for words denoting places or instruments, words denoting sounds, illnesses, colours, or remainders of things. Would it not be a good idea to have a pattern especially for genres?

As a matter of fact, there seems to be precisely such a pattern, which may be algebraically represented as /uR_1R_2ūR_3ah/ (in which R stands for a root consonant). It is found in the following examples: *uqṣūṣah* 'story', *ufkūhah* 'joke, pleasantry', *uḍḥūkah* 'lark, joke' (from a root denoting 'laughter'), *uḥjiyyah* 'riddle',[1] *usjūʿah* 'utterance in rhyming prose', *urjūzah* 'poem in the metre called rajaz', *uḥduwwah* 'camel driver's song', *ughlūṭah* 'sophistry' (from a root associated with error and misleading), *ukdhūbah* 'lie', *uḥlūfah* 'oath', *uḥkūmah* 'juridical decision', *usbūbah* 'vilification, vituperation', *uhjuwwah* 'invective, lampoon', *umdūḥah* 'panegyric, encomium', *usṭūrah* 'fable, legend, myth'. A modern example is *uṭrūḥah* 'thesis, dissertation'.[2] In a recent short article on the pattern, Wolfram von Soden speaks of

> Wörter für Aussagen jeglicher Art, auch irrige Aussagen, Versarten, Dichtungen und Lieder mannigfacher Art, Rätsel, Scherze, Spiele, besondere Arten von Klängen, auch Handlungsweisen usw.[3]

Alas, in practice things do not always work out so neatly. In theory, Arabic is a splendidly 'logical' language in many ways, but as always reality disturbs one's dreams. Most of the words listed above are rare, and in the *discours* about genres many other patterns are employed. It cannot be helped; the same may be observed in the generic systems of some theoreticians of genre, since there, too, the disorder of reality throws a spanner in the works. We know, however, especially since the recent flowering of chaos studies, that chaos often surpasses neat and simple systems in beauty.

1 The "weak" consonant /y/ is responsible for the deviant form.

2 On the pattern, see e.g. Ibn Durayd 1988: 1195; al-Suyūṭī n.d.: ii, 126–27; Abū Ḥayyān al-Tawḥīdī, 1988: iii, 42. A rare form, *uṭnūzah* 'mockery', is used by Ibn Rashīq (Ibn Rashīq 1972: ii, 70)

3 Soden 1995: 137–44, see p. 141. On the same pattern as a plural, see Arioli 1994: 221–32.

1. The relevance of mediaeval Arabic typologies of texts to students of Greek, Latin, or European mediaeval literatures may not be immediately apparent. Yet, in the perspective of comparative poetics it is surely useful to be able to spot differences or parallels. All too often, sometimes even by arabists, the rich tradition of poetics in Arabic is ignored. In 1990 a leading specialist in comparative poetics could still write that "Neither Arabic nor Persian literature has an originative poetics *per se*."[4] In many western general discussions of genre the traditional trinity of epic, lyric and drama still reigns supreme. "Lyric, narrative, dramatic" are called "the most basic modes of literary art" in an entry on genre in Chris Baldick's *The Concise Oxford Dictionary of Literary Terms* (Oxford, 1990), where poetry and prose fiction are dubbed "the broadest categories of composition". In the context of classical Arabic literature the triad of lyric, narrative and drama is questionable, as is the raising of fiction to one of the two "broadest categories". *The New Princeton Encyclopedia of Poetry and Poetics* (Princeton, 1993) devotes considerable space to non-western poetic traditions, yet the entry on genre does not move outside Europe. As a result some arabists have racked their brains in order to solve spurious problems, trying to determine, for instance, whether the pre-Islamic *qaṣīdah* ought to be classified as lyrical or epic, perhaps with some commixture of dramatic elements.[5] The best book about genres known to me is Alastair Fowler's *Kinds of Literature: An Introduction to the Theory of Genres and Modes*;[6] he too restricts himself to western tradition, but his ideas about the ways of formation, transformation, and hierarchies of genres are stimulating, and his distinction of 'kinds' and 'modes' useful.[7] A 'mode' is not connected with an external form, and is best attached to 'kinds' in adjectival form ('comical', 'lyrical', 'satirical', etc.). A 'kind', on the other hand, is a complex of features always connected with a certain external form. In a sense, a 'kind', or historical genre, is formed in a way analogous to the way an Arabic word is formed, as described at the beginning: it is a combination of thematic features (the 'root') and formal features (the 'pattern').

2. In this contribution it is not my aim to apply any existing western theory of genre to Arabic literature. In order to study the system of Arabic genres there is no need for a theoretical underpinning that threatens to secure one's findings in a straitjacket, or at least an ill-fitting costume. Rather, I intend to show how the Arabs themselves have classified their own texts, by giving a survey of the ways of generic classification in classical Arabic literature, in its explicit forms, in more or less theoretical discussions, and its more implicit and practical forms, as in the ways various types of poems and prose texts are arranged in thematically ordered anthologies. This has not yet been done, as far as I am aware, in English; the best (and, one might add, the only) substantial general studies of genre in Arabic literature are in German, and deal with poetry only.[8]

It is true that to the Arabs poetry had (and has) a higher status than prose (apart

---

[4] Miner 1990: 82.

[5] See e.g. Jacobi 1971: 207–12; Wagner 1987: 161–62.

[6] Fowler 1982.

[7] Since the important notion of 'mode' is discussed on pp. 106–7, it may be necessary to mention that in the edition used by me (1985) the unnumbered pages 88 and 106 have inadvertently been exchanged.

[8] Schoeler 1973: 9–55; idem, 1975.

from the Koran, which is deemed *sui generis*) and has received far more attention from theorists; yet there is no good reason to leave out literary genres in prose only because it was discussed less often and because its forms are more diffuse and more difficult to categorise. Nor is it desirable to restrict oneself to 'literary' genres. Although the distinction between literary and non-literary is not pointless – for there are Arabic texts that are unambiguously literary and others that are non-literary – there is a large intermediate area that is not so much grey as multi-coloured, and where a distinction is neither possible nor useful. In this respect it may be useful to look at some western studies on kinds of texts in general, and see whether their models could be applied to mediaeval Arabic genres.[9]

3. In order to give a survey of the Arabic generic classifications one ought to start, ideally, with a description and illustration of many kinds of texts, literary and non-literary, from the oldest pre-Islamic poems dating from the early sixth century CE, including later forms of poetry and kinds of prose, such as orations, sermons, anecdotes, epic narratives, gnomic texts, epistles, essays, treatises, anthologies, and works historical, biographical, prosopographical, theological, mystical, encyclopaedic or scientific; all this over a period of some 1300 years. Instead, I shall give a few examples of the ways in which the Arabs themselves classified texts.

3.1. Poetry being the highest art form and without question the most literary text type according to the Arabs, it is only to be expected that it has received far more attention from critics and theorists than has prose. Traditional Arabic poetry is easily defined in formal terms: it is metrical rhyming speech. All other texts are in prose, including the forms of rhyming prose that have, through the centuries, been used for oracular utterances, aphorisms, orations, epistles, flowery descriptions and some narrative texts. Prose texts cannot be classified as easily as poetry can; consequently, the traditional typology of prose forms is less developed.

Nevertheless, one of the earliest classifications of speech does not seem to be restricted to poetry. It is a statement found in sources from the ninth century onward, and often attributed to the pre-Islamic Iranian Sassanian emperor Parwīz (or Abarwīz):

> All speech (*kalām*) may be summarised as [having one of] four features: either you ask something, or you ask about something, or you command something, or you tell something. These are the pillars of things said (*al-maqālāt*); if a fifth is sought it will not be found.[10]

This looks like a classification of speech acts, as if anticipating J.L. Austin and J.R. Searle. Arabic linguists did in fact use and elaborate this division. Ibn Qutayba (d. 889), who quotes this passage, reformulates it in a work on language: "Speech is four things: command, predication (or report, information, *khabar*), question (or asking for

[9] Of the numerous titles that appeared since the '70s I only mention Gülich & Raible 1972 and Werlich 1975.

[10] Ibn Qutayba 1925–1930: i, 46; Ibn Qutayba 1901: 18; al-Ṭabarī 1965: 179; Ibn ʿAbd Rabbih 1948–1953: ii, 266; al-Ābī 1980-1990: vii, 83.

information, *istikhbār*), and request".[11] A later linguist, Ibn Fāris (d. 1004) expands the list to ten:

> The meanings (or 'functions', *maʿānī*) of speech are ten, according to a scholar: predication, question, command, prohibition, plea (or prayer), request, gentle adhortation, incitement, wish, and [expression of] astonishment.[12]

Such a classification might have been the starting-point of a text linguistics. Just as in traditional western linguistics, however, Arabic grammarians usually restricted their interests to the compass of the sentence; it would be rash to speak here of text typology. But the link between such a classification and one of literary themes or modes was made, already before Ibn Fāris, by the grammarian and philologian Thaʿlab (d. 904). His brief treatise *The Fundaments of Poetry* begins as follows:

> The fundaments of poetry are four: command, prohibition, predication, and question.[13]

Each of these four is illustrated by means of a fragment of two lines of verse. He continues:

> Subsequently these basic elements ramify into panegyric, invective, elegies, apology, love poetry, comparison and telling stories (*akhbār*, plural of *khabar*).[14]

These seven categories are illustrated by means of examples of one or two lines. The author does not attempt to explain precisely how the 'roots' grow into branches; he does not say whether his list is exhaustive. One might be tempted to believe that he is thinking of complete poems, limiting his examples to short fragments in the knowledge that his readers will be acquainted with the rest of the poems. This, however, appears not to be the case. Thus he offers the following single line as an example of 'telling stories':

> Now sweep the winds over all their dwellings: empty they lie,
> as though their lords had been set a time and no more to be.[15]

This is the eleventh line of a famous pre-Islamic poem of 36 lines, which cannot be called a simple telling of a story: it is an elegiac ode with the *ubi sunt* topos as its basis, but it is no narrative. Similarly, the line illustrating 'love poetry' turns out to be taken from a long and complex poem in which 'love' is one of several themes. Thaʿlab's division, and many other thematic classifications from later periods, become clearer when it is realised that what is classified is not so much poems or 'complete' texts as individual lines of verse, or short passages. This also explains the occurrence of 'comparison' as a category on its own, which looks strange at first sight.

---

[11] Ibn Qutayba 1901: 4.

[12] Ibn Fāris 1977: 289 (with elucidation pp. 289–304).

[13] Thaʿlab 1966: 35.

[14] Thaʿlab 1966: 37. The word for 'elements' could be translated as 'roots' or 'tree trunks', which fits the following 'ramifying'. Thaʿlab uses the plural 'elegies' (*marāthī*) presumably because the singular *marthiyah* is less abstract than the other terms, since it refers to a specific poem rather than the 'mode' in general; but he could have used the singular *rithāʾ*, 'elegiac poetry, elegy'.

[15] Thaʿlab 1966: 40, translation by Lyall, 1918: 161.

3.2. This manner of classification is understandable in view of the nature of the *qaṣīdah*, the genre that has by far the highest literary status from the earliest pre-Islamic times throughout the Islamic period. It is a poem or ode of a few dozen lines, occasionally over one hundred lines, in which a number of different themes succeed one another. The beginning is often elegiac, celebrating past love and a former beloved; this may be followed by descriptive passages on a camel or desert fauna. Urban *qaṣīdah* s may have, for instance, a garden description instead. The poem may conclude with vaunting, eulogy of oneself, one's own tribe, or a person; alternatively, or combined with this, one finds invective on opponents. The polythematic structure of such poems has been the subject of many recent studies. The ancient Arab critics obviously highly appreciated such poems as wholes; yet in practical criticism (and, one might add, in Arabic literary appreciation in general) attention is devoted mainly to short fragments that, in a sense, should be considered as 'complete' literary texts. This attitude, which is even clearer in the numerous popular anthological works, is reflected in more theoretical treatises on literary genres. Western ideas on genre, both in the past and the present, are chiefly or wholly focused on larger, or at least 'complete', structures. This does not always work for premodern Arabic literature, where a text such as a *qaṣīdah* has more than one 'mode of existence': as a whole or fragmented, each fragment potentially functioning as a literary text that is just as independent or dependent vis-à-vis the whole poem as the poem is dependent or independent vis-à-vis literature as an intertextual whole.[16]

3.3. In order to get an idea of the different ways of classifying poetry, here are a few passages quoted from an eleventh century manual of poetry, in which the North African critic and poet Ibn Rashīq collects a number of opinions:

> A certain scholar in this field has said: poetry is built on four cornerstones: praise (or panegyric, *madḥ*), blame (or vituperation, *hijāʾ*), love poetry (*nasīb*) and elegy (*rithāʾ*). Others have said: the bases of poetry are four, viz. desire, fear, joy and anger. Panegyric and thanksgiving go with desire, apology and supplication go with fear, passion and delicate love poetry go with joy, and vituperation, threat and hurtful reproach go with anger.
>
> ʿAlī Ibn ʿĪsā al-Rummānī[17] said: the genres (lit. 'purposes', *aghrāḍ*) of poetry are five at most: love poetry, panegyric, vituperation, vaunting and description, simile and metaphor being included in description.
>
> ʿAbd al-Malik Ibn Marwān[18] once said to Arṭāh Ibn Suhayyah, "Will you be making any poetry today?" – "By God!", he answered, "I am neither joyous nor angry; I am not drinking, nor do I desire anything. Poetry only comes with one of these". [...]
>
> ʿAbd al-Karīm[19] said: the kinds of poetry are comprised by four genres: panegyric, vituperation, gnomic verse and light verse. Each kind may be subdivided: to panegyric belong elegy, vaunting and thanksgiving; to vituperation belong blame, reproach and complaining about slowness [in fulfilling a promise]; to gnomic verse

---

16 See van Gelder 1982, esp. pp. 194–203 ("In Search of the Poem").
17 Grammarian and philologian, d. 994.
18 Umayyad caliph, d. 705.
19 al-Nahshalī, critic, d. 1014.

> belong proverbial sayings, renunciation [of worldy pleasures] and homilies; to light verse belong love poetry (*ghazal*), hunting poetry, bacchic verse and obscenity.[20]
>
> Some have said: all poetry is of two kinds: praise and blame. For elegy, vaunting and love poetry go back to praise, as does every favourable description connected with it, such as the description of the deserted campsite and its remains and beautiful comparisons; and also the beautiful representation of ethical qualities, e.g. by means of proverbial sayings, maxims, homily, and renunciation [of worldy affairs]. Blame is the opposite of all this. Only reproach has an intermediate status: it stands at the edge of both kinds. Incitement too is neither praise nor blame. [...]
>
> Diʿbil[21] said in his book: "If you want to make panegyric, then do so by means of desire; if you want vituperation, then with hatred; if you want love poetry, then with passionate love; if you want reproach, then by complaining about slowness [in fulfilling a promise]." As you see, he divides poetry into these four parts, in which elegy, as I have said before, is subsumed under panegyric; he puts 'reproach' in its stead. [...]
>
> ʿAbd al-Ṣamad Ibn al-Muʿadhdhal[22] said: "All poetry is comprised in three words, but not everyone is able to compose them properly: when praising, you say: 'You are'; when blaming, you say: 'You aren't'; when you make an elegy, you say: 'You were'."[23]

Each of the opinions in this selection would deserve some discussion in more detail for which this article lacks the necessary space. Interesting is the classification on the basis of affects such as desire, anger, and fear; later critics have rarely taken this up. Other classifications were elaborated, expanded or refined; they are brave attempts, none of them wholly satisfactory: at times too haphazard a list, at other times too reductionist. The last-quoted statement for instance, on the 'deep structure' of poetry, suggests that a lampoon is basically the exact opposite of an eulogy, and that the distinction between a panegyrical poem and an elegy is in principle nothing but a matter of grammatical tenses. In practice, of course, a lampoon or invective is not simply a eulogy in which all plusses have been changed into minuses. Moreover, the differences between these kinds of verse are not merely thematic but formal. Thus a panegyrical poem often shows the polythematic structure sketched above, with an introduction that could be called 'lyrical', on love for instance, whereas such a preamble is commonly lacking in an elegy. Invective poems may be, but usually are not, polythematic; often they are short epigrams, while panegyrical poems are mostly relatively long.[24]

It is clear that the criteria of classification in the passage quoted above are not so much formal as functional and thematic; they concern 'modes' rather than 'kinds', in Fowler's terminology. Mostly, the categories are directed towards persons, just as the lists of 'speech acts', by Parwīz and his Arab followers, quoted above, were person-directed. Arabic theories of genre take it more or less for granted that each utterance has a purpose which determines its genre or mode. Strictly speaking, each line of

20 Reading *mujūn* for *makhmūr*.
21 Poet and critic, d. 859.
22 Poet, d. c. 854. In Ibn al-Jarrāḥ n.d.: 9 this statement is attributed to ʿAmr Ibn Naṣr al-Qiṣāfī; cf. also Abū Hilāl al-ʿAskarī 1971: 137.
23 Ibn Rashīq (d. 1065 or 1071), 1972: I, pp. 119–23.
24 On invective poems see e.g. van Gelder, 1989; idem, 1990: 14–25. On epigrams, see idem, 1995: 101–40.

verse, which should in principle be able to stand alone and be meaningful, has its own *gharaḍ* 'purpose', 'goal' or 'aim'. A passage dealing with e.g. love, or panegyric, may be said to have a *gharaḍ* too; the polythematic *qaṣīdah* necessarily has more than one *gharaḍ*.[25] This 'aim' is usually a person who is to be praised, urged, threatened, vilified, etc. The term *gharaḍ* (plural *aghrāḍ*) is often to be translated as 'theme'; it resembles what Fowler calls 'mode'. One detects a certain amount of embarrassment among the traditional Arab critics and theoreticians when they have to classify those themes that are not directly aimed at a person, such as purely ecphrastic, descriptive poetry, or narrative poetry, which is very rare anyhow in Arabic, and neglected by the theoreticians. The critics and literary theorists, above all interested in pre- and early Islamic nomadic or quasi-nomadic poetry, were on the whole able to accommodate new urban kinds of poetry in their generic discussions as long as a relation with the old bedouin genres could be established. For instance, the independent love poem or hunting poem posed no problems because love and hunting were important constituents of the traditional *qaṣīdah*; the bacchic poem could also be considered as being rooted in the descriptions of wine and wine drinking in the old *qaṣīdah*, and the congratulatory poem could easily be related to the panegyrical poem. But such a connection could not always be found. As a result some genres are ignored or almost ignored in Arabic poetics, such as narrative poetry. Storytelling, or what we would call fiction, is very much part of Arabic literature but was not considered particularly 'literary' in Arabic poetics and therefore not discussed as such. Any illiterate person could tell stories, it was argued; but that does not amount to literature as long as it not couched in elevated language and diction. Narrative poems, with the appropriate eloquent diction, were produced in Arabic literature, but their status was not particularly high, and if they were discussed by the critics at all it was rarely on account of their narrative aspects. Mystical poetry, or poetry dealing with religious doctrine or philosophy, is also virtually ignored. This did not prevent such poems from being composed.[26]

4. Although the *qaṣīdah* plays a central role in the history of Arabic poetry, this does not mean that much was written on this genre as a form. Speaking about whole poems is not the main concern of traditional Arabic poetics, which is preoccupied with matters of diction and language, and these are mostly studied within the compass of the sentence, the single line or short fragment of verse. A rough distinction is usually made between the polythematic ode (*qaṣīdah*) and the *qiṭʿah*, literally 'fragment, piece', which is a misleading term since often it is a short independent whole that was never part of a larger structure. According to many ancient critics the difference between *qaṣīdah* and *qiṭʿah* is a matter of length only, but there is in fact more to it than that.

The passage quoted from Ibn Rashīq's book on poetry is a rather unordered collection of aphorisms and summarised systems of classification. A few critics developed generic classifications that are more systematic and detailed. One of the more interesting systems is that of the poet and critic Ḥāzim al-Qarṭājannī (d. 1285), who intended to make a synthesis of the Aristotelian-Avicennian tradition of poetics and that of traditional

25 Some scholars use the term *gharaḍ* only for the last part of the *qaṣīdah*; see e.g. Jones, 1996: 87, 92, 98, 194. This is contrary to traditional usage.

26 On such 'shortcomings' of Arabic theory, see the important article by Heinrichs, 1973: 19–69.

Arabic literary criticism and theory. His generic system is utilitarian: the primary goals of poetry are bringing about useful things and warding off harmful things. An elaborate classification of *aghrāḍ* is then made on the basis of further criteria, depending on whether the useful or harmful things have already occurred or have not yet taken place, and depending on whether the nature of this benefit and injury is known or unknown, or whether the identity of the perpetrator is known or unknown.[27] He incorporates the affects (grief, fear, hope, desire etc.) in his system; moreover, in spite of the utilitarian basis and Ḥāzim's dry prose style, he is not blind to the aesthetic aspects of poetry. He is not interested, at least not in this part of his poetics, in formal aspects: he is speaking about poetry, but in principle his system could be applied to prose in various forms.

A classification such as that by Ḥāzim al-Qarṭājannī is possible when studying abstract concepts like 'modes'. In practice, when dealing with concrete texts, the Arabs had to find various solutions, for instance when compiling thematically arranged anthologies or collected poems of a particular poet.[28] A tenth-century redactor of the poetry of the versatile Abū Nuwās (d. c. 200/814) arranged the poems in the following categories: 'flytings', panegyrics, elegies, reproaching poems, invective poems, ascetic poems, bacchic poems, hunting poems, love poetry on women, love poetry on boys, and finally pleasantries and obscene poetry. The categories overlap to some extent; the borderline between erotic love poetry and obscene poetry is not clear-cut, for instance. Moreover, many poems, especially the formal odes or *qaṣīdah*s, are polythematic, so that bacchic or erotic verse is by no means limited to the particular chapters. It is perhaps partly in order to circumvent this problem that in the majority of cases the poems of a poet are arranged alphabetically on the basis of the rhyme (facilitated by the fact that a traditional Arabic poem has only one rhyme throughout).

5. The problem of polythematic poems is less prominent in the numerous anthologies that mostly quote fragments or short monothematic poems. One of these anthologies should be mentioned, since it is one of the earliest and most influential. The *Ḥamāsah* by Abū Tammām (d. 845), himself an important poet, is an anthology of pieces and poems from pre- and early Islamic times, divided into ten chapters.[29] The first and by far the longest, which gave the collection its name, is *Ḥamāsah* ('zeal', 'enthusiasm', 'fighting spirit') and contains heroic verse that would, in other classifications, mostly be categorised under 'vaunting verse' or 'panegyric'. It is followed by 'elegies', then *adab* (usually 'good manners' or 'erudition', here rather referring to gnomic and ethical themes), 'invective poetry', and 'hospitality and eulogy' (in Bedouin society hospitality is the cardinal virtue, next to bravery). Four brief chapters conclude the anthology: 'descriptions', 'nocturnal journey (in the desert)', 'pleasantries' and 'criticising women': a heterogeneous batch which shows that systematic classification did not always have a high priority. Remarkably, the final section, 'criticising women', is separated from that of invective, which is concerned with men only. The difference is not merely a matter of sex: making lampoons on persons or tribes is a serious matter, but mocking and blaming

---

27 Ḥāzim al-Qartājannī, 1966: 336–5. The relevant chapter is translated and studied in Schoeler, 1973.
28 See Schoeler, 1973: 32–53.
29 On this collection, see e.g. Klein-Franke 1971: 13–36 and 1972: 142–78; van Gelder 1985: 610–72. The *Ḥamāsa* was translated into German verse by Rückert 1846.

women, whether they are someone else's relations or one's one, is so improper that it can only be taken as something unserious; hence its following upon a section entitled 'pleasantries', with jokes and light verse.

For poems there are hardly any formal criteria that can be used for the purpose of generic classification. All poetry rhymes, usually in monorhyme. Strophic poetry spread from the tenth century onward. Thematically, these strophic forms tend to favour some of the traditional *aghrāḍ*, such as amatory and bacchic themes, but other themes were also adopted. All Arabic poetry is metrical, each poem having one of the recognised metres. Unlike classical Greek poetry, for instance, there is no clear correlation between the metre and the theme. At most one can say that longer and 'heavier' metres are more often found in formal odes and serious poems, whereas shorter and lighter metres often correspond with lighter genres, but exceptions to this general trend are extremely common. There is one metre, however, that has a special position. *Rajaz*, the oldest and most simple metre, resembling the Greek iambic metre, normally has a lower status than the others. In early Arabic poetry it was used for short occasional verse, often extemporised in the midst of a verbal or physical combat. Soon afterwards it became the metre *par excellence* for long didactic or narrative poems, which replaced monorhyme (*aaaaaaaa...*) with paired rhyme (*aabbccdd...*), so that a length of hundreds of lines is easily achieved if necessary. Such a poem is called *urjūzah* (a word combining the root of *rajaz* with the pattern discussed above). But the boundaries between these 'genres' could be transgressed with impunity: from the seventh century some poets experimented with *rajaz* for the format of the *qaṣīdah*; and the metres with higher status may be used for occasional or didactic poems.

Yet another criterion could be considered in generic classifications. From about the eleventh century a growing quantity of poetry appears which is not composed in the classical standard language but in a form closer to the spoken language. The greater part of this 'vulgar' poetry, as far as it is preserved, is not composed by illiterate poets from the middle and lower strata of society, but by the literary élite. Normally this Neo-Arabic is employed in the lighter genres such as love poetry or jesting poetry; but here, too, barriers are easily broken and one may find panegyrical verse on rulers composed in Neo-Arabic.

6. Classifying poetry or poems may be a difficult matter; things become far more complicated if prose in all its forms is involved. As said before, the Arabs strictly distinguish between poetry and prose; the former, normally called *shiʿr*, is often called *naẓm* 'strung [discourse]' when contrasted with prose (*nathr*, 'unstrung', 'scattered'). Prose includes not only the unembellished diction of everyday speech and factual or scientific texts but also the extremely ornate, even 'poetic', diction of sermons, orations, formal epistles, descriptive purple passages, literary debates, flowery preambles, and picaresque sketches. Many longer and shorter texts – the latter including proverbs, aphorisms, riddles, anecdotes and jokes – participate in both styles, the unadorned and the florid. In addition to the dichotomy poetry vs. prose, the medieval Arab critics often mention a trichotomy: poetry, oratory, and epistle. The three are usually easily distinguished: poetry by its metre and the concomitant special way of recitation; oratory being, in principle, a kind of discourse communicated publicly and orally; and the epistle being, in principle, a kind of discourse communicated personally and in writing. Each discourse has its own domain and functions. It goes without saying that here, too, boundaries are transgressed regularly. A love poem may adopt conventions belonging to epistolography and become a versified love letter; others may compose a sermon in verse, either seriously, like the pious Abū l-ʿAtāhiyah (d. 825), or somewhat irreverently, as did the profligate caliph al-Walīd Ibn Yazīd (d. 744). Some themes that traditionally belong to the domain of poetry, such as vaunting and professing one's love for someone, may occur in prose, in a letter or an oration. The rapprochement of the three kinds is enhanced by the fact that rhyme is increasingly employed in artistic prose and that all literary products, in prose and poetry, tend to become ever more uniform in terms of the use of rhetorical figures and tropes, idiomatic expressions and standardised motifs. A popular literary pastime was the transformation of prose passages into poetry and *vice versa*.

6.1. Parody and satire are the fields *par excellence* in which generic conventions are consciously breached and expectations thwarted. Untrained minds, not only of contemporaries but especially of later ages, may fail to recognise a parody for what it is. The versified sermon referred to above, by a caliph notorious for his dissolute lifestyle, is a case in point.[30] Is it a parody? The content of the poem looks pious and unexceptionable; but it is embedded in a story that reports that the poet-caliph, on a Friday morning, was drinking wine with his friends when, on a sudden impulse, he ascended the pulpit. The poem is a parody for whoever chooses to read it that way.

6.2. In other cases there is less ambiguity, but even here one may find different opinions. A long satirical diatribe against the peasants of Egypt, written by Yūsuf al-Shirbīnī in the second half of the seventeenth century, takes the shape of a quasi-learned philological commentary on a poem in the Egyptian vernacular Arabic, attributed to a poor fellah called Abū Shādūf. To most readers it would be obvious that this poem and its poet are spurious, being fictions of the author. Surprisingly, in recent times several studies by Egyptians – sociologists or historians rather than literary critics – have appeared in which Abū Shādūf is considered to be a real person; these scholars are blinded by their zeal to provide a politically correct reading, in which the poem is a condemnation of the repression and exploitation of the peasants by the non-Egyptian Ottoman authorities, the commentary being a mixture of mockery and compassion coming from an urban Egyptian intellectual who was asked by the rulers to ridicule the rural complaints.[31] Such an interpretation is obviously misguided, but induced by the uniqueness of the work, which combines a very rare theme (peasants are all but absent in classical Arabic literature) with an unusual form (the scholarly commentary parodied).

6.3. Al-Shirbīnī's work is an example of a literary text that makes use of a genre that is not, or not necessarily, literary. This is not to imply that normally there is a sharp distinction between between literary and non-literary texts. A central concept in classi-

[30] Abū l-Faraj al-Iṣfahānī 1927–74: vii, 57-58; Gabrieli 1935: 1–64, see p. 44.

[31] The best introduction to al-Shirbīnī's work is Baer 1982: ch. 1 (pp. 3–47): "Shirbīnī's *Hazz al-quḥūf* and its significance"; an example of a 'politically correct' reading is Abd Al Raheim A. Abd Al Raheim 1975: 245–70.

cal Arabic culture, *adab*, may be rendered as 'good manners, etiquette' or 'erudition', knowledge of the world and of literature in particular. A very large part of Arabic literature shows a nearly inextricable mixture of both *utile* and *dulce*, of *docere*, *delectare* and *movere*, found in countless essayistic, ethico-religious, homiletico-narrative, historiographic or prosopographic works, often compiled in the form of encyclopaedic anthologies. This rough and open-ended enumeration shows that the neat division into poetry, oratory and epistolography mentioned above is unsatisfactory. Western readers will perhaps notice the absence of dramatic texts. Drama did not belong to the traditionally recognised genres; its very existence in pre-modern Arabic literature has been denied. This is not correct: there have been forms of theatre akin to what we would call slapstick comedy, a popular amusement with low status, of which hardly any texts have been preserved.[32] In order to save the western trinity of epic, lyric and drama as a presumed universal criterion in generic systems some rather futile attempts have been made to discover dramatic elements in established Arabic genres.

7. To read Arabic literature correctly there is no need to have a well-defined generic system at one's disposal. The classifications of ancient and modern scholars do give some insight into the minds of these scholars and show at least that they, the medieval Arab critics in particular, were fond of classifications. It is, however, a 'venerable error', as Fowler puts it, to presume that classification is the goal of studying genres; a genre is not so much a pigeonhole as a pigeon.[33] What is essential is to have read many different texts, in order to get an intuitive idea of the various kinds of literature; one should know which characteristics of texts belong together in a specific period – these characteristics include intratextual matters such as language level, register, prosody, stylistics and thematic features, as well as extratextual matters like the situational context of a text; also intertextual characteristics which include quotation, allusion and dependence on other texts or kinds; and finally metatextual matters: a knowledge of generic and typological terminology, which in Arabic (as in any self-respecting literature) is extensive, diffuse and far from systematical.[34] A further prerequisite, apart from knowing these characteristics and being able to recognise them, is the knowledge of their status in a specific constellation of features. To give an example, when someone describes in a poem how he sees to it that a beautiful boy gets inebriated, after which he rapes him (a not infrequent motif) he may offend some puritans, but in appropriate circumstances, recited at a ruler's court or a literary salon, or quoted in a literary anthology, it may not cause the raising of an eyebrow. If, however, the same event, whether fictional or real, would be cast in unadorned first person singular prose, it would be considered highly indecent even when read or quoted on identical occasions. Vaunting, hyperbolical boasting and eulogising or amorous personal effusions are normal and acceptable in verse but reprehensible and odd in straightforward prose. Another example is the concept of fictionality, which in the twentieth century has served as a prime criterion for establishing genres and 'literariness'. As said before, its role in traditional Arabic literature has been a rather minor one. Almost anybody, it was argued, is able to concoct fantastic stories, parables

---

32 See Moreh 1992.

33 Fowler 1982: 37.

34 For a list of the most common terms, see the Appendix.

or fairytales such as may be found in the *Thousand and One Nights* (long deemed an inferior genre, suitable for children, women and schoolteachers); what really counts are matters of poetic and rhetorical style and the invention of clever conceits. Nevertheless, in classical Arabic literature many works of high status are also brimful with stories, anecdotes, reports, legends and other narrative kinds, many of them fictional or at least showing a mixture of fact and fiction. The ancient theoreticians never tried to build systems incorporating terms for narrative, fiction, or the various prose genres. They made some brave attempts particularly with the modes of poetry; the rest they wisely left to theoreticians of a braver new world.

Appendix: *Some Metatextual Terms in Arabic.*[35]

The following is a list, in roughly associative order, of 99 terms (not counting plurals and variants) used for texts of different types and forms. Only pre-modern terms and meanings are given. In some cases related but different terms are found for 'abstract' genres and 'concrete' poems; but often these are used rather indiscriminately.

qawl pl. *aqwāl*, pl. of pl. *aqāwīl*	something said, utterance
kalimah pl. *kalimāt*	word, speech; (sometimes:) poem
kalām	speech, words, utterance, statement
maʿnā pl. *maʿānī*	meaning, motif, topos, idea
gharaḍ pl. *aghrāḍ*	theme, mode (lit. goal, aim, purpose)
fann pl. *funūn*	kind, genre
shiʿr pl. *ashʿār*	poetry, poem
naẓm	versification, poetry
nathr	'unstrung, scattered' speech, prose
sajʿ pl. *asjāʿ*	(text in) rhymed prose
qarīḍ	poetry in monorhyme in high-status metres (not *rajaz*)
rajaz	(poetry in) simple low-status metre
urjūzah pl. *arājīz*	poem in *rajaz*
muzdawaj	text in paired rhyme (*aabbcc...*)
qaṣīd	traditional poetry in *qaṣīdah* form
qaṣīdah pl. *qaṣāʿid*	ode, formal poem, poem (usually polythematic)
qiṭʿah	piece, fragment; short poem, epigram
bayt pl. *abyāt*	line of verse (cf. *āyah* pl. *āyāt* Koranic verse)
miṣrāʿ	hemistich
marthiyah pl. *marāthī*	elegiac poem, lament
rithāʾ	elegy (as a genre)
madīḥ pl. *madāʿiḥ*	panegyrical poem, eulogy, encomium
madḥ	praise, panegyrical poetry
dhamm	blame, condemnation
hijāʾ pl. *ahājī*	invective poetry, vilification, lampoon, satire

[35] [Editor's note: It is perhaps not a coincidence that this list contains 99 items – the same number as that of the names of God which are known to mankind. Only the camel knows the hundredth one.]

waʿīd, tawaʿʿud	threat
fakhr or *iftikhār*	vaunting poetry, self-praise
nasīb	love poetry (usually on past love, at the beginning of a *qaṣīdah*)
ghazal	love poetry, independent love poem (*gh. muʿannath*: on women; *gh. mudhakkar*: on boys)
tashbīb	love poetry
waṣf pl. *awṣāf*	description, ecphrastic or epideictic poetry
khamriyyah pl. *khamriyyāt*	bacchic poem, wine poem
ṭardiyyah (or *ṭaradiyyah*) pl. *ṭardiyyāt*	cynegetic poem, hunting poem
rawḍiyyah pl. *rawḍiyyāt*	garden poem
zahriyyah pl. *zahriyyāt*	flower poem
ʿitāb or *muʿātabah*	reproach
iʿtidhār	apology
tahniʾah pl. *tahāniʾ* (*tahānī*)	congratulation
shukr	thankfulness
zuhd	ascetic poetry, renunciation of the world
zuhdiyyah pl. *zuhdiyyāt*	ascetic poem
mathal pl. *amthāl*	parable, proverb
tashbīh pl. *tashbīhāt*	comparison, simile
lughz pl. *alghāz*, *uḥjiyyah* pl. *aḥājī*, *muʿammā*	various forms of riddle
waʿẓ	homily, paraenesis
mawʾiẓah pl. *mawāʿiẓ*	homiletic, paraenetic text
duʾāʿ pl. *adʿiyah*	prayer, invocation
ḥikma pl. *ḥikam*	wisdom, aphorism, gnomic poetry
mujūn	libertinism, shamelessness, indecent poetry (sex, alcohol, scatology ...)
sukhf	foolishness; obscene or nonsensical poetry
fuḥsh	impudence, obscenity, obscene language or poetry
lahw	distraction, amusement, light verse
jidd	seriousness
hazl	jesting
fukāhah pl. *fukāhāt*	joke, joking
nādirah pl. *nawādir*	anecdote, funny story, joke
mulḥa pl. *mulaḥ*	pleasantry, anecdote, joke
kitāb pl. *kutub*	book, piece of writing
faṣl pl. *fuṣūl*	section, chapter, passage
maqālah pl. *maqālāt*	treatise
qaṣaṣ	narrative, story
qiṣṣah pl. *qiṣaṣ*	story
ḥikāyah pl. *ḥikāyāt*	mimesis, tale, story
riwāyah pl. *riwāyāt*	transmitted account, report, story

ḥadīth pl. *aḥādīth*	news, talk, tale, story (esp. about the Prophet Muḥammad)
khabar pl. *akhbār*	report, account, story
athar pl. *āthār*	trace, report
nabaʾ pl. *anbāʾ*	report, tiding
sīrah pl. *siyar*	conduct, biography
tarjamah pl. *tarājim*	translation, biography, prosopography
maghāzī	res gestae, (account of) military campaigns
malḥamah pl. *malāḥim*	heroic battle, epic
khurāfah pl. *khurāfāt*	fable, fairy tale
munāẓarah pl. *munāẓarāt*	dispute, (literary) debate
munāfarah pl. *munāfarāt*	verbal duelling
mufākharah pl. *mufākharāt*	vaunting match
naqīḍah pl. *naqāʾiḍ*	invective poem in answer to another poem, flyting
muʿāraḥah pl. *muʿāraḥāt*	poem meant to emulate or surpass another poem
muwashshaḥah pl. *muwashshaḥāt*	complex strophic poem
zajal pl. *azjāl*	strophic poem in vulgar Arabic (Neo-Arabic)
bullayq	a *zajal* of satirical content
dūbayt	poem of two lines (four hemistichs) in a special metre (= *rubāʿiyyah*, quatrain)
mawāliyyā pl. *mawāwīl*	poem of four short lines in monorhyme (Neo-Arabic)
kān wa-kān	longer Neo-Arabic poem in monorhyme, in a special metre
musammaṭah	simple strophic poem
mukhammasah/*takhmīs*	a kind of *musammaṭa* (*aaaabccccbddddb*...), often based on an existing poem (*bbbb*...)
khuṭbah pl. *khuṭab*	public address, oration, sermon
risāla pl. *rasāʾil*	letter, epistle, treatise
amālī	(collected) dictations (often philological, linguistic and literary)
muḥāḍarah pl. *muḥāḍarāt*	lecture, discussion
majlis pl. *majālis*	council; (proceedings of a) literary gathering or salon
maqāmah pl. *maqāmāt*	shortish narrative and/or didactic text in ornate prose with poetry, sometimes with a picaresque element
sharḥ pl. *shurūḥ*	running commentary
ḥāshiyah pl. *ḥawāshī*	marginal glosses; supercommentary
tafsīr pl. *tafāsīr*	commentary, exegesis (esp. Koranic commentary)
mukhtaṣar	compendium, epitome
mulakhkhaṣ pl. *mulakhkhaṣāt*; *talkhīṣ*	epitome, résumé, compendium
matn pl. *mutūn*	text serving as basis for a commentary
adab	good manners, education, erudition, 'polite literature'

REFERENCES

Abd Al Raheim A. Abd Al Raheim
1975 "*Hazz al-quḥūf*: A New Source for the Study of the *Fallāḥīn* of Egypt in the XVIIth and XVIIIth Centuries," in *Journal of the Economic and Social History of the Orient* 28: 245–70.

Abū Ḥayyān al-Tawḥīdī
1988 *al-Baṣāʾir wa-l-dhakhāʾir*. ed. Wadād al-Qāḍī, Beirut.

Abū l-Faraj al-Iṣfahānī
1927–74 *al-Aghānī*. Cairo.

Abū Hilāl al-ʿAskarī
1971 *al- Ṣināʿatayn*. Cairo.

al-Ābī
1980–90 *Nathr al-durr*. Cairo.

al-Suyūṭī
n.d. *al-Muzhir*. ed. Muḥammad Aḥmad Jād al-Mawlā, ʿAlī Muḥammad al-Bajāwī & Muḥammad Abū l-Faḍl Ibrāhīm. Cairo.

al-Ṭabarī
1965 *Tārīkh al-rusul wa-l-mulūk* VI . Cairo.

Arioli, Angelo
1994 "*Ufʿūl*: forma rara di plurale arabo," in *Rivista degli studi orientali* 68/3-4: 221–32.

Baer, Gabriel
1982 *Fellah and Townsman in the Middle East: Studies in Social History*. London.

Fowler, Alastair
1982 *Kinds of Literature: An Introduction to the Theory of Genres and Modes*. Oxford.

Gabrieli, Francesco
1935 "Al-Walīd Ibn Yazīd: Il califfo e il poeta," in *Rivista degli Studi Orientali* 15: 1–64.

Gelder, Geert Jan van
1982 *Beyond the Line: Classical Arabic Literary Critics on the Coherence and Unity of the Poem*. Leiden.

1985 "Against Women, and Other Pleasantries: The Last Chapter of Abū Tammām's *Ḥamāsa*," in *Journal of Arabic Literature* 16: 61–72.

1989 *The Bad and the Ugly: Attitudes Towards Invective Poetry* (Hijāʾ) *in Classical Arabic Literature*. Leiden.

1990 "Genres in Collision: *Nasīb* and *Hijāʾ*," in *Journal of Arabic Literature* 21: 14–25.

1995 "Pointed and Well-Rounded: Arabic Encomiastic and Elegiac Epigrams," in *Orientalia Lovaniensia Periodica* 26: 101–40.

Gülich, Elisabeth & Raible, Wolfgang (Hgg.)
1972 *Textsorten: Differenzierungskriterien aus linguistischer Sicht.* Frankfurt am Main.

Heinrichs, Wolfhart
1973 "Literary Theory: the Problem of Its Efficiency," pp. 16–69 in G.E. von Grunebaum (ed.), *Arabic Poetry: Theory and Development* (Third Giorgio Levi Della Vida Biennal Conference). Wiesbaden.

Ḥāzim al-Qarṭājannī
1966 *Minhāj al-bulaghā'*. ed. Mohamed Habib Belkhodja. Tunis.

Ibn ʿAbd Rabbih
1948–53 *al-ʿIqd al-farīd*. Cairo.

Ibn al-Jarrāḥ
n.d. *al-Waraqah*. ed. ʿAbd al-Wahhāb ʿAzzām and ʿAbd al-Sattār Aḥmad Farrāj. Cairo.

Ibn Durayd
1987–88 *Jamharat al-lughah*. ed. Ramzī Munīr al-Baʿlabakkī. Beirut.

Ibn Fāris
1977 *al-Ṣāḥibī*. ed. al-Sayyid Aḥmad Ṣaqr. Cairo.

Ibn Qutayba
1901 *Adab al-kātib*. ed. Max Grünert. Leiden.
1925–30 *ʿUyūn al-akhbār*. Cairo.

Ibn Rashīq
1972 *al-ʿUmdah* ed. Muḥammad Muḥyī l-Dīn ʿAbd al-Ḥamīd, repr. Beirut.

Jacobi, Renate
1971 *Studien zur Poetik der altarabischen Qaṣide*. Wiesbaden.

Jones, Alan (ed., tr. and comm.)
1996 *Early Arabic Poetry, II: Select Odes*. Reading.

Klein-Franke, Felix
1971–72 "The Ḥamāsa of Abū Tammām," in: *Journal of Arabic Literature* 2: 13–36; 3: 142–78.

Lyall, Ch.J.
1918 *The Mufaḍḍalīyāt: An Anthology of Ancient Arabian Odes, II: Translation and Notes*. Oxford.

Miner, Earl
1990 *Comparative Poetics: An Intercultural Essay on Theories of Literature*. Princeton, NJ.

Moreh, Shmuel
1992 *Live Theatre and Dramatic Literature in the Medieval Arabic World*. Edinburgh.

Rückert, Friedrich
1846 *Hamâsa, oder die ältesten arabischen Volkslieder*. Stuttgart.

Soden, Wolfram von
1995 "Die Nominalform *ufʿūla/ufʿūl* im Schriftarabischen," in *Welt des Orients* 26: 137–44.

Schoeler, Gregor
1973 "Die Einteilung der Dichtung bei den Arabern," in *Zeitschrift der Deutschen Morgenländischen Gesellschaft* 123: 9–55
1975 *Einige Grundproblemen der autochthonen und der aristotelischen arabischen Literaturtheorie*. Wiesbaden.

Thaʿlab
1966 *Qawāʿid al-shiʿr*. ed. Ramaḍān ʿAbd al-Tawwāb. Cairo.

Wagner, Ewald
1987 *Grundzüge der klassischen arabischen Dichtung, I: Die altarabische Dichtung*. Darmstadt.

Werlich, Egon
1975 *Typologie der Texte*. Heidelberg.

RIGID READINGS OF FLEXIBLE TEXTS
The Case of Sixteenth Century Comic Drama[1]

Femke Kramer

0. *Prologue*

A well-known phenomenon among scholars in literary history is their inclination towards methods which are supposedly typical for biologists. Nature, in particular living nature, must be a very attractive metaphor for literature: texts and textual traditions are often described as if they were organisms that reproduce, grow, flower, wither and die. The tendency to use zoological or botanical jargon shows up most strikingly when the literary historian deals with generic problems and classifications. Genres, in the hands of the literary classifier, become species and the specimens are the individual texts which belong to them. Unfortunately, the biological paradigm conceals some annoying flaws – the ineradicable differences between the (pro)creation of living creatures and of texts is a striking instance. Moreover, most literary historians who call upon biological terminology when dealing with genres turn out to be taxonomists of an outmoded, pre-Darwinistic kind which in late twentieth-century biology is, so to speak, an extinct species: the type of biologist who went out in the jungle to collect unknown specimens, and put them in natural history museums as representatives of newly discovered species. They categorised them in the taxonomy of the Kingdoms of Plants and Animals to represent the unchanging, everlasting 'Order of God's Creation'. The basic idea was that a species could be described and defined in terms of essential, exemplary characteristics. These characteristics were attributed a prescriptive value for the species as a whole; deviations were either accidental flaws of the divine order, or a cause to install a newfound (sub)species. Present-day biology has abandoned this way of thinking about species as transhistorical phenomena in favour of a perspective in which evolutionary and procreational aspects are taken into account. An important factor in defining a group of specimina as a species is the common descent of its members, and their capability of reproduction.[2]

It is tempting to think about texts and genres – or, in fact, about any form of intertextuality – in terms of relationships between living creatures; yet a sonnet is not a sonnet because its mother and father are. Texts do not procreate; a literary or dramatic text is a man-made thing. Of course, the human author of a literary or dramatic text refers to already existing texts and traditions, but intertextuality is not the same as intercourse, and generic features are not the same as genetic characteristics.

In this paper I discuss several ways in which literary historians treat generic aspects of late mediaeval drama, farces in particular; a troublesome 'taxonomic rank' because of the seemingly disorderly way in which the authors labelled their texts, and because

1 I wish to thank dr. Eric Saak for commenting upon earlier drafts of this paper.

2 Hickman, Roberts & Larson 1993: 258–71.

explicit contemporary poetical information, such as handbooks describing or prescribing the nature of genres is lacking. This problem obviously does not occur exclusively in the field of late mediaeval drama. Many other historical groups of texts cause classification problems as well. Hence my observations perhaps also apply to other fields of literary history.

In addition to the problem of classifying texts, there is the recognition that such classifications are determined by the taxonomy of the classifier. As a taxonomist of the species 'literary historian', I distinguish two main subspecies: the top-down-classifiers, and the bottom-up-systematisers. Their points of departure are opposite to each other, but they both aim at a taxonomy of impermeable classes of drama texts, an objective which inevitably implies the neglect or the 'correction' of the original generic namings. The pursuit of a conclusive system of exclusive groups is, as I will explain, precisely the weakness of these methods of approach.

Yet there is a much smaller third subspecies of literary historians: those who do not care for rigorous taxonomies, but rather accept the generic 'chaos' as it is. They prefer an approach of genres as dynamic phenomena which are subject to change, innovation and experimentation. Texts, in their view, are made by people who not merely reproduce generic conventions, but may also break the rules knowingly or unconsciously. Authors may have 'crossbred' generic features, created hybrids and launched new genres on the edge of, or even outside the realm of the genre they practised – for "indeed, late medieval drama as a whole was a veritable laboratory of generic experimentation."[3] These literary historians represent an approach which acknowledges the importance of the original naming of the texts for our understanding of them. It is an approach based on the awareness of the fact that the meaning of texts, particularly of performance texts, largely *depends* on their generic identity.

1. *The chaos: an impression*

I will start with an impression of the disarray of generic naming in the fifteenth- and sixteenth-centuries. Wim Hummelen's authoritative repertory of the dramatic production of the so-called *rederijkers* – non-professional poets, playwrights and actors, who dominated the cultural life in the fifteenth- and sixteenth-century southern Low Countries – includes a 'provisional classification' of the material listed in his book.[4] The farce corpus marked out by Hummelen includes 79 texts, labelled with ten different generic names. The labels the authors and copiers used most frequently in Hummelen's farce corpus, *esbatement* (29), *clucht* (23), *spel* (5), and *tafelspel* (7), also occur elsewhere in the corpus of *rederijkers*' drama as denominations of texts belonging to other genres, such as the *tafelspel* (short plays to be performed at special occasions such as weddings and festive meals) and the *spel van sinne* (morality play): the well-known play *Van sMenschen Sin en Verganckelijcke Schoonheit* ('Of Man's Desire and Fleeting Beauty'[5]), for example, which is an almost prototypical *spel van sinne* as most literary

---

[3] Knight 1983: 2.

[4] Hummelen 1968: 341.

[5] *Een esbatement van sMenschen Sin*, 1967; for an English translation of this play, see Potter and Strietman 1986: 53–107. Potter and Strietman translated *esbatement* as 'comedy', a generic name not used by the *rederijkers*, though its present-day connotation probably comes closer to *esbatement* than does 'morality

historians agree, is labelled as an *esbatement*. Nor is this the only play showing an unexpected relation between generic naming and content. There are 24 *esbatementen*, 3 *cluchten*, 96 *spelen*, and 85 *tafelspelen* which according to Hummelen do not belong to the class of farces. Moreover several texts are named *clucht* and *esbatement*, or *clucht* and *esbatement* and *tafelspel*, or bear different combinations of two or three generic names. In the case of collections of texts, the nomination in the table of contents often differs from that of the individual text itself. And sometimes, when more than one copy of a text has survived, the copies are labelled differently. The farce about the *enfant terrible* Tielebuijs, for instance, who is made to believe that he was 'born too early' (a figurative expression for lunacy), and who therefore desires to be carried in the womb again, is labelled as *cluijt* (*clucht*), as *esbatement*, and as *kamerspel*.

Late mediaeval French drama shows a similar generic irregularity. Many texts seem to have been labelled at random as *farce*, as *moralité*, or as *sottie*. An intermezzo in the hagiographical play about St. Martin, for instance, is entitled *Moralité de l'aveugle et du boiteux*, but appears to be a farce. In it, two disabled persons first find each other in a fruitful cooperation – the blind man walks while the cripple, sitting on his back, navigates – , but they end up squabbling about the question whether or not to attend a procession in honour of the Saint. Suppose they will be miraculously cured from their disabilities and thus forfeit their source of revenue! After some hilarious skirmishes the procession passes by and the powers of St. Martin heal both the blind man, who is grateful, and the cripple, who curses the Saint for depriving him from his source of income.

We are obviously dealing with a farce here, and a blasphemous one at that, outrageously mocking the holy benefactor, as Louis Petit de Julleville maintained. Entitling this play as a *moralité* must be a mistake. Others on the contrary have claimed that the play is rightly called a *moralité*. It is only superficially farcical; underneath this veneer it contains a deeper layer of moral sense, presented in the guise of commonness, which enabled the audience to apply the hagiographic story to their own lives. To a large extent this phenomenon finds an analogy in the likewise superficially farcical *Second Shepherds' Play* of the Wakefield Cycle, in which the facetious elements are subordinated to the message about the coming of the Saviour.[6] This is a plausible reading of the play, taking into account its original generic naming. But if it were not for this seemingly erroneous generic name, and if it were not for the hagiographical context in which the play is embedded, no one would ever claim this play to be anything other than a farce. Realising this, one may wonder if there is any intrinsic difference between *farces* and *moralités*, or, for that matter, between *farces* and *sotties*. Literary historians cannot manage to agree on the question whether or not the terms *farce* and *sottie* stand for one and the same genre.[7] Perhaps intrinsic elements are not decisive as far as generic identity is concerned? This is a question to which I will return below.

Clearly, late mediaeval authors did not use a highly systematised generic taxonomy to qualify their pieces – or, put differently, present-day literary historians are not capable of detecting their system.

---

play'.

6 See Knight, 1983: 61.

7 See, for example, Porter 1959: 89–123 and the review of this article by Cigada 1960: 123–4. The discussion intensified further in a debate between Porter and Cigada in *Studi Francesi* 4 (1960): 486–7.

3. *Structuring chaos: two approaches*

How to deal with this apparent chaos? Few literary historians bend their minds to the ontological status of genres, and ask themselves what a genre is, and where and how it exists. Is it a transcendant extra-textual, transhistorical essence; is it a reconstructable set of features in the texts; is it something in the minds of those who write and perform plays; or in the minds of those who categorise them? Some critics have radically repudiated the whole concept of literary classification, or advocated a lenient attitude towards the generic disorder; but most literary historians consider it to be their duty, if not vocation, to sort out and rearrange the performance texts properly:

> Que les poètes du XVe et du XVIe siècle n'aient pas toujours distingué nettement entre ces deux genres [*farce* and *sottie*], cela n'exige point du tout que nous soyons contents en affirmer docilement qu'il n'y en avait pas,

as Lambert Porter's slogan goes. I discern two approaches: one operates top-down, and the other bottom-up.

3.1. *Top-down*

The top-down way of tackling generic problems invariably yields a vertically represented taxonomy, usually suspended from a twofold top level; drama classifiers show a remarkable penchant for thinking in binary terms. Well-known examples are the supposed antipodes *serious drama* vs *comic drama* (Louis Petit de Julleville, Eugène Lintilhac) and *religious drama* vs *secular drama* (Jean Frappier, Jean-Claude Aubailly).[8] These main categories cover subcategories which are either named after original generic appellations (*farces* and *sotties*) or are specified with newly devised definitions (e.g. *dramatic monologue*, *biblical plays*, *hagiographical plays*). Many plays, however, seem to resist being categorised in such clear-cut dichotomies, and keep hovering between categories and subcategories, while literary historians continue to argue about their 'correct' identity. The quarrel about the degree to which the play about the cripple and the blind man mentioned above is serious or humorous, religious or profane is a case in point.

The basic problem of both top-down systems seems to be located in the use of non-mediaeval terminology. Serious vs comic and religious vs secular reflect categories or oppositions which are alien to late mediaeval culture. As a consequence, groups of plays that present themselves as a genre, have to be split up to fit in the modern classification.

The dividing line in a more recently proposed diptic is defined in terms of *fiction* vs *history* (Alan Knight, followed by Wim Hüsken).[9] This system claims to be rooted in mediaeval thought – or, to be more precise, in Augustinian philosophy. This way of thinking is aimed at two objects: study of God as manifested in the past, whereby man comes to know his origin, and study of the soul, whereby man, via introspection, learns to know himself. Knight recognises this twofold concern in late mediaeval culture, literature, and drama. Some of the cultural phenomena are aimed at commemoration of the past, and accordingly at the knowledge of God (e.g. in church: liturgy; in literature: epic; in drama: historical, biblical, and hagiographic plays), while others are aimed at moral guidance (sermons, respectively fictional literature: exempla, novels, romances

[8] Knight 1983: 5–15.
[9] Knight 1986: 17–40 and Hüsken 1987: 42–44.

etc., and fictional drama: morality plays and farces). It may be somewhat surprising to find farce among the genres that provided late mediaeval men with moral guidance. According to Knight, however, the contradiction between farce and ethics is a paradox. Farces may be invariably populated by inveterate villains and harlots who cheat on each other and who are after each other's blood, the only rule in this a-moral world being *à trompeur, trompeur et demi*; but the fact that

> farce is a mimesis of the fallen world where time neither expiates nor brings to fruition, where it has neither past nor future, and where the characters, as a consequence, are condemned to an endless repetition of the same errors[10]

does not imply that there is no lesson to be learned. Farce world in its entirety, Knight asserts, should be understood as a metaphor of precisely the opposite of the moral ideal, as a metaphor of moral folly, with an indirect, world-upside-down-impact. The lesson taught by this ethical jungle is: let our own world be a better place.

The dichotomy history/fiction may be a fruitful one, though rather as a global profile of mediaeval culture than as a means to understand genres of fifteenth- and sixteenth-century drama. Besides, Knight's interpretation of farce as a genre with primarily moral aims hides some serious bias. It seems as if he feels it necessary to legitimise the humour of farce by giving it a superior function,; i.e. as if humour cannot be an aim in itself. In the words of one of his reviewers,

> [t]he major defect in his analysis derives from [Knight's] high-minded and over-solemn view of all fictional drama as exemplary, which obliges him to reject a function of 'true' farce as entertainment ...[11]

3.2. *Bottom-up*

Turning to the bottom-up approach, we find that the starting-point is not an abstract pair of antithetical categories, but the surviving textual material itself, and the generic contours outlined in this tradition. In fact, the above-mentioned classification of Dutch *rederijkers'* drama by Wim Hummelen is a good example of the bottom-up approach. In the corpus of *rederijkers*' drama in its entirety Hummelen discerned certain differences and similarities between texts, and on the basis of these observations he proposed a division of the texts in categories which he either named after the members of the category (as in the case of the farces: this category is called *kluchten*, the modern Dutch form of *cluchten*), or invented a name (for instance: a sub-category of the *spelen van sinne* is called *historiaalspelen*, on the basis of the historical subject matter treated in these pieces).

Bottom-up constructed systems are usually organised more loosely than top-down ones. For lack of a general covering principle reflecting twentieth-century thought, they are not *per se* hierarchically organised. In terms of respect for historical categories, a bottom-up approach appears to be preferable to a top-down way of categorising, but this respect is deceptive. In practice, the consideration for original namings and historical notions is limited to those aspects that concur with the presuppositions of the modern categoriser. Instead of representing some sort of 'natural' order in which

[10] Knight 1983: 169.
[11] Evans 1986: 193.

the material presents itself, bottom-up systems often implicitly reflect the prescriptive criteria used by the literary historian for distinguishing the texts. Usually these criteria relate to intrinsic features of the texts that in some cases conflict with 'external' features, such as generic naming. Moreover, the decisive characteristics are hardly measurable quantities. The criterion Hummelen used for distinguishing farces from other sorts of texts, for instance, is casually expressed in the formula 'comical drama with an intrigue'.[12] Obviously humour and intrigue are highly elastic notions; accordingly both the definition itself and the corpus marked out on the basis of such a definition are debatable.

The flaws of the bottom-up approach appear even more clearly in a study by Patricia Pikhaus about another *rederijkers* genre, the so-called *tafelspelen*. Pikhaus describes the way she established the corpus for her study in great detail: from the entire corpus of 92 texts labelled as *tafelspel*, she removed those texts which contained no *tafelspel* characteristics. Then, she added texts which were labelled differently (*arguaties*, *disputaties*, *esbatementen*, *farces*, *cluchten*, *samensprekingen*, and *spelen*) but *did* show *tafelspel* characteristics. Eventually she arrived at a corpus of 113 *tafelspelen*.[13] So, even before the whole inquiry into the genre of *tafelspelen* and its characteristics had started, Pikhaus already applied a definition of the genre in at least two stages of the process of establishing her corpus. Everything deviating from some sort of greatest common denominator which is in keeping with a preconceived notion of the genre is excluded, and texts that are named differently but do match this notion are included on the basis of this denominator. It follows that it must have been Pikhaus' own, twentieth century (and rather narrow) definition of a *tafelspel* which determined the identity of the genre and its features, and not the genre as it presents itself.[14] Pikhaus' rigorous operation appears to be inspired by her endeavour to establish the *tafelspel* as an independent, autonomous genre. In doing so she overlooks the possibility that genres may overlap; that one text possibly belongs to more than one genre at the same time; that not all genres are of the same order; finally, that some generic nominations may apply to intrinsic features, whereas others (such as the term *tafelspel*) relate to aspects in the field of performance conditions, and others – for instance the term *esbatement* – refer to the intended impact of the performance on the audience.

The effect of preconceived notions on the various stages in this circular process of building a corpus and understanding a genre becomes even clearer when one realises the differences between the existing definitions of farces. Various definitions and, correspondingly, varying lists of the genre are in current use. Any definition modern literary historians can think of is in one way or the other violated by unruly specimens that refuse to fit in. For Barbara Bowen, for instance, the essence of the genre is its "esprit gai, grossier, réaliste et débordant de vie."[15] Farces, in her opinion, are slices of life, displaying the common ups and downs of the lives of ordinary people. Satirical, obscene, moral, or political elements do not suit the name of farce, and plays containing such elements are excluded from Bowen's farce list. Halina Lewicka on the other hand considers the occurrence of such features to be no adequate cause for ruling out texts from the farce

[12] Hummelen 1968: 13.
[13] Pikhaus 1988–89, vol. 1: 12–15.
[14] For a review of various ways of *Korpusbildung* see also Hempfer 1973: 128–136.
[15] Bowen 1964: 3.

corpus. To her, subject matter, structure and "le type et le rôle du comique" are more important criteria, though at the same time she is aware of the fact that these factors can hardly be used as distinctive characteristics. Accordingly, Lewicka's list of farces is much longer than the one established by Bowen.[16] Correspondingly, genre studies based on either of the two lists yield considerably differing views of the genre. And even if more or less the same corpus is used to obtain insight in the essence of the genre, present-day scholars arrive at diverging notions of the farce. Knight's portrayal of the farce as "a mimesis of the fallen world" as cited above is based on a moralistic view of the genre which is completely absent in Bernadette Rey-Flaud's definition of the farce as "la mise en jeu des divers mécanismes de la ruse dans une machinerie aux rouages".[17]

A profile of mediaeval Dutch farce which is in some aspects similar to Bowen's standard of French farce can be found in J.J. Mak's somewhat restorative typology of the genre. Mak considers what he calls the historicising and moralising developments in sixteenth century farce (due, in Mak's opinion, to the Dutch Revolt) to be a serious corrosion of the mediaeval essence of the genre. In his eyes it transformed the humour of the early farce into crude satire.[18] The result of Mak's judgment is a disqualification of almost the entire farce production by the *rederijkers*. Hummelen, as I have mentioned above, loosely considered the presence of humour and an intrigue to be the typical characteristics of the genre. An attempt to establish more measurable criteria for distinguishing farces from morality plays has been made by Wim Hüsken. He proposes the percentage of allegorical characters as a gauge for this distinction. In texts labelled as farce in which more than 50 per cent of the characters carry allegorical names, a *utilitas* aspect prevails and therefore they cannot be counted as specimens of the farce genre, in which *delectatio* ought to have the upper hand.[19] There is no need to argue that, apart from being difficult to apply, this criterion is highly artificial and arbitrary.

4. *An alternative*

4.1. *Keynotes*

> Nous serions porté à croire qu'un même texte pouvait, au gré des acteurs, être farce ou sottie ... En relisant la littérature du XVe siècle, on est obligé de constater que l'on glisse imperceptiblement d'un genre à l'autre et que la distinction que nous voudrions établir n'existait pas plus dans l'esprit des auteurs que dans celui des acteurs et des spectateurs.[20]

With these words, Eugénie Droz took a stand against her colleagues staking out genre demarcations, whereas the surviving material hardly gives any cause for doing so. Anticipating the debate between Lambert Porter, cited above as an adherent of sharp definitions, and Sergio Cigada, who considers Porter's endeavour to be "una battaglia coi mulini a

16 Lewicka 1974: 9–17 and 136–147.
17 Rey-Flaud 1984: 291.
18 Mak 1950: vi.
19 Hüsken 1987: 43.
20 Droz 1935: lxviii-lxix.

vento", about whether or not to draw sharp dividing lines between *farce* and *sottie*,[21] she argued that such dividing lines are untenable, because in many cases one and the same text could be *used* as both. Intrinsic textual characteristics have very little probative value as far as the generic identity of a performance text is concerned: "La différence essentielle résidait vraisemblablement dans le style du jeu et de l'interprétation."

Droz correctly emphasises the status of a performance text as an inherently and essentially incomplete 'semi-manufacture', which exercises little control over the way in which it is performed, and which, as a matter of principle, leaves open an infinite number of staging options. In terms of the communication process, the recipient of a performance text is not the final audience but the troupe performing the play. Unlike many of her colleagues, Droz is aware of the fact that the realisation of a performance involves more than a change of materiality from written signifiers to sounded and visual ones; that those who are involved in a stage production – director, actors, designers, technicians – contribute to it actively and creatively. As a matter of principle they can do with their written material whatever they want; their possibilities are countless, and they are continuously making choices. Precise generic namings, however, reduce the number of alternatives a performance text offers to its interpreters to a manageable frame, indicating the way in which the performance text wants to be interpreted. In other words, a generic name may be regarded as a strategic device by means of which a text indicates the way in which it wants to be read – a view even more important when dealing with *drama* from a distant past. Genre, in the case of performance texts, is an overall, general stage direction, guiding the readers of the 'text' – that is, those involved in a stage production – in the process of making choices in the sphere of acting style, mise en scène, costume and set design etc.

This is the reason why Droz' observations and conclusions, as lenient towards generic chaos as they may be, do not invalidate the existence of genres, nor the importance of studying genre – quite the opposite. They oblige the literary historian to reflect upon the ontological status of genre, and upon the role genre and generic namings ought to play in our understanding of literature from the past. The outcome of such a reflection is that genres and generic names are vital for our understanding of this literature, but that they are hardly appropriate as classificatory principles in the traditional sense of establishing exclusive text groups. Genres are not destined for literary classification, but for the interpretation of texts, primarily to those who originally wrote, read, directed and performed them, but no less to present-day literary historians who wish to understand them. In the words of Alastair Fowler:

> ... genre is much less of a pigeonhole than a pigeon, and genre theory has a different use altogether, being concerned with communication and interpretation ... When we try to decide the genre of a work ... our aim is to discover its meaning.[22]

This notion implies the urgency of taking original namings seriously. If genre is not so much a classificatory category as an interpretative principle, the neglect of original namings is a violation of the historical understanding of literature.

Paradoxically, some keynotes of this theoretical point of departure are articulated by

---

[21] See above, note 7.
[22] Fowler 1982: 37–38.

a romanist whom I mentioned earlier as an exponent of the top-down way of thinking. Before going into the dichotomy of history vs fiction, and while disregarding his theoretical principles, Alan Knight marks the problem of recovering the original meaning of texts from a distant past as one of the most difficult problems that mediaevalists have to deal with. One single text, he justly asserts, carries multiple meanings:

> One reason that so many possible meanings do not lead to a breakdown in communication is that they are organised at a higher conceptual level into larger units of meaning, or genres. A genre is thus a conceptual frame that limits and orders the possible meanings of a text.[23]

4.2. *Implications*

Literary historians who are in search of historical meanings of performance texts ought to be looking for the meanings of these conceptual frames rather than to determine the texts according to their intrinsic features – or, at least, to understand generic names *before* determining texts in such a way. Knight proposes a threefold research program for the inquiry into historical generic systems focused on three "areas *extrinsic to the fictions*: titles [generic namings], historical documents, and theoretical writings".[24] This approach of historical reflection on genre obviously cannot uncover genre notions in their entirety, if only because we are not able to look into the minds of the fifteenth and sixteenth century people. But even if we have to reckon with unreliable, limited, and distorted information, this approach implies more consideration with historical intentions of the texts than do the top-down or bottom-up approaches I dealt with above.

In the case of the Dutch *rederijkers*' drama, three main groups emerge from such 'metatheatrical' sources: *spelen van sinne*, *tafelspelen* and *esbatementen*.[25] These terms, the historical sources suggest, refer to aspects which are not of the same order. The term *spel van sinne* appears to relate predominantly to subject matter and representational style. It can be loosely characterised as the allegorically fashioned dramatic exposition of an argument on an ethical, ideological, political, or religious (etc.) issue. The term *sinne* is rather vague; the possible meanings of the word vary from 'sentence', 'sense' and 'intention' to 'desire' or 'lust',[26] and it may also relate to the couples of devilish *sinnekens* who invariably appear in *the spel van sinne*, exerting their perfidious influence on the main character of the play.[27] The term *tafelspel* on the other hand refers to performance conditions: these plays were deemed fit for short performances at festive occasions.[28] As

---

23 Knight 1983: 1.

24 Knight 1983: 42-3 (my italics, FK).

25 See for instance the only poetical treatise that has survived from the sixteenth century Low Countries, viz. Castelein 1555: stanza 155. However, we have to reckon with the fact that in other contexts different systems may have existed. In the documentation of the *rederijkers*' theatre contests, for example, the *tafelspel* is lacking, whereas other genres, such as the *factie* (street theatre?) and the autonomous *prologue* are frequently mentioned.

26 Some contemporary records referring to the genre with a different though almost homophonic term (such as spel van *sene* in the Brussels records I will mention below) give the impression that these etymologically established meanings of the word *sinne*, perhaps gradually, lost their force, and that the generic name became a more or less void *nomen*, to be associated with common knowledge about the genre rather than with the various meanings of the word *sinne*.

27 On the *sinnekens* in the *spel van sinne*, see Hummelen 1958.

28 This aspect is an important component of Pikhaus' definition; see note 13. Pikhaus, however, does not consider the possibility that a play which does not have typical *tafelspel* features could still become a

for *esbatementen*, the sources invariably mention one vital characteristic: an *esbatement*, the sources unanimously state, is a play which causes laughter, without, however, being rude or offensive.[29]

A significant source of information for fifteenth- and sixteenth-century notions of the *esbatement* consists in the written invitations sent out by *rederijkers*' chambers when they organised theatre festivals. At such festivals, companies competed in presenting theatre performances in several categories. The invitations clearly and unanimously articulate the principal criteria for judging *esbatementen* and other types of plays. Thus the first prize at the Antwerp *Landjuweel* of 1496 was awarded to the company performing the

> ... most amusing, cheerful and funny *esbatement* which can provoke the most laughter in the audience, without displaying any disgrace, reproach, or indecent language (... plaisanste 't vreughdelijcxste ende vremste esbattement ... meest beruerende 't volck tot lachene sonder eenigh vylonie verwijt oft oneerbaer redenen daer inne te verhaelene...)[30]

In other words, the essential feature of a performance text called an *esbatement* relates to the effect a performance ought to have on the audience on the basis of such a text – a strategic device, indeed. The choices made by a fifteenth- or sixteenth-century company during their preparations for the performance of a play labelled as an *esbatement* were all likely to be aimed at this object.

Yet it may have been realised that the *esbatement* in question was fit for a performance at some festive (*tafelspel*) occasion. An exceptionally detailed source of information about *rederijkers* theatrical practice, viz. the proceedings of the interrogation of several *rederijkers* who had been involved in the performance of allegedly blasphemous plays in Brussels in 1559, gives the impression that such generic 'changeovers' were common indeed, and that they caused interpretative confusion *then* as well.[31]

The most striking example of the multiple possibilities of single texts in these proceedings is offered by the case of the *esbatement* of *Lichtgelaeyen, Selden Rust en Beswaert met Laste*. The play as such has not survived, but the records of the hearing repeatedly refer to it as an *esbatement*. The incident which caused the hearings was as follows. After having been present at a rehearsal of this *esbatement* at the chamber *Den Boecke*, land surveyor Leon de Fuytere engaged the three junior *rederijkers* who had performed this play to give performance at the wedding party of his brother, where he (de Fuytere) was to act as master of ceremonies. Since the three were young trainees, a senior member of the chamber proposed to have the performance preceded by a prologue specially tailored to introduce a beginners' play. In this prologue, 'Dame Rhetoric' complains about the disparagement and contempt she has to suffer, but a 'Friend in Distress' comforts her by telling her that many young people are still attracted to her, and still dedicate themselves to her service – a statement substantiated by the juniors' performance, which thereby became more or less a play within a play. We may already

tafelspel by being used as such. In other words, she does not distinguish between *intended* and *actual* playing conditions.

29 See also Coigneau 1991: 204–15.

30 Autenboer 1978–79: 143–49.

31 These proceedings and several of the texts they concern are conserved in Brussels, Royal Archives, Manuscrits divers no. 182, ff 116r-137v; 224r-263r. See also Eeghem 1937: 73–96, and Kramer 1996: 283–92.

conclude at this stage of the events that an *esbatement* could easily become (part of) a *tafelspel*, merely because it could be *used* as such. After having performed the prologue and the *esbatement* at the wedding, the chamber might well have decided to store the two plays together as a *tafelspel* – if it had not been for the subsequent events, that in themselves show even more clearly the flexibility of performance texts. As it happened, one of the actors of the *esbatement* was unable to appear on stage at the day of the wedding: he had witnessed a murder, and was summoned to remain sequestered. De Fuytere, lest the wedding guests would be deprived of the expected entertainment, begged for an alternative for the *esbatement*. The chamber *Den Boeck* decided to send out the prologue about Dame Rhetoric and Friend in Distress combined with another play they had in the repertory, to be performed by three other actors, two of whom also figured in the prologue. This other play was about three fools. There is no specific Dutch name for this type of play; in fact, only a few fool's plays have survived in Dutch. In French, however, one would label this play unhesitatingly as a *sottie*! The play in question, which has survived, is highly critical. In it, a 'simulated fool' (*gemaicten sot*) provokes a boasting scholar and a hypocritical clergyman into unmasking each other as, respectively, a 'conceited fool' (*opgeblasen sot*) and a 'clerical fool' (*gheestelycken sot*). Both of them eventually perceive their own foolishness and decide to change their demeanour.[32]

The combination of these two plays turned out to be highly unfortunate. Perhaps the audience did not catch the layered structure of the performance, with Dame Rhetoric's complaint framing the fool's play; perhaps they did not grasp the split identity of the double roles of two of the actors. Or, perhaps, they expected an *esbatement*: during the hearings several of them refer to the performance they had seen as an *esbatement*. Perhaps Leon de Fuytere had announced the play before he knew that the junior actor would be prevented from performing. In the expectation of one integral laughter evoking play, Rhetoric's complaint may have been directly connected to the activities of the clergyman. The audience may have thought that, in this '*esbatement*', Rhetoric's deplorable situation was imputed to clerical foolishness – whereby the *esbatement* ignored the ban on defamation and disgrace. One may wonder why the *rederijkers* had not been more cautious in this respect. Particularly in those dangerous days of reformation and counter-reformation, representing members of the clergy as objects of ridicule could have serious consequences. At any rate, some of the (clerical!) wedding guests misunderstood the performance and the (moral) intention of both the outer and the inner play, and took it as an insult against clergymen. This caused them to press charges against the chamber.

If performance texts were indeed so easily – though not with complete safety! – adaptable to multiple circumstances, it is not up to us, twentieth century scholars, to reject the identities they are given by their authors *and* contemporary interpreters. A play may be *tafelspel* as well as *esbatement*. These terms, after all, do not primarily refer to intrinsic features but to other, various aspects of the play-in-performance. Moreover, the events that probably took place in Brussels clearly demonstrate the interpretative weight of generic information. Generic information not only directs the interpreters who stage a play, but, when the audience is aware of what will be shown, also governs their expectation and interpretation. Obviously, things can go terribly wrong in this stage of

32 On this play, see also Hüsken 1996: 130–32.

the communication as well.

The definition of *esbatement* as a genre which was aimed at provoking laughter in the audience is to a high degree in keeping with the comical aspect of Hummelen's definition. In one important respect, however, there is a flaw in this definition and especially in its application to the surviving material. This flaw is the fact that it is based on the sense of humour of a twentieth-century scholar, and this scholar may overlook the humorous potential of some of the *esbatementen* he excludes from the genre. But humour, like genre concepts, is not a transhistorically stable category. Besides, actors and directors, even if they lived in the late Middle Ages, should not be underrated in their ability to make seemingly solemn subject matter into laughing matter.

5. *Epilogue*

To sum up, I would argue for the use of the concept of genre in a way other than as a classificatory principle. Contrary to the premises of most current approaches of literary genres – either top-down or bottom-up –, genres are not the same as biological species. There is no such thing as an everlasting Order of Texts; each culture and each period has its own generic systems and, though looked at *a posteriori* they may seem fossilised and unchanging categories, these systems have been continually subject to change, either by gradual development or by deliberate experimentation.

Generic terms are not merely meant for classification; they largely determine the meaning of the texts they cover. In a sense – and particularly when dealing with performance texts – they reflect a strategic device by means of which the text makes an assertion about the way in which it wants to be read; an all-encompassing stage direction limiting the infinite number of options the interpreters have as to style, atmosphere and purport of their production.

The approach of literary genre as an interpretative principle, and of generic names (and, for that matter, other sorts of extrinsic characteristics associated with specific genres, such as styling, lay-out, etc.) as categories that carry meanings, also allows for the recognition of the possibility of playing and experimenting with genre and generic expectations. Parody, pastiche, or other ways of deliberately challenging the audience's anticipation have always been a preoccupation of authors, pre-modern as well as modern and post-modern. After all, late mediaeval drama, as Knight put it, was a laboratory for generic experimentation.

Therefore generic names ought not to be neglected or 'corrected', but to be taken seriously. Instead of replacing them by 'proper' names, it is the literary historian's task to try to understand these terms and their relation to the texts they cover, not just by recording the intrinsic features of the texts, but rather by looking for contemporary reflection on the terminology, even if the outcome may yield groups that considerably overlap and that contradict presupposed images of a genre.

REFERENCES

Autenboer, E. van
1978–79 "Een 'landjuweel' te Antwerpen in 1496?" in *Jaarboek de Fonteine* 29:143–49.

Bowen, Barbara C.
1964 *Les caractéristiques essentielles de la farce française et leur survivance dans les années 1550–1620*. Urbana.

Castelein, Matthijs de
1555 *De const van rhetoriken* [..]. Gent [facs. Oudenaarde 1986]

Cigada, Sergio
1960 [Review of Porter 1959] in *Studi Francesi* 4: 123–24.

Coigneau, Dirk
1991 [Review of Hüsken 1987] in *Spiegel der Letteren* 33: 204–15.

Droz, Eugénie
1935 *Le recueil Trepperel. Les sotties*. Paris.

Eeghem, Willem van
1937 *Drie schandaleuze spelen*. Antwerpen.

Een esbatement van sMenschen Sin
1967 *Een esbatement van sMenschen Sin en Verganckelijcke Schoonheit*. Nederlands instituut der Rijksuniversiteit Groningen. Zwolle.

Evans, Daffyd
1986 [Review of Knight 1983] in *French Studies* 40:193.

Fowler, Alastair
1982 *Kinds of Literature. An Introduction to the Theory of Genres and Modes*. Cambridge.

Hempfer, Klaus W.
1973 *Gattungstheorie. Information und Synthese*. München

Hickman, Cleveland P., Larry S. Roberts & Allan Larson
1993 *The Integrated Principles of Zoology*. St. Louis.

Hummelen, W.M.H.
1958 *De sinnekens in het rederijkerdrama*. Groningen.
1968 *Repertorium van het rederijkersdrama 1500-ca.1620*. Assen.

Hüsken, Wim N.M.
1987 *Noyt meerder vreucht. Compositie en structuur van het komische toneel in de Nederlanden voor de Renaissance*. Deventer.
1996 "The Fool as Social Critic: The Case of Dutch Rhetoricians' Drama," pp. 112–45 in C. Davidson (ed.), *Fools and Folly*. Kalamazoo.

Knight, Alan
1983 *Aspects of Genre in Late Medieval Drama*. Manchester.

Kramer, Femke
1996 "Staging Practice in Brussels, 1559: Lawsuit Reports Concerning *Het esbatement van de bervoete bruers*," pp. 283–92 in Francesc Massip, (ed.), *Formes teatrals de la tradicío medieval* (Actes del VII Col.loqui de la Société Internationale pour l'Étude du Théâtre Médiéval, Girona, Juliol de 1992). Barcelona.

Lewicka, Halina
1974 *Études sur l'ancienne farce française*. Paris.

Mak, J.J.
1950 *Vier excellente kluchten*. Amsterdam/Antwerpen.

Pikhaus, Patricia
1988–89 *Het tafelspel bij de rederijkers*. 2 vols. Gent.

Porter, Lambert C.
1959 "La Farce et la Sotie," in *Zeitschrift für Romanische Philologie* 75: 89–123.

Potter, R. & E. Strietman
1986 "Man's Desire and Fleeting Beauty. Sixteenth-Century Comedy," in *Dutch Crossing* 28: 53–107.

Rey-Flaud, Bernadette
1984 *La farce ou la machine à rire. Théorie d'un genre dramatique 1450–1550*. Genève.

MEDIAEVAL HISTORIOGRAPHY:
About generic constraints and scholarly constructions.[1]

Bert Roest

0. From classical Antiquity onwards the problem of genre has held a central place in the theoretical discourse on literature. In the ancient, mediaeval and early modern *artes poeticae* generic stability was regarded as necessary, and the adherence to generic boundaries was seen to be a necessary precondition for both poetic production and proper understanding by reader or audience. This predominantly prescriptive view of genre, which even in this century has staunch defenders – hence Hirsch's dictum that "All understanding of verbal meaning is necessarily genre-based"[2] – only quite recently partly gave way to several other forms of generic criticism. In this century alone, according to the survey of Thomas O. Beebee, we have seen generic criticism which deals with genre as a biological species (complete with the metaphors of origin and decay); the formalist and structuralist approaches of Propp c.s., concentrating on specific textual features at different levels, by which genres can be determined – which would find its structuralist apogee in the work of Zumthor;[3] readers' response criticism, by which genres are assigned to texts by the community of readers; postmodernist approaches which opt for conventionalist positions and not seldom regard the use of universalist generic qualifications as an obstructive imposition on 'true' literature (which thrives on generic instability); the view that genre and typological classification is the outcome of the 'social function' of the text (Juri Lotman's cultural semiotics); and finally the opinion that genre should be defined as the "use value of a discourse" (Beebee's own position).[4]

1. In the theoretical discourse on history, which is the area of philosophers of history and intellectually inclined historians, the situation is somewhat different. Although history for over a century has been a label for several related, predominantly academic kinds of writing, it has not always triggered such deep concerns for its generic statue or its generic aspects. To be sure, as true scholars, historians and philosophers of history have been more than willing to define history and its methods over against the social sciences, and to engage in more or less exhaustive classifications, or rather inventarisations of the historical craft and its results. We might, for instance, point at the classifications by subject matter or the inventories which list the approaches taken to connect the

[1] This study originated as a lecture for a COMERS seminar on (literary) genres and typological problems in pre-modern culture. Thanks to the generous support of NWO (Nederlandse Organisatie voor Wetenschappelijk Onderzoek) and the Royal Dutch Academy of Arts and Sciences I was able to rework this lecture during my stay at the Fondazione Ezio Franceschini in Florence, Italy.

[2] Hirsch 1965: 76.

[3] Zumthor 1972: 157–85.

[4] Beebee 1994: 3–29.

historical facts themselves. The former delivers well-known lists like political history, military history, history of religion, institutional history, economic history, social history, history of science and intellectual history (to which nowadays we should add cultural history, and the history of mentalities). The latter, pursuing and refining the classic inventory of Bauer,[5] provides us with annalist history, referential or narrativist history, pragmatic or educational history, genetic history, and comparative history.[6]

1.1. Exhaustive as these inventories may seem, in the eyes of many historians they have more to do with the object of research and with the research strategies themselves than with the generic qualities of the end product, the so-called narrative substance, as Frank Ankersmit would call it. And it is questionable to what extent historians see the differences between these forms of history in generic terms, even though Bauer's inventory has strong generic features. Genre consciousness of a different kind is growing among historians, since the by now more than three decades old 'linguistic turn' of the historical discipline through the seminal works of Louis O. Mink, Hayden V. White and their so-called 'narrativist' successors. By focussing on the properties and the nature of the historical narrative itself, and particularly on the literary and fictional aspects of historical writing (both as an activity and as a substratum), rather than on the approaches taken in historical research (although Hayden White would object against this distinction), the critical vocabulary of literary criticism became feasible. Hence much has been written recently on the fictional nature of historical discourse itself and its tropological qualities, giving rise to questions concerning stylistic conventions, modes of plot construction and the power of ideology, as well as on the problem of generic overflow, that is the problem of the fuzzy boundaries between history and literature and between history and mere works of art.[7]

1.2. In the light of these discussions one might almost forget that issues like generic instability and the problem of assigning historical writing its proper place have always been central in studies devoted to mediaeval historiography, much more so than in the study of modern historiography, which, after all, is predominantly an easily recogniseable product of an acknowledged academic activity. Scholars writing about the historiography of the middle ages, however, deal with a far more alien subject matter and an often stubborn corpus of (sometimes barely legible) manuscript sources, that have to be differentiated and to be defined over against other, often intersecting corpora, such as epics, romances, fables, travel stories, and exegetical literature.

Yet even as a mere analytic tool the typology of mediaeval historiography has never been without its problems. Inspired by nineteenth-century historicism and a universalist and normative conception of genre – in which genre is a system of rules for writing as well as for the evaluation of what is written – historians and philologists who are editing historiographical sources have tried to delineate and to judge 'existing' mediaeval historigraphical genres by comparing mediaeval titles, utterances of mediaeval historians, and the content of their writings. On this basis many traditional typologies of mediaeval historiography distinguish between *gestae*, *annales*, *chronicae*, *historiae*, *genealogiae*,

5 Bauer 1921.

6 See for instance Slicher van Bath 1978: 19–28.

7 See especially White 1978: 81–100; 1987: 1–82; Ankersmit 1989: 150–200.

vitae etc. – mediaeval terms which at first sight seem to signify different genres or subgenres of historical writing. Interpreted in this way they can be assigned exclusive definitions and generic properties, which can then be projected on the surviving sources in order to classify and so evaluate them.[8] This has not only enabled historians to sketch seemingly objective generic developments, but also helped them to assign many untitled works and works which overtly had the 'wrong' title in their surviving manuscript versions to their 'proper' generic place. This procedure, which was not challenged up till the 1970s, has led to a predilection for eleventh and twelfth century historical writings, as they seemed to provide the best *specimina* of the identified historiographical genres, and to a negative verdict of later mediaeval chronicles, which apparently did not abide by the generic rules.

Historicist inspired as this may seem – it could, after all, be defended as a source-based procedure – several mediaeval generic claims to 'history' were nevertheless challenged with implicit or explicit recourse to essentially nineteenth-century conceptions concerning the proper object of history and its proper mode of representation. Hayden White has shown that from the late eighteenth century onwards

> the subordination of historical narrative to the deliberate mode of the middle style entails stylistic exclusions, and had implications for the kind of events that can be represented in narrative. Excluded are the kinds of events traditionally conceived to be the stuff of religious belief and ritual (miracles, magical events, godly events) on the one side, and the kinds of'grotesque' events that are the stuff of farce, satire, and calumny, on the other.[9]

In consequence, historians writing about mediaeval historiography have tried to marginalise history dealing with the miraculous – such as saints' lives and chronicles abounding in miracle stories –, condemning it as bad history or as something that did not really belong to mediaeval historiography 'properly speaking'.[10]

1.3. Because mediaeval generic terms in themselves were not sufficient to fully stratify the mediaeval historiographical output, other normative generic categories have been added for heuristic purposes. Hence we nowadays also work with seemingly objective labels like Universal History, *Gegenwartschronistik*, *Volksgeschichte*, Family History and *Stadtgeschichte* or Urban History, alongside of and not seldom in combination with mediaeval terms as *gestae* and *annales*, used as supplementary stylistic qualifications. On the basis of important analytical studies of Anna Dorothea von den Brincken in particular, we nowadays even distinguish in a genre such as Universal History (*Weltgeschichte*) several subgenres: the *series temporum* (ordered by decades or *regna*), the *mare historiarum* (which breaks through the annalist scheme to depict history more fully in a reflective manner), and the *imago mundi* (an encyclopaedic form of universal history, in which history is presented as part of a bigger encyclopaedic whole).[11] This

8 Grundmann 1978: 7–51; Caenegem 1978: 17–54.

9 White 1987: 66.

10 Sometimes editors refused to edit fabulous or miraculous episodes present in mediaeval chronicles, or they wrote condemning editorial remarks about these materials which clearly 'did not belong' to history. On the relationship between hagiography and history, see Schmale 1985: 105–11.

11 Brincken 1969: 47–57. See also Grundmann 1978: 18–24, 45–8; Caenegem 1978: 18–22, 26–9.

suggests that we are dealing with different types or subgenres of universal history with determinable characteristics. However, further analysis quickly reveals the difficulty of distinguishing between all these genres, or, put differently, the substantial generic overflow between them, as can be inferred from articles by medievalists as Hans-Werner Goetz and Peter Johanek.[12]

Insightful as these heuristic categories and labels are from a modern research point of view, they are indeed fundamentally modern, and need to be handled with care in case of evaluative purposes. Whereas they seem to be the outcome of purely 'objective' research, it can be argued that not a few of these labels – for instance the label *Volksgeschichte* – have their origins in romantic and even nationalist scholarly projects; therefore they carry with them a specific ideological agenda and do not simply contain statements about mediaeval generic developments.

2. As long as the study of mediaeval historiography remains a scholarly activity, we will always have to use these kinds of modern analytic typologies, because they do provide us with necessary discriminating elements. However, since the early 1970s one can observe a renewed interest in mediaeval (pseudo-)generic terms and conceptions of history, which is perhaps inspired by earlier developments in Romanist studies and rising conventionalist positions in literary criticism in general. Romanists have discussed the implications of the fact that mediaeval titles (such as *fabliau*, *dit*, *estoire*, *lai*) in themselves were not straightforward generic indications and could not function directly to identify generic categories.[13] The presence of these mediaeval titles in mediaeval manuscripts, even when inconsequently used, nevertheless betray the existence of a mediaeval genre-consciousness of some kind.

These observations, combined with the idea that generic subscription was important for the interpretation of mediaeval works both by mediaeval readers and by modern scholars, also seemed to inspire mediaevalists dealing with mediaeval historiography. These latter scholars therefore re-entered the generic arena with the conviction that

> toute œuvre médiévale en général, et toute œuvre historique médiévale en particulier, se situe dans un genre, et ne peut être jugée et comprise que par rapport aux lois de ce genre.[14]

The problems surrounding the generic qualifications of mediaeval historiography further stimulated scholars to re-evaluate the character of mediaeval historiographical writing itself, either on the analytic lines provided by Von den Brincken, or on the basis of a new scrutiny of the mediaeval terminology. With some simplification this latter activity appears to take three somewhat different, though overlapping approaches.[15]

3. An important step has been the attempt to determine the place of history in the mediaeval edifice of arts and sciences.[16] Apparently, history during the middle ages was

---

12 Johanek 1987: 287–330; Goetz 1991: 247–61.

13 Zumthor 1972: 158–59.

14 Guenée 1984: 3.

15 For a very enlightening introduction to these problems see Schmale 1985: 105–23.

16 See in particular Boehm 1965: 663–93; Goetz 1985: 165–213; idem 1989: 695–713.

not an independent *ars* in itself. Aristotle already argues in his *Poetics* that history lacks form and universality, two necessary ingredients of each proper *ars*. Later antique and mediaeval rhetoricians had repeated this, and therefore mediaeval *artes historicae* did not exist. But on the basis of (pseudo-)Ciceronian and other late antique handbooks on the liberal arts, it can be proposed that throughout the middle ages *historia* in the broad sense of the word was seen (1) as a way of knowing (either depicted as an activity: *historia est videre vel cognoscere*; or as the medium by which is known: *narratio per quam ea, quae in praeterito facta sunt, dignoscuntur*); (2) as something like a literary genre (*a narratio rerum gestarum*); or (3) as the object of cognition itself (*res verae quae factae sunt*).

As a *narratio rerum gestarum, historia*, though not an *ars* in itself, could be assigned a position in several arts of the *trivium*. Going back to (pseudo-)Cicero (*Ad Herennium* and *De Inventione*), history could be presented as a genre of prose writing, namely as one of the main three parts of *narratio*, alongside of *fabula* and *argumentum*. In contrast with these other two forms of *narratio, historia* was characterised by its truthfulness, its clearity, its brevity, and its probability.[17] As such it could be assigned to grammar (Alcuin) or to Rhetorics (Honorius Augustodunensis and others),[18] and it could further be divided in different subcategories. Hence Isidore subdivides the *genus historiae* in *Diarium, Kalendarium, Annales* and *Historia*, depending on the timespan used as underlying structure, viz. days, months, years or a *multitudo annorum vel temporum*. Further attempts, for instance by Bede, to identify history on the basis of stylistic grounds, could lead to the identification of a specific historical style, a 'genus commune vel mixtum', in which the author's voice is intermingled with the voices of literary persons, a style history shared with the epos but also with many biblical books.[19]

For mediaeval religious authors these biblical books were in fact the true examples of historical writing, insofar as they contained the normative *narratio rei gestae, per quam ea, quae in praeterito facta sunt, dignoscuntur*. For the Bible taught true history concerning the creation of the world, the vicissitudes of God's chosen people, and the redemptive work of Christ on earth by Himself and through his apostles. Therefore, the Bible was the *historia* par excellence, the *Historia Sacra*, which from Eusebius and Jerome onwards was incorporated in almost every universal chronicle worthy of the name. And Moses, the divinely inspired author of the Pentateuch, became the prototype for mediaeval historians.[20]

But the meaning of *Historia Sacra* – its doctrinal, moral and eschatological message – went beyond the level of the *res gestae* presented in it. History therefore also became

---

17 Cicero: "Fabula est, quae neque veras neque veri imiles continet res, ut eae sunt, quae tragoedis traditae sunt. Historia est gesta res, quae tamen fieri potuit, velut argumenta comoediarum.."; "Namque historia et brevis esse debet in expositione et aperte et probabilis." Q. Fabii Laurentii Victorini, *Explanationum in Rhetoricum M. Tullii Ciceronis Libri Duo*, ed. K. Halm, *Rhetores Latini Minores* (Leipzig, 1863), 203. Comparable statements can be found in the rhetorical works of Martianus Capella and in mediaeval works inspired by these late antique rhetorical traditions.

18 Alcuin, *Grammatica*, PL 101, 858a; Honorius Augustodunensis, *De Animae Exsilio et Patria*, PL 172, 1243a.

19 Knape 1984: 61f.

20 Note also the identification of truly historical books of the Bible: John of La Rochelle, "Deux leçons d'ouverture de cours biblique données par Jean de la Rochelle", ed. F. Delorme, *La France Franciscaine* 16 (1933), 345–60; Bonaventure, *Breviloquium*, ed. J. Bougerol (Paris, 1965), Prologus, 90–92; Klauck 1974: 71–128.

identified with the first literal sense of the biblical word, as starting point for further spiritual exegesis on the moral, allegorical and anagogical levels. In this context, beyond the conceptual world of grammar and rhetorics, *historia* became a term for and a level of exegetical practice in biblical hermeneutics.[21]

The attempts of religious authors like Eusebius, Jerome and Bede to synchronise biblical events with events in pagan history also caused a sincere interest in matters of chronology and calculation, an aspect of history called *chronologia*, which during the early and high middle ages was taught predominantly in the context of the quadrivium. It was this concern for chronological matters that to a large extent shaped the format of mediaeval chronicles, in that the flow of years and the determination of the ruling years of emperors, popes and kings with respect to Christ's incarnation and with respect to the chronology of the history of the world as a whole became the most common structuring device for large-scale historical writing, and the chronological skeleton to which the other res gestae could provide additional tissue.

3.2. These ventures into the character of mediaeval history by means of an investigation of its place in the edifice of learning are complemented by a slightly different approach by scholars who engage in an exhaustive scrutiny of mediaeval sources for terms like *historia*, to arrive at a sort of phenomenological 'Begriffsgeschichte', which also sheds light on the generic status of mediaeval history and its various subbranches. The outstanding work of Joachim Knape, together with A. Seifert the most important representative of this approach,[22] confronts the reader with the "Inkonsequenz, mit der mittelalterliche Autoren oder Schreiber ihre Texte benennen".[23] This should make us wary of using words like *gesta*, *chronica*, *annales* etc. to construct our own normative generic superstructures of mediaeval historical writing. A closer look at the terminology used in surviving mediaeval catalogues reveals that one and the same work – say the chronicles of Eusebius – over time could be and was referred to as *historia*, *chronica*, or *gestae*. Yet in most cases the word *historia* seems to be the broadest generic term, both more frequent than other terms by which works of history are labelled in the sources, and more broadly used. Actually, the term has such a wide range of meanings in mediaeval sources, that

> Gemessen an bestimmten Dichtungsgattungen, für die seit der Antike strenge Maßstäbe galten, deren Kenntnisse auch in den mittelalterlichen Schulen vermittelt wurden, war der 'Gattungsbegriff' *historia*, wenn man von einem solchen sprechen will, vom hohen Allgemeingrad.[24]

In its most general meaning, *historia* as *narratio rerum gestarum* could subsume every truthful prose narrative, ranging from chronicles, biblical books, exempla collections, saints' lives and biographies to liturgical offices and excerpt collections of canon law

---

[21] Captured in the famous dictum: "littera/historia gesta docet, quod credas allegoria, moralis quod agas, quo tendas anagogia." For an exhaustive treatment of these aspects of mediaeval biblical hermeneutics see Lubac 1961.

[22] Knape 1984, esp. pp. 93–212. The work is a real encyclopaedia for those dealing with conceptual and generic aspects of mediaeval and early modern historiography, and also contains very valuable surveys of the work done thus far. See also Seifert 1977: 226–284.

[23] Knape 1984: 95.

[24] Knape 1984: 195.

decrees. Terms like *chronica*, *gestae*, *annales*, *biblia*, *exempla* etc. to a large extent were interchangeable and related to *historia* more or less metonymously. As the broadest generical term, *historia* often was accompagnied by more closely defining terms, to make better identification possible for the reader (hence titles as *Historia Sacra*, *Historia Satyrica*, *Historia Scholastica* etc.).

It appears then that it is not possible to use mediaeval terms like *historia* to create exclusive generic distinctions. These terms were used in a very flexible way. This might indicate that during the middle ages these generic distinctions themselves were also fluent and based on mere convention. Coercive, rule-based generic distinctions in the field of history only appeared in the Renaissance under the influence of treatises such as *De Historicae Conscribendae Forma* (1446) of Guerino Guarini and works by other humanists.[25] Yet the mediaeval authors do not seem to have been at a loss. Not only did they recognise what they were dealing with; they actually engaged in several revealing differentiating discussions.

3.3. While *historia* as such was a wide generical term with many different connotations, there was at the level of historical writing properly speaking a more specific core meaning of the word *historia* in opposition to and in interaction with the word *chronica*. Gert Melville and Bernard Guenée in particular point at the ways in which mediaeval historians on this level used these two terms in a more or less generic sense to define their own work.[26] The *locus classicus* of this distinction, which in essence goes back to Isidore, is the prologue of Gervase of Canterbury's *Chronicon*. For Gervase the *historicus* uses a specific narrative prose (which illustrates the well known rhetorical view of history as a form of *narratio*) to relate in a truthful manner the events that have happened, whereas the *chronicus* concentrates first and foremost on the flow of years (the computational concerns dealt with within the context of the quadrivium). Gervase immediately concedes that this distinction is often discarded in practice:

> Sunt autem plurimi qui, cronicas vel annales scribentes, limites suos excedunt, nam philacteria sua dilatare et fimbrias magnificare delectant. Dum enim cronicam compilare cupiunt,historici more incediunt, et quod breviter sermoneque humili de modo scribendi dicere debuerant, verbis ampullosis aggravare conantur.[27]

However, Gervase nevertheless did find it worth while to abide by the distinction. During the middle ages, it somehow was a functional topos, or an "appareil formel de l'énonciation", if only to enable mediaeval historians and their readers to map out and to justify their own position against the background of current historiographical practice. The same distinction reappears again and again over the centuries, for instance in the works of Geoffrey of Viterbo (twelfth century), Thomas of Pavia (mid thirteenth century) and Paulinus of Venice (early fourteenth century). Often the emphasis is on the *brevitas* and simple style (*stilus humilis*) of the *chronica* or *chronografia* and on the *prolixitas* and the ornate style of the *historia*, therewith discarding the old rhetorical urge to maintain a plain and simple style for the historical *narratio*. Statements like these enabled Melville and Guenée to distinguish two main ideal types or archetypes of mediaeval historical

25 Landfester 1972.
26 Melville 1975: 33–67, 308–41; For Guenée see note 13. See also Schmale 1985: 105–10.
27 *Chronicon*, ed. W. Stubbs, I: 87–88.

writing properly speaking, namely *chronographia*: "Eine Geschichtsaufzeichnung, die das historische Geschehen schlechthin grundsätzlich in einer linearen Zeitlichkeit fixieren wollte"; and the *historia*: "das komplexe Geschehen, das sie durch die notwendige Ausführlichkeit in seiner eigenstandigen Thematisierbarkeit erfassen will."[28]

3.4. It would be naïve to seek these ideal types in the works of history themselves. Yet the distinction was a formative conceptual tool, which certainly in the thirteenth and fourteenth century enabled historians to make fundamental choices about forms of presentation and about the actual format of their historical writings. When Thomas of Pavia announced that he wanted to write *gestae* which would strike a virtuous mean between chronical *brevitas* and historical *prolixitas*, he was not merely evoking a worn-out topos.[29] The distinction was the leading guideline behind the organisation of his chronicle. This might not be apparent from the existing partial MGH edition, but it certainly shows in several manuscripts which contain versions of the work,[30] which makes it possible to consider the text and its organisation as a whole, for it shows that Thomas, on the basis of a strong dual chronological matrix (a series of emperors and a series of popes) actually struck a mean between the short chronological list and the exhaustive historical narrative, and that he compiled a highly organised middle size chronicle of the world from the times of Christ to his own period, with substantial but restrained historical digressions wherever he thought them necessary for his purpose.

The chronicles of Paulinus of Venice also adhere to the distinction between *chronographia* and *historia*. Not only did Paulinus refer to this distinction in several of the prologues of the *Chronologia Magna* (ca. 1326) and the *Satirica Ystoria* (ca. 1334);[31] it also shines through in the overall organisation of his works. Thus the *Chronologia Magna* tries to combine the benefits of history and chronology, while avoiding their set-

---

[28] Melville 1975: 313.

[29] "Scripturi gesta imperatorum sublimium nec non et pontificum Romanorum brevitatem ac prolixitatem devitare concupimus, eo quod brevitas nimia nubilum obscuritatis inducit et famem desideriumque sciendi non minuit, set incendit; sicut si aliquis multum esuriens modicum in cibum assumat, non famem extinguit, set excitat potius et incendit; et ipsa prolixitas nimia, debito moderamine non frenata, fastidium legentibus sepe parit, quia et nimium famescente superfluus cibus sumptus nauseam generare probatur. Nos ergo inter paucum et nimium via media incedentes et dicemus utilia, quantum expedire videbimus, et superflua relinquemus. Nam nimia brevitate sunt usi plerique, qui cronicas conscripserunt; set prolixitas vitium ut plurimum incurrerunt, qui conscripserunt historias. Itaque invocato Deo ab Octaviano cesare, qui primus universale Romanorum est dominium assecutus, sub quo et mundi salvator Christus, pontifex noster summus, est temporaliter de sacratissima virgine natus, narrationis nostre initia capiamus." Thomae Tusci Gesta Imperatorum et Pontificum , ed. E. Ehrenfeuchter, MGH, Scriptores, 22 (Hannover, 1872), 483–528, 490.

[30] Such as MS Bibl. Medicea laurenziana Plut.12.dex.11, which contains a very fine fourteenth century specimen.

[31] "...omnium enim ystorias scribencium bipartitus est ordo. Aut enim ystoriografi sunt, rerum ystorias seorsum vel separatim continuantes sed negligentes earum contemporaneitatem, aut cronographi econtra gestarum rerum contemporaneitatem notantes, sed ystoriarum continuacionem omictentes, ita ut frequenter difficile sit lectori, una parte ystorie conspecta, consequentem invenire. Sic utrique deficiunt in modo scribendi. Cupientes autem huius amovere defectus, ut tocius universi decorem clarius monstrare possimus, distinctam per lineas in longum et transversum summam libri premictimus, in qua sequencia pene universa conspicimus, sed sicut segetem in semine et arborem in radice. Et primo quidem per lineas in longum protractas partes dicendorum que subsistentes in se conspicimus, in eis enim ystoriographi modi invenies quas enim ystorias inchoant, ad finem usque perducunt. Secundo per lineas transversales earum connexionem in toto advertimus, quia omnia inter transversales lineas comprehensa contemporanea sunt (...) Tercio proportionem ipsarum adinvicem et contingencia regnorum et regum et provinciarum et gentium inter se tota libri prosecutio seriosius manifestat." *Compendium*, Prologue (version of MS Vat. Lat. 1960), ed. Heullant-Donat, 1993, p. 438.

backs. This amounts to a systematically arranged complex of synoptic historical tables around a central *linea regularis*, which is reminiscent of the works of Martin of Troppau and John of Mailly, but on a much larger scale. The *Satirica Ystoria* on the other hand, though written for brevity's sake,[32] presents history in a seemingly more conventional manner. Following as a consequent ordering principle the generations of patriarchs, judges, kings and emperors, it is ordered in chapters (*capita*) – one for each ruling 'generation' -, and subordinated paragraphs (*particulae*), dealing with the main events of that particular generation, including the history of contemporary rulers, scholars, important political, military, religious and natural events.

As has been said before, these archetypal distinctions between *historia* and *chronica* do not, as a rule, lead to a clear-cut typological stratification of mediaeval historical writing. The vocabulary in mediaeval sources varies considerably, and so do form and content of mediaeval works of history themselves. The loose way in which mediaeval authors and compilers interpreted terms like *historia*, *chronica*, and a range of related ones are an indication of the authors' or compilers' flexible attitude towards typological matters. This flexibility made it possible for mediaeval historians to adapt their texts to their own specific needs, and to those of their implied audience; to deal with specific, even exotic subjects, or to comply with the latest trends in compilatory writing. Some examples may suffice.

4. The Satirica Ystoria mentioned above allegedly was written

> ad informacionem morum ut actus virtutum maxime in gestis sanctorum; ad illuminationem intellectui maxime in ystoria evangelii et veteris testamenti, et flosculis doctorum; ad cautelam futurorum periculorum maxime in ystoriis pasaziorum romanorum bellorum et aliorum regnorum.

This meant a great variety of information, which also appears from the title itself. As Heullant-Donat rightly observes, the adjective *satirica* in the title of the chronicle ultimately derives from the noun *satyra* or *satura*, which in classical times meant 'mixture' or 'variety'. Used as a typological category in classical literature, *satyra* could refer to texts composed of several other texts on different subjects, or to texts dealing with different topics.[33] And encyclopaedists like Isidore of Seville and Gratian legitimised their activities with recourse to the so-called *lex satirica*, referring to the principle of creating a satisfactory compilation on the basis of many different and heterogeneous sources.[34]

The chronicle therefore not only contains large excerpts from the *Historia Sacra*,

---

32 "...Ideo ex innumeris quasi voluminibus electissima tamen collegimus exemplo illius sollennis theorici [namely John the Evangelist] qui evidentiora de Christo scribens in fine evangelii sui ait [Joh. 21:24] *multa alia fecit Iesus que non sunt scripta in libro hoc que si scribantur per singula nec ipsum arbitror mundum capere eos qui scribendi sunt libros*. Et IIo Machabeorum IIa capitulo [II Mach. 2:24–25] dicitur *a Iasone v libris conprehensa temptavimus uno volumine breviare considerantes enim multitudinem librorum et difficultatem volentibus agredi narrationem ystoriarum propter multitudinem rerum* ut facile possint memorie commendare hoc opus brevitandi causa suscripsimus." MS Vat. Lat 1960, f. 49ra.

33 Heullant-Donat 1993: 415 note 107.

34 In the *Decretum*, Gratian, following Isidore of Sevilla, remarks: "Satyrica vero lex est, que de pluribus simul rebus eloquitur dicta a copia rerum et quasi a saturitate: unde et satyram scribere est poëmata varia condere; ut Oratii, Iuvenalis et Persii." *Decretum Magistri Gratiani*, I, Dist. ii, Cap. vii.

alongside of *res gestae* of secular origin, but also a careful selection of philosophical excerpts, geographical descriptions of the world, saints' lives, including almost the complete *Legenda Aurea*, and a wide range of educational and meditational abstracts (for instance of the famous *Meditationes Vitae Christi*). All these materials are included in the historical narrative, disclosed together with additional treatises and the rest of the chronicle by a carefully thematically organised group of alfabetical tables. Whereas several of these materials did not belong to history in our narrow sense of the word, they could be subsumed under *historia* taken broadly, as long as it dealt in a narrative manner with truth, or at least with matters of an exemplary nature. Paulinus, writing in the context of the Neapolitan court culture of Robert of Anjou – the pious, Franciscan oriented *rex praedicans*[35] – therefore could present his maecenas under the guise of history with a full-blown encyclopaedia of historical, geographical, political, moral and religious learning, fitting for and adapted to the erudite forensic and diplomatic ambitions of the Neapolitan ruler and his court.

In a different context we can point at the *Ystoria Tartarorum* of John of Piancarpine (ca. 1247). John, coming back from an ambassadorial mission from the Mongols, wrote it to inform the West about the Mongol military strength and to make Europeans aware of the imminent danger of a Mongol invasion. He therefore gave in his *Ystoria Tartarorum* a meticulous account of Mongol history, the Mongol mentality and the structure of Mongol society. By using the terminology and the format of a *historia*, John wanted to express the truth value of his observations, which implies that *historia* here has the classical sense of a reliable eyewitness report. Contrary to the view of many modern scholars, who tried to assign this work to ethnography, geography or travel literature, all this could be subsumed under history.[36] Only quite recently, following a re-evaluation of the fact that several mediaeval historians fully incorporated such travel accounts in their own chronicles, there is more willingness to accept the mediaeval "Tendenz, Werke der Reiseliteratur mit Chroniktexten – vorwiegend Weltchronikkompilationen – und pseudohistorischen Romane zu verbinden."[37]

Finally, new compilatory fashions – aspects of which we did in fact already encounter in the works of Thomas of Pavia and Paulinus of Venice – also lead to the smooth incorporation of history in the wider 'genres' of *speculum* and *florilegium* literature, which became so very important in the later twelfth and thirteenth centuries in the wake of more formalised modes of scholastic learning and new pastoral objectives in mendicant circles.[38] Works of history like the anonymous Franciscan *Flores Temporum*, the chronicle of Martin of Troppau, and the *Speculum Historiale* of Vincent of Beauvais, to name but some of the most famous examples, are a clear indication of the flexibility of the mediaeval historical craft and the willingness of mediaeval historians to rethink their historiographical parameters in view of new developments.[39]

---

[35] Pryds 1993: 231–54.

[36] On the work of John, see in particular Schmitt 1961. Not surprisingly, many itineraries and travel accounts present in later mediaeval chronicles, such as in John Marignola's *Cronica Bohemorum* (ca. 1354), therefore were severed from their 'insignificant' historical context and edited separately "...like unexpected fossils in a mud-bank." Yule 1913–1916, III: 177.

[37] Bremer 1992: 349. See also Richard 1981: 25; Guzman 1974: 287–306.

[38] For these new developments, see in particular: Parkes 1976, esp. pp. 119–120; Minnis 1979: 385–421; Rouse 1981: 116–18; Le Goff 1994: 24–39.

[39] Brincken 1986: 77–103; idem 1987: 195–214; Meier 1992: 157–75.

5. In view of all this, it seems necessary to depend on something like Beebee's 'use value of discourse' in order to arrive at a phenomenology of the historiographical output within various literary communities. It also seems necessary to revise our ingrained negative verdicts on generic overflow. Modern scholars have a hard time in trying to clearly delineate the late mediaeval historiographical genre – to distinguish between historiography proper and biblical exegesis, itineraries, meditational writings, fables, exempla, theological distinctions, or historically organised canon law compilations; look for instance at the chronicles of Martin of Troppau, or at the chronicle of Erfurt – or to distinguish between different historiographical subbranches. Even when we consistently stick to modern typologies the problem of generic overflow and generic instability remains.

Although it will never be possible to arrive at an exhaustive and stable typology of mediaeval historiography, certainly not for the later mediaeval period, it seems that we can gain some insight in the generic dynamics which actually underly the success of mediaeval historiography in many different contexts altogether. The flexibility of generic concepts like *historia* (as a form of knowing, as a form of writing, and as the object known), as well as the lack of coercive generic rules, which had so much more influence in the production of 'high' literature, made it possible for history to appear almost everywhere. This seemingly uncontrolled pervasiveness remains hidden as long as we concentrate on the rule books in formalised educational settings like the schools and the universities, from which history seems absent. History could not be assigned a specific place in the mediaeval curriculum, because it was everywhere, in even so many disguises. And when we look at the combined expectations of compilers and their intended public, informed by their own re-interpretation of received literary traditions, their not seldom multi-focussed practical concerns, and their often not clearly articulated ideological goals, we might be able to track down the use value of the historical discourse within specific contexts, and therewith come to a better understanding of form and content of later mediaeval historical narratives.

REFERENCES

Ankersmit, Frank R.
1989 *De navel van de geschiedenis. Over interpretatie, representatie en historische realiteit.* Groningen.

Bauer, W.
1921 *Einführung in das Studium der Geschichte.* Tübingen.

Beebee, Thomas O.
1994 *The Ideology of Genre. A Comparative Study of Generic Instability.* University Park.

Boehm, Laetitia
1965 "Der wissenschaftstheoretische Ort der historia im frühen Mittelalter. Die Geschichte auf dem Wege zur 'Geschichtswissenschaft'," pp. 663–93 in Cl. Bauer, L. Boehm & M. Müller (eds.), *Speculum historiale. Geschichte im Spiegel von Geschichtsschreibung und Geschichtsdeutung.* Munich.

Bremer, Ernst
1992 "Spätmittelalterliche Reiseliteratur - ein Genre? Überlieferungssymbiosen und Gattungstypologie," pp. 349–60 in Xenja von Ertzdorff & Dieter Neukirch (eds.), *Reisen und Reiseliteratur im Mittelalter und in der frühen Neuzeit* (Chloe, Beiheft zum Daphnis 13). Amsterdam.

Brincken, A.-D. von den
1969 "Die lateinische Weltchronistik," pp. 47–57 in A. Randa (ed.), *Mensch und Weltgeschichte. Zur Geschichte der Universalgeschichtsschreibung.* Berlin.

1986 "Inter spinas principum terrenorum. Annotazioni sulle summe e su i compendi storici dei mendicanti," pp. 77–103 in C. Leonardi & G. Orlandi (eds.), *Aspetti della letteratura latina nel secolo XIII* (Atti del primo convegno internazionale di studi dell'Associazione per il Medioevo e l'Umanesimo Latini [AMUL]). Spoleto.

1987 "Anniversaristische und chronikalische Geschichtsschreibung in den 'Flores Temporum' (um 1292)," pp. 195–214 in H. Patze (ed.), *Geschichtsschreibung und Geschichtsbewußtsein im späten Mittelalter* (Vorträge und Forschungen 31). Sigmaringen.

Caenegem, R.C. van
1978 *Guide to the Sources of mediaeval History* (Europe in the Middle Ages: Selected Studies 2). Amsterdam.

Goetz, Hans-Werner
1985 "Die 'Geschichte' im Wissenschaftssystem des Mittelalters," pp.165–213 in Schmale 1985.
1989 "Von der *res gesta* zur *narratio rerum gestarum*. Anmerkungen zu Methoden und Hilfswissenschaften des mittelalterlichen Geschichtsschreibers," in *Revue Belge de philologie et d'histoire* 67: 695–713.
1991 "On the Universality of Universal History," pp. 247–61 in J.-Ph. Genet (ed.), *L'historiographie médiévale en Europe*. Paris.

Grundmann, Herbert
1978[3] *Geschichtsschreibung im Mittelalter. Gattungen-Epochen-Eigenart*. Göttingen.

Guenée, Bernard
1993 "Histoire et chronique. Nouvelles réflexions sur les genres historiques au moyen âge," in D. Poiron (ed.) *La chronique et l'histoire au moyen-âge* (Culture et Civilisation Médiévales II). Paris.

Guzman, G.G.
1974 "The Encyclopedist Vincent of Beauvais and his Mongol Extracts from John of Plano Carpino and Simon of Saint-Quentin," in *Speculum* 49: 287–306.

Heullant-Donat, I.
1993 "Entrer dans l'histoire. Paolino da Venezia et les prologues de ses chroniques universelles," in *Melanges de l'École Française de Rome, Moyen Age - Temps Modernes* 105: 381–442.

Hirsch, E.D.
1965 *Validity in Interpretation*. New Haven.

Johanek, Peter
1987 "Weltchronistik und regionale Geschichtsschreibung im Spätmittelalter," pp. 287–330 in H. Patze (ed.), *Geschichtsschreibung und Geschichtsbewusstsein im späten Mittelalter* (Vorträge und Forschungen 31.) Sigmaringen.

Klauck, H.-J.
1974 "Theorie der Exegese bei Bonaventura," pp. 71–128 in *Bonaventura 1274–1974* (Volume 4). Rome.

Knape, Joachim
1984 *Historie in Mittelalter und früher Neuzeit. Begriffs- und Gattungsgeschichtliche Untersuchungen im interdisziplinären Kontext* (Saecula Spiritualia 10). Baden-Baden.

Landfester, R.
1972 *Historia Magistra Vitae. Untersuchungen zur humanistischen Geschichtstheorie des 14. bis 16. Jahrhunderts* (Travaux d'Humanisme et Renaissance 123). Genève.

Le Goff, J.
1994 "Pourquoi le XIIIe siècle a-t-il été plus particulièrement une siècle d'encylopédisme?," pp. 24–39 in M. Picone (ed.), *L'enciclopedismo medievale. Atti del convegno 'l'encyclopedismo medievale', San Gimignano 8–10 ottobre 1992*. Ravenna.

Lubac, Henri de
1961 *Exégèse médiévale. Les quatre sens de l'écriture*. Paris.

Meier, Ch.
1992 "Vom Homo Coelestis zum Homo Faber. Die Reorganisation der mittelalterlichen Enzyklopädie für neue Gebrauchsfunktionen bei Vinzenz von Beauvais und Brunetto Latini," pp. 157–75 in H. Keller (ed.), *Pragmatische Schriftlichkeit im Mittelalter. Erscheinungsformen und Entwicklungen*. Munich.

Melville, Gert
1975 "System und Diachronie," in *Historisches Jahrbuch der Görres Gesellschaft* 95: 33–67, 308–41.

Minnis, A.J.
1979 "Late-mediaeval Discussions of Compilatio and the Role of the Compilator," in *Beiträge zur Geschichte der deutschen Sprache und Literatur* 101: 385–421.

Parkes, M.B.
1975 "The Influence of the Concepts Ordinatio and Compilatio on the Development of the Book," pp. 115–41 in J.J.G. Alexander & M.T. Gibson (eds.), *Mediaeval Learning and Literature. Essays presented to Richard William Hunt*. Oxford.

Pryds, Darleen
1993 "Rex praedicans : Robert d'Anjou and the Politics of Preaching," pp. 231–54 in J. Hamesse (ed.), *De l'homélie au sermon. Histoire de la prédication médiévale. Actes du colloque international Louvain-la-Neuve, 9–11 juillet 1992*. Leuven.

Richard, Jean
1981 *Les récits de voyages et de pélerinages* (Typologie des sources du moyen âge occidental 38). Turnhout.

Rouse, R.H.
1981 "Développement des instruments de travail au xiiie siècle," pp.116–18 in G. Hasenohr & J. Longère (eds.), *Culture et travail intellectuel dans l'occident médiéval*. Paris.

Schmale, F.J.
1985 *Funktion und Formen mittelalterlicher Geschichtsschreibung. Eine Einführung*. Darmstadt.

Schmitt, Cl.
1961 *Jean de Pian Carpine, histoire des mongols* (Aventuriers de l'Evangile 2). Paris.

Seifert, A.
1977 "Historia im Mittelalter," in *Archiv für Begriffsgeschichte* 21: 226–84.
Slicher van Bath, Bernard
1978 *Geschiedenis: Theorie en praktijk*. Utrecht-Antwerpen.
White, Hayden V.
1978 *Tropics of Discourse. Essays in Cultural Criticism*. Baltimore.
1987 *The Content of the Form. Narrative Discourse and Historical Representation*. Baltimore.
Yule, H.
1913/1916[2] *Cathay and the Way Thither*. London.
Zumthor, Paul
1972 *Essai de poétique médiévale*. Paris.

BOUNDLESS PAPYRI.[1]

Monique van Rossum-Steenbeek

0. This contribution deals with an aspect of generic studies that is essentially practical, technical and heuristic: what is the importance of the context when we attempt to allocate an incompletely preserved papyrus to a definite genre? Understandably, I will treat only of Greek papyri,[2] but the matter is assumed to apply to other written traditions as well.

Most Greek papyri were and are found in Egypt, where they were written by Greek immigrants roughly between the third century BCE and the sixth century CE. Weather, water, worms or the commercial interest of dealers are responsible for the incomplete preservation of the majority of these papyri. It is extremely rare to find a complete papyrus roll, which can be several metres in length. In fact, we think ourselves fortunate when we find some ten columns of text. In most cases the papyri come to us as small fragments or snippets. The task of the papyrologist is to decipher these fragments and then locate the text within the literary corpus and its generic system.[3] The *context* has an important role in this proceeding; and by context I mean the larger environment in which the text was found. This larger environment can itself be divided into three areas; we can distinguish a literal, a material, and a historical context. These will be treated in reverse order.

1. What conclusions concerning the generic location of a given fragment can be drawn from its *historical context*, defined as the *findspot* of the fragment combined with the *time* when it was written?

1.1. The majority of papyri are found in rubbish-heaps, and therefore are unable to inform us about their original owner or even contents. On the other hand, when a papyrus is found inside a school building or the like, the decipherer will in the first instance look for possible links with those compositions that were used generally in education, such as the Homeric epics, Euripides' tragedies, sentences from Menander as represented in the anthologies etc. The *findspot* of a fragment will influence our view of a text.

It must be noted that the archaeological expeditions in the late nineteenth and the

[1] [*Editors' note*: When the topic was submitted to the organising committee the original title: "Papyri without genre" ('genreloos') was misread as 'without bounds" ('grenzeloos'). Since internal boundaries are an important feature of any generic system, the author preferred to keep the misreading. It is a pity that English cannot adequately reflect the phonic dimension of the involuntary pun which results in Dutch. At the same time it should be observed that what happened is an illustration of W. Empson's fifth type of ambiguity ('fortunate confusion'; Empson 1947: 184ff.)]

[2] Obviously, the term 'papyrus' can refer to the writing material, made of the papyrus plant. In this contribution, however, the term 'Greek papyrus' refers to a Greek *text* written on papyrus. For general introductions to Greek papyri, see Turner 1968 and Rupprecht 1994.

[3] This paper will deal only with literary material. Non-literary texts are not taken into consideration.

early twentieth century attached but small importance to findspots. The aim of most archaeologists was simply to dig up as many objects, including papyri, as possible; the exact location where these were found was deemed to be irrelevant. It is only since the thirties of this century that archaeologists have become interested in revealing and/or reconstructing the life pattern of a settlement.[4]

Furthermore, it is not only the local findspot, such as a living room or a temple room or the like, which is important. In larger towns, such as Oxyrhynchus, Arsinoe or Hermopolis – all three are a kind of provincial capital – a greater variety of texts of different levels will be found than in a smaller village such as Karanis.[5]

The findspot can also be important for the possibilities of dating the fragment. Literary papyri, which are generally very difficult to date on internal evidence, may be more confidently dated when found as parts of an archive which contains dated official, juridical or economic documents.

1.2. What inferences can be drawn from the *time* in which the fragment was written? Some genres, such as epic and drama, came into being very early and they never disappeared. But there are others which show a definite *terminus post quem*. Thus the political biography is effectively a Roman invention. We do not find it earlier than the late republic (145–44 BCE): see Suetonius and Plutarchus.[6] Also, in the words of Stephens and Winkler, "novels do not seem to emerge as a form before the late Hellenistic or early Roman period (between the first century B.C.E. and first century C.E.".[7] Obviously there are no Christian texts before the first century CE. And finally a commentary on any text or author has a built-in *terminus post quem*.

Therefore, if a papyrus can be dated with certainty in, for instance, the second century BCE, we can confidently exclude certain genres.

2. Another feature determining our view of a fragment and its genre is the *material context*. This material context includes the writing material, the lay-out of the text, and the script.

2.1. At the outset it should be noted that papyrus is not the only *writing material* in Egypt. Texts were also written on stone, ostraca, wooden or wax tablets (tabulae) and parchment, aside from inscriptions on goblets, jewelry, weapons etc. The properties of these materials codetermine the kind of texts which will be written on them. In a

---

4 See van Minnen 1994.

5 For a survey of Greek literature in Egypt see Wouters 1975; for a general discussion of the literary culture in Roman Upper Egypt, see Parca 1991: 95–112. Most information on individual authors, scholars and scribes can be had from Oxyrhynchus (see Turner 1968 and 1975; Krüger 1990).

6 Suetonius: first half second century CE; Plutarchus: late first, early second century CE. [*Editors' note*: this is strange in a way, for the genre of political biography was well known in the Ancient Near East, albeit that it usually takes the form of (pseudo)autobiography or annals. See e.g. in general Greenstein 1996; in Hittite (Güterbock 1978, 217–24; van den Hout 1996), Egyptian (Perdue 1996), Akkadian (Tremper Longman 1991)]

7 Stephens & Winkler 1995: 12. The oldest text, which contains a fragment of *Ninus* is first century CE. It should be noted that the Greek translation of something which looks like an Egyptian novel, viz. the *Dream of Nectanebus*, assigned to the third century BCE, is not regarded as belonging to the genre of the ancient novel.

region where wood is scarce, a wooden tablet is an expensive object. Therefore it is not surprising that these tabulae were not used for writing down for once and for all time a passage from an epic or a drama, but rather for all kinds of exercises which could be erased again and again. Also the modest dimensions of an ostracon predispose it for the writing of short texts, such as exercises, notices, memoranda and the like. More than half the ostraca therefore are found in the context of schools.[8] Writing on another material – stone – is traditionally taken not to belong to the field of papyrology. Yet writing on stone provides us with a very good illustration of what is at stake. This material is manifestly unfit for letters, or drama, or the epic. Conversely, it is eminently appropriate for texts which had to be accessible to everyone over a long period of time, such as laws, funerary inscriptions, votive inscriptions on donations and buildings etc. Thus the earliest examples of the epigram are found on stone.

In short, the textual type will be different according to the material which is used; the conditions of the material will limit the textual types, and thereby the generic repertory. Papyrus can carry any type of text or any genre; in this sense papyri can be said to have no limits or boundaries.[9]

2.2. The general *lay-out* of a papyrus roll is such that the text is written in succeeding columns which may vary in width, height and margin justification. The external format of texts often betrays immediately whether the text is in prose or poetry. In poetry the length of the verse determines the length of the line; each verse is normally written on a new line. Because verses are not equal in length, the right hand side of the column is not justified. But even within the poetic discourse we can go further. To generalise, a text with uniformly long lines will probably consist of dactylic hexameters – the metre of epic poetry with Homer as its most important representative. A regular alternation of longer and shorter lines probably indicates elegiac poetry, such as an epigram, which uses hexameters and pentameters.[10]

When the text has the appearance of a regular block, wherein every line begins and ends at approximately the same vertical line, the text will be in prose. The only possibility for variation then resides in the length and width of the columns and the vertical and horizontal margins. One type of text, the commentary, is known to be written in broad columns. There is also the long-standing opinion of papyrologists that oratory is written in columns that are much narrower than those used for philosophy and history.[11] But William Johnson has recently shown that this opinion properly belongs to the genre of the fable.[12] A number of case studies has indeed shown that professional writers wrote prose texts of different genres, such as history or oratory, in exactly the same columns. The lay-out of a text can therefore be used to determine the genre of the text only to a limited extent (or rather width).

---

8 See Cribiore 1996 for more precise information about the relationship between the writing materials and the texts they contain.

9 Yet the roll of papyrus also has its limits, and for longer texts it is far from user-friendly. In the second century CE therefore the papyrus codex was invented. Despite the many advantages – it can take more text, it is less vulnerable; it is easier to handle – the codex took a long time to oust the roll. There is one type of text, however, which used codices from the start: the Christian text (see Turner 1968: 10–11).

10 See e.g. Turner 1987 pl. 45, representing part of an epigram of Posidippus.

11 Turner 1987: 7: "Oratory is often written in narrower columns than history or philosophy".

12 Johnson 1992: 108 and § 3.7.1.

There are some other *prima facie* features which can be used to determine the genre. The Greek texts that we use nowadays show capitals, spacing, punctuation, and accents – all of which are accessories to help us read the text. Since these accessories are present on the papyri only in a limited number of cases, their presence often provides information about the nature of the text. To sketch a simplified picture, a papyrus which abounds in dicolons is probably a tragedy or a comedy, because the dicolon indicates a change of speaking person. When the text uses accents and marks of long and short quantity[13] we may assume a poetic, more specifically a lyrical text. School texts are a special case, in that they regularly use spacing between words and even syllables, and, in the case of poetry, also accents in order to facilitate reading.

Abbreviations too can be very informative, because they are used predominantly in two types of text, viz. commentaries or learned treatises[14] on the one hand, and Christian texts on the other.[15]

This overview of signals which allow us to recognise the typology of texts and genres has obvious pendants in modern conditions. We use comparable signals: letters, diaries, comics, catalogues or newspapers are immediately recognisable by their lay-out. The main difference is that nowadays there are far more techniques for materially defining types and genres of texts; graphic designers have an almost unlimited choice of fonts, of extent, nature and colour of the material.

2.3. A last kind of material context is the *handwriting*. The hands of beginning scribes, of students, of teachers – whose hands are often notable by the big size and the clearness of their letters – and those of professional scribes are easily recognisable. Although we may meet all kinds of genres in diverse kinds of hands, the handwriting does have a prognostic value for our interpretation of the textual type. Suppose we find a badly constructed oration; the interpretation of this text will be influenced by the type of script. If it is in a student's hand we will probably qualify the text as an exercise; if it is a professional hand we will classify it without much doubt simply as a piece of (bad) oratory. This does not mean that the hand changes the text from one genre to another; but it does mean that the text changes in status.[16]

3. Lastly, there is the text as discourse. The text itself can show its *literal* context. The presence of a title and/or the name of the author will create a pattern of expectation when we set about deciphering the text. Assume we have before us a simple prose text which tells the following story: Theseus, king of Athens, has a son Hippolytus from a former marriage. Phaedra, Theseus' second wife, falls in love with her stepson and attempts to seduce him. Hippolytus is not interested; Phaedra writes a letter accusing him of rape, and then commits suicide. Theseus believes the accusation and curses his son, who dies wretchedly.

If we find this text or a portion of it with the superscript "hypothesis of Euripides'

---

[13] See Turner 1987 pl. 15b.

[14] Such as Aristotle's *Constitution of Athens*, see Turner 1987, pl. 60.

[15] See the contractions of the *nomina sacra*: ΚΣ for Κύριος, ΘΣ for Θεός, and ΙΣ for Ἰησοῦς. See Turner 1987, pl. 63.

[16] And effectively such a text will indeed be classified differently in an inventory such as Pack 1965: in the first case as a school text; in the second case as oratory.

Hippolytus" we know immediately that this fragment belongs to a well-defined genre, viz. 'a summary of the tragedy Hippolytus by Euripides'. But if we have the same text without the superscript we may well decide that what we have is just a story about persons from mythology. We will then be much more hesitant to assign specific generic properties to the text.

Furthermore, in the first case our decipherment and restoration of gaps in the text will be strongly influenced by our ideas about the tragedy as a genre in general, and by our knowledge[17] of the contents and structure of this specific tragedy in particular. Suppose that our fragment also mentions another woman, who cannot be clearly identified. Going by our knowledge of the genre, we will assume that this woman can be a nurse or a goddess, but never a hetaere, a kind of woman that does appear in comedy. Also our eventual reconstruction and interpretation shall have to take into account formal matters such as peripeteia and the unities of place, time and action.[18]

In most cases, however, such superscripts are lacking, so that we will have to use other means to identify the text. And this works much as does determination in plant biology: the smaller the fragment, the more numerous the possibilities. And it becomes very difficult when we have to deal with a text that belongs to one genre but which is used in a text belonging to another genre. Suppose we find four verses of Homer; our first idea almost automatically will be that we are dealing with the epic genre. But this is not the only possibility, for we may meet quotes from Homer in other genres or types, such as the ancient novel,[19] in an anthology or in a commentary, in Plutarchus' biographies, in Plato's philosophical prose, in Strabo's Geography etc.

A second example is again about the Hippolytus story. I have found it three times in a comparable prose text, but with a completely different background. The first case I have already mentioned: it is the hypothesis or summary of Euripides' tragedy,[20] and it appears in a collection of hypotheses which are classified alphabetically according to the first letter of the title of the tragedy. Second, the story is told in the *Bibliotheca*,[21] a mythographic manual by Pseudo-Apollodorus from the second or third century CE. And finally we meet the story among a collection of prose stories connected to Homer by means of *lemmata*, (parts of) Homeric verses. Words (often proper names) of these lemmata serve as starting point to tell stories about mythical persons, adventures, foundations etc. The Hippolytus story is coupled to the quotation *Odyssey* 11, 321, which mentions Phaedra.[22] Thus we find the same story in three very different contexts, and although it is quite possible that all three texts are ultimately derived from the tragedy, it

[17] Such as from *testimonia* or existing fragments.

[18] This pattern of expectation influences not only the reconstruction of classical texts which had to obey strict formal rules – for which one must keep in mind Horace and the normative interpretation of genre – but also applies to modern generic problems. When we find a fragment of a detective novel which is located in England, the possibilities are still unlimited. But if the fragment shows that the author is Colin Dexter, and contains the title of the work, we will approach the text in a much more concrete and constructive way: we will be able to reconstruct individual passages by means of our knowledge of stereotype elements, the chief among which is the main actor, chief inspector Morse, of whom we know that he is a bachelor, knowledgeable in literature, music and art, lover of fine wines and beers.

[19] See e.g the quote Ilias 18, 22–24 in *Chariton* 1,4,6.

[20] Ed. Diggle 1984: 204–05; *P.Mil. Vogl.* 2, 44 (*ed. pr.* Vandoni 1961: 29–31).

[21] Epit. 1, 18–19.

[22] Ed. Dindorf 1855: 504. A few lines of the story are also found in *PSI* 10, 1173 (*ed. pr.* Coppola 1932: 131-40). On the collection of stories written by the so-called Mythographicus Homericus, see Montanari 1995 and van Rossum-Steenbeek 1997, chapter 3.

has lost all formal characteristics of that genre. We are left with stories 'without genre', which may be gathered under the name of 'mythography': a crucible of mythological stories derived from different genres, which have preserved only the contents, and not the form.

4. In conclusion I would like to stress that the less we know about the context – any or all of the three types of context – , the more prudent we must be in allocating the text to a definite genre or type. This seems obvious and logical; but experience shows that it is far from being general practice. From the plethora of possible examples I have chosen a papyrus which is now in Vienna.[23] Here we find some forty-odd verses taken from *Iliad* 6 followed by a prose text. This text has led Nachtergael to posit a new genre, the "Homeric anthology", which would consist of an anthology of Homeric passages linked together by prose.[24] In his view these prose passages would summarise the intervening Homeric text. As much as with the other papyri adduced as illustrations of this genre, this identification of the Vienna papyrus is imaginary.[25] The prose passage which follows the quote, and which was supposed to summarise the rest of book 6 of the *Iliad* consists of two mathematical problems. Experience and practice show that papyrologists – and not only they – often are too eager to distinguish all kinds of textual and generic types, to delimit them and and to classify them under 'appropriate' predicates. But all too often this process is guided not by the facts but by boundless subjectivity.

---

[23] *P.Vindob. Gr.* 26740 ed. Oellacher 1938: 133–35. The mathematical problems were identified and reedited by Bruins et.al. 1974.

[24] See Nachtergael 1971.

[25] See van Rossum-Steenbeek, forthc.

REFERENCES

Bruins, E.M. , P.J. Sijpesteijn & K.A. Worp
1974 "A Greek Mathematical Papyrus," in *Janus* 61: 297–312.

Coppola, G. (ed. pr.)
1932 *Papiri greci e latini*. Firenze.

Cribiore, R.
1996 *Writing, Teachers, and Students in Graeco-Roman Egypt* (American Studies in Papyrology 36). Atlanta.

Diggle, J. (ed.)
1984 *Euripidis Fabulae I*. Oxford.

Dindorf, W. (ed.)
1855 *Scholia Graeca in Homeri Odysseam II*. Oxford.

Empson, W.
1947 *Seven Types of Ambiguity*. London.

Greenstein, E.L.
1996 "Autobiographies in Ancient Western Asia," pp. 2421–32 in J.M. Sasson *et.al.* (eds.), *Civilizations of the Ancient Near East*. New York

Güterbock, H.G.
1978 "Hethitische Literatur," pp. 211–53 in W. Röllig (ed.), *Altorientalische Literaturen* (Neues Handbuch der Literaturwissenschaft 1). Wiesbaden.

Johnson, W.A.
1992 *The Literary Papyrus Roll: Formats and Conventions. An Analysis of the Evidence from Oxyrhynchus*. Dissertation Yale University.

Krüger, J.
1990 *Oxyrhynchos in der Kaiserzeit. Studien zur Topographie und Literaturrezeption*. Frankfurt am Main.

Nachtergael, G.
1971 "Fragments d'anthologies homériques," in *CE* 46: 344–51.

Oellacher, H. (ed. pr.)
1938 "Griechische literarische Papyri aus der Papyrus-sammlung Erzherzog Rainer in Wien," in *Études de Papyrologie* 4: 110–41.

Pack, R.A.
1965 *The Greek and Latin Literary Texts from Greco-Roman Egypt*. (Second revised and enlarged edition). Ann Arbor.

Parca, M.G.
1991 *Ptocheia or Odysseus in Disguise at Troy (P. Köln VI 245)* (American Studies in Papyrology 31). Atlanta.

Perdu, O.
1996 "Ancient Egyptian Autobiographies," pp. 2443–54 in J.M. Sasson *et.al.* (eds.), *Civilizations of the Ancient Near East*. New York.

Rupprecht, H.-A.
1994 *Kleine Einführung in die Papyruskunde*. Darmstadt.

Stephens, S.A. & J.J. Winkler
1995 *Ancient Greek Novels. The Fragments*. Princeton.

Tremper Longman III
1991 *Fictional Akkadian Biography. A Generic and Comparative Study*. Winona Lake.

Turner, E.G.
1968 *Greek Papyri. An Introduction*. Oxford.
1975 "Oxyrhynchus and Rome," in *HSPh* 79: 1–24.
1987 *Greek Manuscripts of the Ancient World* (Second edition revised and enlarged by P.J. Parsons). London.

van den Hout, Th.P.J.
1996 "Khattushili III, King of the Hittites," pp. 1107–20 in J.M. Sasson *et.al.* (eds.), *Civilizations of the Ancient Near East*. New York.

Vandoni, M. (ed. pr.)
1961 *Papiri della Università degli Studi di Milano 2*. Milano.

van Minnen, P.
1994 "House-to-House Enquiries: An Interdisciplinary Approach to Roman Karanis," in *ZPE* 100: 227–51.

Montanari, F.
1995 "The Mythographicus Homericus," pp. 135–72 in J.G.J. Abbenes *et.al.* (eds.) *Greek Literary Theory after Aristotle. A Collection of Papers in Honour of D.M. Schenkeveld*. Amsterdam.

van Rossum-Steenbeek, M.E.
1997 "Mythographicus Homericus," chapter 3 in *id. Greek Readers' Digests? Studies on a Selection of Subliterary Papyri*. Leiden-New York-Köln.
forthc. "The So-called 'Homeric Anthologies'," in *Akten des 21. internationalen Papyrologenkongresses in Berlin 1995* (Beiheft zum *Archiv für Papyrusforschung*).

Wouters, A.
1975 "De literaire papyri en de Griekse literatuur," in *Kleio* 5: 6–29.

THE FABLE IS DEAD; LONG LIVE THE FABLE!
IS THERE ANY LIFE AFTER GENRE?
A personal essay and a plea

Anda Schippers

0. This contribution treats the concept and theory of genre in the first instance within the confines of the Middle Dutch fable. But in this connection I also want to suggest some ideas concerning the concept of *genre* as such in a broader context (but limited to historical, i.e. really existing, texts). The central question is whether and in how far the concept of genre still has relevance for contemporary literary-critical research, and what kind of concept might eventually replace it.

1. In my dissertation I analysed Middle Dutch fables. This should have resulted in a catalogue of fables preceded by a study of the genre. The shining example ought to have been Dicke and Grubmüller's catalogue of German fables.[1] For this catalogue, an ultimate definition of the genre 'fable' had been designed, and therefore my task seemed a bed of roses. All I had to do was to imitate – in Dutch – German *Gründlichkeit*. But roses are notorious for having thorns, which I soon became entangled in. The basic problem is simple: historical genres cannot be grasped by modern definitions.

1.1. The usual procedure is as follows: one takes the texts which have been traditionally regarded as fables; one tries to discover an underlying structure and common features; on this basis one defines the genre; then one tackles the corpus identified by tradition. Here comes the first complication: according to our construed definition a number of texts which tradition has always regarded as fables should be discarded. It is as if one takes a basket full of eggs; on this basis one defines 'an egg'; and then one throws away a number of eggs. In other words: we try to *adapt the material to the definition*, and not the other way around.

1.2. This brings us to the second complication: definitions of genres tend to be *normative*. They describe the ideal fable and often function as a criterion with which one may (or must?) measure the quality of individual fables. Many researchers have a vision of the ideal form of the one true fable – often without being aware of this or in any case without an explicit description of this ideal form. Their language use is often revealing: they mention the *battle* against wrong interpretations of fables, or the *falsification* of fables, or the *flowering* or *decline* of the *real* fable and much more in that vein. Reinhardt Dithmar,[2] to give just one example, thinks that only those fables

[1] Dicke & Grubmüller 1987.
[2] Dithmar 1972.

that were written in connection with a real, historical, social or political event and that contain a measure of combativity can be called *real* fables. In this case, the corpus of Middle Dutch fables would be reduced to a single unit.

1.3. Modern definitions of a genre, however scrupulously they are formulated, always have as a consequence that texts which according to historical perception certainly belong to a given genre suddenly find themselves excluded. This is the third complication. Is it not an obvious procedure to use historical definitions of a genre when studying historical genres? This has been observed before, but researchers often feel that the historical terminology (and therefore real historical genre awareness) is not adequate for modern scholarship. Hugo Kuhn's *Dichtung und Welt im Mittelalter*[3] is very perceptive and discriminating on the problem of historical genres; yet he concludes – sadly – that the terminology which is handed down in German literary practice cannot lead to a generic system, since the terms are not used consistently. To my mind another conclusion is much more plausible: the lack of consistency in the terminology points to the absence of a generic system in the modern usage of the word. It follows that searching for such a system seems not a good use of time and effort. The much admired – and I am one of the admirers – specialist Klaus Grubmüller arrives at a conclusion very similar to Kuhn's in his *Meister Esopus*.[4] Mediaeval terminology for genre lacks modern precision and is therefore useless. This seems very logical and attractive. Modern western society does not hang criminals in public; when we are ill we prefer our doctor to use modern precision instruments instead of the rusty tongs and saws of yore. But on the other hand it seems also obvious to question the sense of differentiating in a highly detailed way between animal fable, animal allegory and animal simile, or between fable, parable and likeness, while we know that these differentiations were not made in the Middle Ages, and that they are therefore manifestly absent from the mediaeval corpus.

2. All these modern procedures are meant to force the Middle Dutch fable in a straitjacket and so to reduce the object of research to manageable proportions. The rationale is then that "one is forced to make limitations, so one cannot accept every stray text that bears some resemblance to a fable into the corpus". At this point I realised that I did not want to follow this path. But what was I to do then? And, which is just as important, how could I justify another approach? For as long as one keeps to the beaten track nobody expects any deep theorising; but if you want to go your own way, you are obliged to legitimise.

To summarise the problem: I felt that modern genre definitions were more of a hindrance than a help in understanding Middle Dutch fables; and I felt the need for a methodological and theoretical framework, which could solve these problems and show me the right path to take.

3 Kuhn 1959.
4 Grubmüller 1977.

3. Both points are closely interrelated at every level, but I shall treat them in sequence.

3.1. A study of the Middle Dutch terminology for fables and perceptions of the genre 'fable' shows that the mediaeval approach to genre was radically different from ours, and most importantly that this old terminology is much more than a genre classification which is far too untidy for our taste. What then are these differences? First, it appears that Middle Dutch texts contain no definitions of the genre; therefore there are no normative descriptions. On purpose I have not used the statements on genre theory from the Latin tradition, not only because the time gap between that tradition and the late mediaeval period is too large, but also because the compulsion to classify – a compulsion which modern research ascribes to the Middle Ages and which was presumably based on Latin theory – is noticeably absent from our material. True, certain features of fables are listed and explained, often stressing at the same time that fables have a literal and figurative meaning wherein the literal meaning is *untrue* and the figurative meaning is *true*. So it seems that for an understanding of the genre the 'meaning' and the possibility of more than one meaning in a text is more relevant than a precise definition. This becomes clear from the fact that the nomenclature for the 'smaller genres' (itself another modern term) such as fable, exemplum, parable, likeness etc. in most cases overlaps in different ways. This is possible because all these smaller genres fulfill the same sort of function: they present the reader/hearer with a message which is dressed up in a certain manner which he must do his best to penetrate. This special dressing up means that the reader's attention is caught, that he can therefore understand the message better, and remember it for a longer time. These features are much more relevant, and much more characteristic, than the questions of whether the personages must always be plants, animals, or things (they must not); whether the fable always has a moral; whether the structure is always that of the sequence 'situation-action-reaction'; whether a personage from a fable can also appear in a fairy tale etc. It is thanks to the overriding feature of the 'specially dressed message' that the Middle Dutch fable can take on many forms and formats – which aspect of the genre is mostly lost sight of in the traditional generic approach. Mediaeval collections of fables present us with pieces which we would not accept as fables; but it is stated explicitly that they are. On the other hand, there are texts which conform on all points to modern definitions of fables; but they are called *figure*, *bijspel*, *exempel* etc. Middle Dutch fables show an enormous variation, in actors, in length, in formal features (such as rime or prose), in language register and in the contexts in which they are found (sermons, fable collections, animal epics, collections of poems, chronicles, *vorstenspiegels* etc.). What is more, it is not only the individual fables which can be so different from each other; also the six Middle Dutch collections which have been preserved can be compared only with great difficulty. They come from diverse traditions and periods. Even the fact that two relatively voluminous collections were composed during the Middle Ages proper, and therefore are not a reworking of the classical Aesopic fables, and therefore show a totally different character, has not prevented researchers from lumping all Middle Dutch fables with Aesop.

The provisional conclusion then is this: the *variation* which is so characteristic of Middle Dutch fables and kindred texts is lost when the matter is approached in the traditional manner. Also the mediaeval stress on (manifold) *meaning* is in danger of disappearing if we keep treating it with preconceived definitions.

3.2. The second point is that of a methodological/theoretical framework. The allusions to semiotics and to (post)structuralism in the above are clear: different levels of meaning, appreciation of variations, emphasis on *différence/différance*. This is not the occasion for a discussion of the finer points of poststructuralism but some points relevant to the problem at hand may be usefully made. However fruitful and, indeed, necessary, structuralism was, the poststructuralist reaction pointed to its somewhat fixed and formal approach of texts, since it assumed that (textual) structures have a central point which defines the rest of the structure without itself being defined by that structure. Derrida[5] has stated that such an 'immovable mover' as the centre point of a structure is logically impossible, for one cannot be completely part of something and completely not be part of it at the same time. According to Derrida structures consist of ever changing elements, that have therefore ever changing relations to each other. It follows that also the meanings within a text are subject to constant variation; and the same applies to groups of texts: the underlying relationships cannot be subjected to a single static structure – which is what a 'universal' definition of a genre tries to do.

This can be seen in the practice of fable research. Grubmüller[6] argues that we ought to describe the fable on the basis of its *Bildteil*, its narrative part. The other parts, such as introduction, title, moral and illustration are subject to changes and influences. Thus it happens that in a fable's moral we may find a point-to-point allegorical explanation; but this is not as it should be... The narrative part, according to him, is the stable, unchangeable feature of a fable, thus precluding blending with other genres. Yet this argument is easy to refute. The collection *Twispraec der creaturen* uses in its narrative parts many elements from mediaeval natural science, such as *bestiaria*. Here we do have a clear case of commixture with another genre; and since the collection has 122 fables, this evidence has some weight.

As to 'meaning', the fact that this also is not a stable element appears already from the general observation that words do not take their meaning from the thing they refer to, but from their relation to other words. Thus the meaning of words is arbitrary and dependent on the context in which they are used. Also, language as such is not a neutral instrument, but it is coloured by many conditions: culture, ideology, age, gender... It follows that meaning can never be unitary or neutral. Semiotics has introduced the concept of 'denotation' and 'connotation' for respectively the 'first' or obvious meaning, and a number of 'secondary meanings' in the background.

Poststructuralism is interested in the processes underlying the construction of meaning. An example of such a process is oppositional thinking. In order to control it, Western man tends strongly towards the division of the perceived universe into contradictions, such as male-female, culture-nature; young-old. Also, structuralism states that textual structures are based upon oppositions. But Derrida[7] has shown that we have a tendency to value only one half of such an opposition, and to undervalue the other half. Many texts treating of 'Man'(mankind) treat in fact only of man (male). In science also we find this tendency. Precision is highly praised; imprecision is not. This explains why so many researchers find the mediaeval genre terminology and classification unusable

[5] Derrida 1967: 409–28.
[6] Grubmüller 1977.
[7] Derrida 1967.

for their work, forgetting that the equivalence precision = scientific is ideological, not natural.

Summing up, I have tried to show that mediaeval *and* modern theory point to the fact that the traditional genre approach to Middle Dutch fables is neither fruitful not logical. When I put together my fable corpus I have therefore tried to adhere to criteria that I thought to find in the Middle Dutch texts themselves.

4. But one may well ask where, in these conditions, I found the courage to compile a corpus anyhow. Apart from easily inferable practical considerations, I have tried to justify my catalogue by emphasising that this is not a sharply delimited, nicely rounded corpus, but a kind of instantaneous view of a group of texts that is constantly in movement, and of which group many texts could just as easily and justifiably be put in another corpus. Whether a fable is a fable depends for the better part on the context in which it appears. The same text can be a fable at one occasion, and something else at another moment in historical time. 'The' fable does not exist anymore; neither does 'the' corpus of fables. What remains is a collection of texts that at a certain point in time share a number of features, which features do not even have to be the same ones every time.

Although I think my corpus can be defended in the contexts of mediaeval and poststructuralist theory, I have given thought to a genre-free approach to Middle Dutch studies. Such an approach could give space to much other work of high potential and might break through a deadlock situation. Of course, returning to the original point of departure, the researcher in fields like this faces a jungle of different texts, and somehow he has to put some order into this jungle. But we must remain aware of the fact that we *create* this order; we do not *discover* it. This order is not present in the natural state of the texts, or at any rate hardly present. Of course, texts can be related to each other, and can react upon each other. Precisely this datum of 'intertextuality' will have to play a major role in a new approach to Middle Dutch studies; and I am convinced that the texts themselves must be the point of focus. One should start again with studying the texts as texts - which procedure seems to have gone out of fashion in the field. The recently published *Handgeschreven Wereld*[8] is a good example. Although not intended as a scholarly publication the book states that it is still a kind of depository of current scientific opinion and practice in the field of Middle Dutch. It is a fine book; it is nice to read and has many beautiful illustrations. But it makes one's hair stand on end to read on page 7 that the cultural-historical context within which the authors want to present Middle Dutch literature is defined as follows: "For which audience and in which circles did the oldest preserved literary texts of our linguistic area function?" This presumes a point-to-point relation between mediaeval texts and mediaeval reality, which can never be justified from literary (or any other) theory. This audience and these circles have to be derived from the texts; afterwards this cultural historical context is used to interpret the texts. I am convinced that looking for rhetorical strategies in a text, for denotation and connotation, or for places where the text destroys its own logic (deconstruction) – or all these together – makes a lot more sense.

[8] Hogenelst & Van Oostrom 1995.

5. One can find an illustration of such analysis using the concepts of denotation and connotation in the dissertation of Arie Jan Gelderblom.[9] In the chapter "*De maagd en de mannen*" he discusses the use of the personification 'woman' or 'virgin' for cities in seventeenth century poetry. The obvious meaning, the denotation, is that the city is praised by means of this personification. By describing a woman one describes the city. But close reading for *connotations* of certain key concepts results in totally different readings. Nor does the researcher have to resort to subterfuge in order to do so: the connotation of verses like

> Aan d'Amstel en het IJ, daar doet zich heerlijk open
> Zij, die als keizerin de kroon draagt van Europe[10]

is perfectly obvious. Gelderblom has shown how such connotations indicate subdued conflicts between male and female. The power ascribed to 'woman as city', and with which she devours and crushes many men, is of course in crass contradiction to the power men would be apt (and willing) to ascribe to women in seventeenth century 'reality'.

Having analysed the texts in this way, the next step might be a study of the text in its immediate textual context, for this defines for the better part the meaning of the text *in this place*. In this way, one has already isolated two levels of meaning: significations which are governed by text-internal features, and those that are governed by immediate context. There is bound to be a degree of interaction between those levels; it follows that that interaction must be analysed as well.

A third step is the search for intertextual relationships. The links may be very small or very large; and they can operate on different levels. Of course, we must ask ourselves whether it is possible to link texts from different periods and cultures to each other, or not. In this kind of comparative analysis a 'genre' can come into being, that is to say a group of texts composed for the occasion, and which from a certain point of view share a number of features. This can be associated with John Reichert's definition of the concept genre : "any group of works selected on the basis of some shared features"[11] Maybe the similarity consists in their having nothing in common. Intertextual research is also important for texts that present themselves as a group, such as a compilation manuscript or a collection.

6. Of course, I realise that I have not quite solved the problems surrounding the study of historical texts and different kinds of texts. Many questions remain that I could not easily answer. What about historical genre-awareness? To put it simply: when an author sat down to write a nice fable, did he or she have a clear image in mind of how a fable should look? And when a reader took up a collection of fables, did he have a clear image of what he was in for (Jauss's *Erwartungshorizont*[12])? They probably did; but I think we are no longer able to find out. It may well be that texts cannot be analysed in the same way they originated; and the fable material that has been preserved does not

[9] Gelderblom 1991: 78–93.
[10] Lit.: 'Along the Amstel and the IJ, she opens herself royally, she, who as empress wears the crown of Europe'
[11] Reichert 1978: 57–79.
[12] Jauss 1977: 327–58.

show a unitary genre awareness. Part of the mediaeval fables consists of reworkings of a selection of classical Aesopic fables. These reworkings do not show that the authors based their selection on any perception of what made some fables better or worse than others. And the two collections originating in the Middle Ages (in about the same period) do not only differ greatly from the Aesopic collections, but also among themselves. This does not seem to point to a strongly felt awareness of the fable as a genre.

7. I have attempted to show that applying modern genre systematics to historical texts is not very useful. This approach does not relate to the way in which texts were grouped and produced in the Middle Ages. It might be preferable to apply the mediaeval generic system. But the texts seem to show that the authors and audiences did not think overmuch in terms of genre. If there was a clear awareness of genre, we can no longer reconstruct it. What we do find are statements about the genesis and the function of meaning in texts. Also, the way in which the text addresses the reader is important; and this does relate to modern literary theories. Therefore I think that for Middle Dutch studies it is preferable and more fruitful to give attention to the diverse levels of meaning in Middle Dutch texts, and the ways in which meaning(s) can be assigned to texts, *viz.* by means of text-internal, text-in-context and intertextual research.

8. I remarked earlier that the life in research is not a bed of roses, although it sometimes looks like one. As a consolation and a closure I would like to present you, unavoidably, with a fable called 'Of the rosebush and the partridge'.

A rosebush full with beautiful blooms stood in a pretty bower.
A partridge passed by. He looked at the rosebush, trampled
some roses and walked up to the rosebush, saying:
"O flower above all flowers, give me some of your roses, so that I may
refresh myself with their sweet smell."
The rosebush replied: "Come to me, my dearest brother, and from my
blossoms take the prettiest and enjoy it as much as you like."
Thereupon the partridge flew up to the rosebush to pick roses, and the
thorns pricked him even in his bones and over his whole body,
so that he flew away from the bush without a single flower,
and said:
"Though roses be pretty and costly,
they are also hard and tart."

REFERENCES

Derrida, J.
1967 "La structure, le signe et le jeu dans le discours des sciences humaines," pp. 409–28 in id., *L'écriture et la différence*, Paris.
1972 *Marges de la philosophie*. Paris.

Dicke, G. & K. Grubmüller
1987 *Die Fabeln des Mittelalters und der frühen Neuzeit. Ein Katalog der deutschen Versionen und ihrer lateinischen Entsprechungen*. München.

Dithmar, R.
1972 *Fabeln, Parabeln und Gleichnisse. Beispiele didaktische Literatur*. München.

Gelderblom, A. J.
1991 "De maagd en de mannen," pp. 78–93 in id., *Mannen en maagden in Hollands tuin*. Amsterdam (Diss.).

Grubmüller, K.
1977 *Meister Esopus. Untersuchungen zu Geschichte und Funktion der Fabel im Mittelalter*. München.

Hogenelst D. & F. van Oostrom
1995 *Handgeschreven wereld. Nederlandse literatuur en cultuur in de middeleeuwen*. Amsterdam.

Jauss, H.-R.
1977 "Theorie der Gattungen und Literatur des Mittelalters," pp. 327–58 in id., *Alterität und Modernität der mittelalterlichen Literatur. Gesammelte Aufsätze 1956–1976*. München.

Kuhn, H.
1959 "Gattungsprobleme der mittelhochdeutschen Literatur," pp. 41–61 in id., *Dichtung und Welt im Mittelalter*. Stuttgart.

Reichert, J.
1978 "More than Kin and Less than Kind: the Limits of Genre Theory," pp. 57–79 in J.P. Strelka (ed.), *Theories of Literary Genre*. Philadelphia.

Schippers, A.
1995 *Middelnederlandse fabels. Studie van het genre, beschrijving van collecties, catalogus van afzonderlijke fabels*. Nijmegen (Diss.).

‘I CAN PUT ANYTHING IN ITS RIGHT PLACE’
Generic and Typological Studies as Strategies for the Analysis and Evaluation of Mankind’s Oldest Literature.

H.L.J. Vanstiphout

0. *Introductory remarks.*

The statement figuring as title to this contribution is an indirect quote[1] from one of the delightful Sumerian texts we refer to as ‘School Dialogues’. These poetical compositions date roughly from between 1900 and 1800 BCE. They consist of a dialogue between a father and his son, or a student and a teacher, or a pupil and his mentor (an older student) etc.. They treat of the life and tribulations of the pupil at the school, or Eduba in Sumerian.[2] But most importantly, they often give us many details of the curriculum used in school and even now and then some indication of the methods used.[3]

The aptness of this quote for our business may be thought to be obvious: to be able to put everything in its correct place is one of the literary skills the student has to acquire. As Sjöberg remarked quite some time ago,[4] this means the identification of text quotes. Now this would work perfectly well on the level of the explicit and active mastery of the Sumerian scholarly literature *in toto* – which is feasible in the light of the stupendous feats human memory is capable of. But it is important to note that this can hardly be expected from a junior scholar, and also that the education of a junior scholar is an education in writing, first and foremost. Therefore it is reasonable to assume that the intention of the requirement is to develop an ability to ‘place’ a line or a fragment in a composition on the grounds of its formal, semantic and stylistic poetic properties.[5] This, in turn, means that the formal properties of the ‘unknown’ line or fragment are used to reconstruct, as it were, its immediate literary context – much as we do today when we try to solve the puzzles in the *Times Literary Supplement*. Ultimately, this ability at least initially depends upon a sense of a clear and unequivocal generic system: the first thing you do is to look for features which can place the line or fragment in a few broad classes which may then be refined into more precise types etc. Our quote therefore implies three things:

(a) it indicates the use of a generic system;
(b) a grasp of this generic system is part of the ‘scribal arts and sciences’;[6]
(c) it follows that such a generic system must be consciously and explicitly present.

1 For the curious, its antiphrase is found in Sjöberg 1975: 163. Those who know the author will have suspected anyway.
2 For the school see most handily Sjöberg 1975; for the tablet as an educational tool, and its implications for the curriculum etc., see Veldhuis 1996 and this volume.
3 For some examples of the genre see Vanstiphout 1997a.
4 Sjöberg 1975: 172.
5 See van Rossum in this volume.
6 nam-dub-šar-ra in Sumerian; *ṭupšarrutu* in Akkadian; the most correct translation seems to be ‘tabletology’.

The last observation is of specific importance. It is an axiom that every linguistic community has an intuitive or implicit sense of a generic system, or at the very least a typological grid. It does not matter very much whether the literature in question is oral or written, or even whether we are dealing with poetic 'texts' in a strict sense or not. But the implications as listed above indicate that this is not the case here. To the contrary, the chances are very much that we are in the presence of an explicit, conscious and articulate generic system. The urgent questions then seem to be:

i: How explicit is this system?
ii: In what manner is the validity or function of this system perceived?
iii: What does the system look like?

1. The literature of the Ancient Near East – mankind's oldest literature – is in the happy circumstance of being free from the procrustean bed of classical generic theory on chronological grounds alone. Unless one assumes classical theory to be universal, which tended to happen in the Western European classicist and romantic periods,[7] and which still applies in a sense to Northrop Frye's criticism,[8] it would be starkly anachronistic to proceed otherwise. Therefore I think it would not be a sensible use of time to try and reduce the Ancient Near Eastern poetry to say the Horatian system, or to the system falsely and naively ascribed by the Romantics to Aristotle. This is not so much because I would somehow doubt the reality of the classical system as it is represented to us – which by the way I do[9] – but because in Ancient Near Eastern literature it makes no sense at all to construct a normative, *ante rem* , system to which the historical data should be made to conform.[10] We have not the slightest indication of the existence of such a thing in the Ancient Near East; what is more, there are plenty of indications of something completely different. This does not mean that I refute normative generic systems, or *ante rem* guidelines for the creation of texts. There are a number of literary periods in Western Europe where such principles were certainly important on some level. But it did not exist in the Ancient Near East.

This state of affairs has led modern scholars of the Ancient Near East too often to take a *soi-disant* 'pragmatic' position, which orders the literary material into discrete groups according to modern insights, or to single features.[11] This is basically a *post rem* taxonomy. The embarrassing thing is that no two classifiers agree, and, which is worse, that almost no individual work, upon close reading, seems to fit the categories. The reason is that texts are grouped usually according to one or a very few features. These features then are taken to identify the class as such over against another class,

[7] See Genette 1977.
[8] See e.g. Frye 1951 and 1957.
[9] This calls for a qualification. Surely the classical system has reality value; but this classical system is not precisely what we suppose it to have been. It fulfilled other needs; it was first and foremost a pragmatic guide, based upon a parental model and expressed in craft terminology, and far less a theory of genre. In fact, abstract thought or reflexion is either about external effect or intention rather than about poetic features (as in Aristotle's 'theory' of tragedy), or non-existent, as in Horace. I find myself much in agreement with Rosenmeyer's conclusion that "the availability of the parental model helped to forestall the recognition of any need for an authentic theory of genres" (Rosenmeyer 1985: 82).
[10] See Edzard 1994a, who defines the Gilgamesh stories as 'fairy tales' on the basis of the definition of 'fairy tale' in a modern, i.e. post-Grimm German handbook.
[11] An example is Longman 1991, which is otherwise a very fine study.

which again shares a single or very few properties. Moreover, the features are chosen because of their easy identification, not because of their dominant character in the text or group. Lastly, the 'identity' of the identifying features across texts or groups sometimes turns out to be a mirage rather than reality. All this brings to mind Borges' *Celestial Emporium of Benevolent Knowledge*:

> On those remote pages it is written that animals are divided into (a) those that belong to the Emperor, (b) embalmed ones, (c) those that are trained, (d) suckling pigs, (e) mermaids, (f) fabulous ones, (g) stray dogs, (h) those that are included in this classification, (i) those that tremble as if they were mad, (j) innumerable ones, (k) those drawn with a fine camel's hair brush, (l) others, (m) those that have just broken a flower vase, (n) those that resemble flies from a distance.[12]

It is a cause for worry that too often our own classification schemes do not really take us much beyond this point. I do not mean that the classifications we use are worthless: from a practical point of view they are very useful; indeed they are often indispensable. The point is that only in recent years some of us[13] have tried to reach out beyond this stage.

Finally, the unalterable fact that the Mesopotamians never explicitly formulated a framework for their generic system, let alone handed it down, does not mean that it did not exist. By the same reasoning one might as well say – as some Assyriologists still do – that they did not have a theory of language, of writing or of mathematics, which is demonstrably false. Nor does the lack of such an explicit theory necessarily condemn us to mute passivity or nihilistic acceptance. On the contrary, as I see it we have a duty to try to find the answers to our problems in the textual material itself, which means *in re*. I realise that this principle applies to any literary system, including those that have superimposed an explicit genre theory over their historic products. In the case of Mesopotamia we are fortunate in that the material by its very materiality is better preserved than much later literature.

2.1. To start we can infer the existence and the operation of an active generic consciousness from a number of *indirect indications*, such as the quote which heads this contribution. There are many more of those, and close reading of the texts from the Academic environment – when they finally appear in definitive editions – will reveal many details.

But there are also a number of *direct indications*. Best known are the *catalogue texts*.[14] These are lists of incipits of literary compositions, the majority of which we know to have been much studied in the Old Babylonian[15] schools. There are a number of these catalogues, and while some may have been simple inventories of the personal

---

12 Borges 1974: 708.

13 Vanstiphout 1986a; Michalowski 1989: 4–8 ; Longman 1991: 3–21 and 39–48; Dobbs-Allsopp 1993: 15–26; Edzard 1994; and more recently Tinney 1996: 11–25. In the summer of 1995 the Department of Semitic Languages and Cultures of Groningen University organised a workshop on genre in the Mesopotamian Literatures, the proceedings of which are forthcoming.

14 See the entry 'Kataloge (literarische)' in the *Reallexikon der Assyriologie*.

15 The term 'Old Babylonian' is purely chronological. It refers to the first two or three centuries of the second millennium BCE (more precisely this is Early Old Babylonian) which gave us the bulk of standard Sumerian literature, mainly from the schools in Nippur, Ur, Kish and Sippar.

library of a teacher or even a private person, there are a small number of them[16] that manifestly go beyond this, in having grouped the incipits according to subjest matter, mode (in the Fowlerian sense), and observable formal properties of the pieces in question. Taken together these criteria might well qualify as generic distinctions. Thus we find in these catalogues a number of longish hymns, followed by the longer narrative texts representing the cycles of Uruk and of Gilgamesh, some of the narrative texts about the deeds of the gods, some of the literary debates and even the school dialogues etc. Although there are some deviations, the lists as such with regard to their articulation and grouping are essentially the same[17] on the three main exemplars – which come from three different cities.

Also there is the matter of *tablet formats* and their *distribution*. Our material is so bountiful that we can with some degree of assurance relate the manner of publication to certain literary types. Some works we find only in a few copies. In other cases we have many very popular works,[18] which exist in a range of different formats: complete 'library' copies,[19] series of extracts,[20] and 'exercise' tablets.[21]

This threefold distribution, which generally shows more well-written *extract series* than exemplars of the two other types (that is, complete editions on one tablet, or exercise tablets containing random extracts), seems to be typical for three genres: the great hymns, the great heroic narratives, and the great divine stories.

There are also *unica*, i.e. compositions which are found in only one copy. The hypothesis that this is to be attributed to the fortunes of excavation is now no longer tenable, excepting some notable cases.[22] These *unica* represent an interesting but as yet unsolved problem; provisionally it might be pointed out that *unica* often represent elegiac or erotic poetry. This may well lead to the not unreasonable assumption that these pieces were composed for specific and unique events at the royal court or the temple, and that they therefore did not make the Academic canon.

What is more, these *unica* sometimes appear on *compilation tablets*, i.e. tablets containing more than one composition. These relatively large tablets are another indication

[16] See e.g. Kramer 1942, 1943, 1961 and 1980. See also Hallo 1982.

[17] Although the *order* is not, which seems to prove my point.

[18] Thus the Nippur Lament has been reconstructed from 31 tablets from Nippur alone. See Tinney 1996: 90–94.

[19] Contrary to expectation the complete 'library' copies are not generally the best texts! See e.g. Cooper 1983: 41.

[20] See Cooper 1983: 45; Heimpel 1981: 71–72; Tinney 1996: 88–89. Often, but not always, one can arrange these extract tablets into different series containing the whole composition and written by the same hand. The most usual formats contain 50, 60, 70 or 80 lines (i.e. 25, 30, 35 or 40 lines per face) and are traceable by 'catch-lines': tablet no. 2 starts by repeating the last line of tablet no. 1. For an example see Vanstiphout 1987. For a possible relevance of numbers of lines of the extracts, see Vanstiphout 1986b. There are also 'half' or 'third' tablets, which contain more than one column per side, and have divided the long composition into two or three parts. This format practically *always* represents complete editions on several tablets. Actually 'extract' is a somewhat unfortunate term; it is almost certain that we should be thinking along the lines of 'editions' comprising several 'volumes' – i.e. tablets – which together form the complete edition.

[21] The real exercises, which can often be recognised by clumsy handwriting, mistakes and generally careless preparation of the tablet show no regular division in line numbers, as the 'extracts' do. They can contain any number of lines, from 3 to 20, and no 'preceding' or 'following' tablets are found. They are also few in number for the major compositions.

[22] Such as the *Marriage of Martu* (semi-mythological heroic/divine story) and possibly the Sargon Legend (heroic story), for which compositions see Klein 1997 and Cooper & Heimpel 1983 respectively. There is no apparent reason why these poems should exist in only one exemplar. The first poem is actually present on a catalogue tablet from the city of Ur, while the only *exemplar* we have comes from the city of Nippur.

of the generic approach. They generally contain between three and ten relatively short compositions. In a number of cases these contain erotic poetry, in which case the term 'anthology' might be more fitting, especially since as I indicated above these pieces are often found only there. In other cases, however, they may contain an assemblage of proverbs,[23] fables, exempla, and short didactic pieces including versions of some of our 'school dialogues' and the like. Since these texts are generally well known from other sources and in other formats, the term 'chrestomathy' seems to apply here. This is interesting, since the procedure illustrates a grouping and subdivision of the literary material as conceived and applied by the Mesopotamians themselves, which makes sense as to content and structure of the texts, and which is also expressed materially. In one way or another the same can be said of the other considerations of format and distribution as mentioned above.

While it is realised that such considerations apply in many other literatures as well, and that the matter should be investigated in much more detail in our case, the point I am trying to make is that these formal phenomena are manifestly based on a recuperable generic consciousness, or even intention.

What is more, the range of preferred formats highlights at least one of the applications[24] of the generic system: it runs parallel to what we can reasonably infer as the structure of the literary curriculum.[25] Therefore the articulation into several preferred formats, reflecting an articulation into distinct genres, is used *also* for its *function in the Academy*. A reconstruction of the articulation over time of the literary curriculum along the following lines seems not too unreasonable, although it is presented here with many reserves and hesitations.

1st grade:	Proverbs, exempla, fables, short didactic pieces.[26]
2nd grade:	'School texts',[27] longer didactic pieces,[28] debates.
3rd grade:	Hymns, odes, performative texts.
4th grade:	Major hymnic, lyric or 'historical' texts[29] (possibly also performative).
5th grade:	Major narrative poems about heroes or gods; reflective poems.

However provisional this scheme is, the first two 'grades' are based more or less firmly on two considerations. First grade texts occur on compilation tablets, sometimes together

23 As in most independent proverb collections, these are grouped thematically.

24 I use the term 'application', because at present I do not regard as probable the radical solution which would have it that the function in the curriculum is the basic or only *fons et origo* of the generic system. But Tinney's remarks on ethnic versus critical genre (although not applicable as such to the matter at hand) may yet force me to reconsider (Tinney 1996: 11–15 and 16–24). On the other hand, the Sperber-Wilson approach (Sperber & Wilson 1995), insisting among other things upon the cognitive aspects of genre and type might be more appropriate and, which is more important, more fruitful in our case.

25 A provisional overview of the literary curriculum is found in Molina Martos 1996.

26 The short didactic pieces may be disguised as 'other genres', but their true function is betrayed by their distribution, which in turn gives powerful hints for their stylistic and structural analysis. Thus one of the first running texts to be studied for 'Sumerian 001' – still now – appears as an ode to king Lipit-Eshtar (1934–1924 BCE). See Vanstiphout 1978, 1979 and 1980.

27 I.e. texts about the school.

28 These can be practical or ethical in nature: thus we have a kind of georgica , but also 'ethical instructions'. See Civil 1993 and Alster 1974 respectively.

29 Such as the 'historical lamentations', about which more later.

with lexical teaching material.[30] Second grade 'books', if short enough, will also appear in compilations, sometimes together with first grade material. Both grades show a preponderance of exercise tablets over 'master copies' or complete editions. The three subsequent grades can be distinguished as to the falling off of the percentage of exercise tablets and the increase of well-executed complete editions.[31]

Thus it seems clear that the Academic function as well reflects a conscious generic system. But it is important to note that this is merely a reflection: the Academic function is not identical or even isomorphic to the generic system,[32]

2.2. Our material, again by its very materiality, also allows us to trace the *origin* of certain genres. A genre can come into being in different ways. I will mention here only these cases which are more or less easily detectable in our material.

2.2.1. First there is the traceable evolution of distinct genres by *spontaneous development from concrete situations*. In an excellent study of the matter, Todorov has illustrated how in Luba (a Congolese language) the simple and concrete situation of a meeting followed by an invitation has led to a specific kind of panegyric appellation or salutation poetry.[33] In Mesopotamia something comparable seems to have happened, in the following way. We possess a great volume[34] of praise poetry which we collectively refer to as 'hymns'. A very rough subdivision can be made as to the object; that is:

(a) odes to the king, mainly in his functions vis-à-vis gods, temple, and city;
(b) odes to the king as such;
(c) hymns and/or prayers to gods, temples and cities.

From very early on we find inscriptions, mainly on parts of temples or other important buildings in a city or even smaller but precious objects, identifying a ruler (or high priest) as the person who has dedicated the object or built the structure. These inscriptions are very short; in general they simply identify the donator, his donation and sometimes the occasion of his act. Gradually these simple, non-poetic inscriptions grow by accumulation. The identification becomes longer, since the ruler wants to get in as many of his titles as possible; these titles again can be parallelled by his personal characteristics. Thus a high-flown titulature evolves. This in turn has led, in a much freer style, to *odes* extolling the king as such. These odes may be put in the first person (the 'original' mode) or in the second, implying that then it is the population that praises the king in his functions and/or for his personal properties.

Now the reason for the dedicatory inscription in the 'original' form was usually a building activity. This leads to a first variant type, the *building hymn*. Again in a much

[30] See Veldhuis in this volume.

[31] Three additional remarks seem in order. (a) The division between grades 4 and 5 is at this moment merely an impression; it may turn out to be imaginary. (b) Grades 4 and 5 are represented on the major literary catalogues. (c) Individual genres can apparently straddle grades: thus some disputations might be placed in grade 2 on account of their appearance in compilations tablets together with clearly first grade material; on the other hand, they may appear on the major literary catalogues as well.

[32] As illustrated in the preceding footnote.

[33] Todorov 1976.

[34] In fact, M. Civil estimates that about 25% of Standard Sumerian poetry belongs to the specific type of royal odes alone. A succinct presentation of the hymnal genre is Edzard 1994b.

freer style this type praisingly tells of the occasion for the construction work, of the ruler's building activity itself, but also of the consequent excellence of the building. Sometimes this happens at great length.[35] A third variant type, insisting on the typical Mesopotamian notion of the endurance and supremacy of temples and cities, concentrates on the temple or city itself, thus completely disregarding the builder. It is not impossible that the great collection[36] of short *Temple/City hymns*, a kind of model for this type, also had a function in the temple cult.

Lastly there also had existed since time immemorial an independent type of *Hymn to the gods*. In a number of cases the 'pure' divine hymn becomes contaminated, as it were, by either the royal ode, so that a hymn (or ode!) is addressed to the king as much as to his tutelary deity; more often the divine hymn becomes mixed with the temple/city hymn: one of the greatest of divine hymns, appropriately dedicated to the chief deity Enlil, is as much a hymn to his city Nippur as it is a hymn to Enlil in person.[37] In fact it is possible to represent the development as a hypothetical series of steps[38] in the following way:

(1) King Ur-Namma[39] has built the temple E-kur[40] for his god Enlil in the city of Nippur for his life.[41]

(2) Great and mighty king Ur-Namma, who is the favourite of the goddess Inana, who was chosen by the god Enlil, who is a powerful warrior, who loves justice, at the occasion of his victory over his enemies has built the splendid temple E-kur, adorned it with the choicest material, and made it into a terrifying sight for the unsubmissive foreign countries, for his god Enlil, who has always supported and succoured him, so that he (the king) and his people may rest in peace.[42]

(3) O king Ur-Namma, proud king, enthroned prince,
most fit offshoot of kingship,
who walks like Utu, brilliant light of the Land,[43]
who is lofty in nobility,
who settles the four quarters,
favoured by Enlil, beloved by Inana;
true youth with shining eyes:
Truth and justice you make manifest;

---

35 In fact, one of the masterpieces of Sumerian poetry is the partly narrative hymn dealing with the building by Gudea (ab. 2125 BCE) of the great temple of the god Ningirsu. The hymn was written on three cylinders, of which one is now lost. They can be seen in the Louvre. The text is laid out in columns of 25 to 30 (short) lines each. Cylinder A, the original middle cylinder, has 30 such columns; cylinder B has 24. The best modern translation is Jacobsen 1987, 386–444.

36 Edited in Sjöberg 1969. The same volume contains an edition of one of the major city hymns. The difference between temple hymn and city hymn is minimal, and probably modern at that.

37 See Jacobsen 1987: 101–11.

38 Which are not to be taken as chronological beyond step two!

39 A historical king, effective founder of the new national state in the Ur III period. He reigned from 2112 to 2095 BCE. The following examples are not 'real', in the sense that they do not translate extant inscriptions or texts. But all expressions (and also the structures) have been taken from real texts.

40 The name of the main temple of Enlil in Nippur. Literally 'mountain-house'.

41 This formula has endured long after it was first used in third millennium Sumer! It still occurs as a stock phrase in Aramaic votive inscriptions in the Greco-Roman period. A thorough study of the formula as used in Palmyra is Dijkstra 1992.

42 This 'text' clearly embroiders upon the simple formula of stage (1).

43 Utu, the all-seeing sun god, is thereby also the god of justice.

Your goodness covers even the horizon,
To Nippur you are its scribe,
to the E-kur, Enlil's house,
you are its provider
...

(4) Temple, your façade is like a giant; from your midst springs bounty;
your treasury is a mountain of wealth;
your fragrance is like (that of) a mound of herbs;
your (divine) overseer is foremost among the gods
...

(5) The lord Enlil, surpassingly great in heaven and on earth,
knowing counsellor, wise, broad of insight,
settled in Duranki,[44] and in Nippur built himself a house.
The front of the city was a terrifying halo;
its walls soared into the impenetrable heaven;
the inner city, a sharp dagger,
was a trap to the rebel lands.
No one spoke irreverent words in it,
or quarrelsome insults leading to lawsuits
...[45]

Thus we see how a relatively simple and practical kind of non-poetical text (which, by the way, continues its life as an independent type, and within its own bounds evolves into highly sophisticated later forms which then also attain literary status[46]) can evolve into a number of related poetical types, and by affiliation to an independently existing type enrich the register of the genre as such.

2.2.2. The last example used above already illustrates a second way in which 'new' genres develop. This way may be said to be *poetical and structural* in nature. One example may suffice. One of the most intriguing and enjoyable Mesopotamian genres are the debates. To date we know about[47] sixteen examples, ten in Sumerian and six in Akkadian. As is not often the case, the (older) Sumerian material is on the whole more plentiful and better preserved than its Akkadian counterpart. These pieces all share the following common features:

(a) they are poetic dialogues between two non-human contenders, the bone of contention being their relative value;
(b) the quarrel is put into a setting, which may or may not havequasi-cosmogonic 'aetiological' overtones;
(c) the matter is decided in every case by a divine or royal judge;
(d) the verdict of this judge is reached much more on the strength of the rhetoric used by the contenders than on the value of the argument;

[44] A 'kenning'-like epitheton for the E-kur or Nippur. Literally it means 'bond between heaven and earth'.
[45] These lines are in fact taken from the great hymn to Enlil, for which see above fn. 37.
[46] An excellent anthology of these 'official inscriptions' of the older periods, up to and including the Old Babylonian period, is Sollberger & Kupper 1971.
[47] The identity of some pieces is not altogether certain.

(e) in any case, the judge usually states that, after all, both are worthies in their own right.

This genre,[48] which as a matter of fact endures till the present day in many cultures, shows a surprising scale of variations in the Sumerian material alone.

Mostly, but not exclusively, the contenders are animals. This obviously makes for a relationship to fables, the more so since there also animals are usually presented as possessing the faculty of speech. It should be kept in mind that the fable is essentially a narrative form, while the debate is by its nature a rhetorical form;[49] yet the affinity on those grounds (speaking animals in a conflict situation) has in some cases led to an evolution by combination of distinct features. The result is a mixed form, between or perhaps better astride the Debate and the Fable. Let us compare three texts, *viz.*

(A) *Ewe and Grain*,[50]
(B) *The Lion and the Goat*,[51]
(C) *Bird and Fish*.[52]

A is a straightforward debate, in which the contenders are simply arguing their merits for humanity – in fact for a banquet at which both will 'serve'! B is just as straightforwardly an almost classical Aesopic fable, in which a clever goat outwits a stupid and vain lion by playing upon his vanity, pampering to his greed, and a clever pun.[53] But C is hard to classify. It starts off as a simple debate. Fish is convinced of its own superiority, because it is dour, earnest and useful, and does not hold with frivolities like beauty and charm and songs. But bird does not even try to meet these arguments; it revels in the pleasure it gives to mankind, including the king, by its beauty and its music. At this superciliousness and aloofness fish becomes so insensed that it destroys bird's nest and tramples its eggs. Now bird is furious, and takes fish to court. Fish, still convinced that its 'moral superiority' entitles it to behave as it did,[54] is punished for its criminal violence instead of being just the looser in a debate. In this instance, significantly, the judge does not state that both contenders are really equivalent. Thus in A the discourse develops simply and straightforwardly as a give and take of opposing arguments; in B the story is the essential feature; the spoken word is a ruse used by the goat to influence the sequence of events; in C the validity of the opposing arguments is doubled by the narration, which shows which of the parties is bound to be declared the victor! Still,

---

48 For a presentation and some translations see Alster 1990, Ponchia 1996, Vanstiphout 1984, 1990, 1991, 1992a, 1992b. Reinink & Vanstiphout 1991 contains a number of studies from different (oriental) cultures as well as an ample bibliography.

49 This basic distinction is not always preceived: Lambert 1960 publishes most of the Akkadian debates under the heading 'Fables', while the true fables are found under 'Proverbs and Sayings'! For the Fable in Mesopotamian literature, see Falkowitz 1984, Krispijn 1993 and Vanstiphout 1989.

50 See Alster & Vanstiphout 1987, or, for easy reference, Vanstiphout 1997b.

51 See Vanstiphout 1988: 19–20.

52 See Vanstiphout 1997c.

53 The story (which takes about ten lines) runs as follows: A lion had caught a helpless goat. The goat begs: "Release me, and I will hand over to you my friend, the ewe!" The lion answers: "I'll let you go if you tell me your name." Goat replies: "Do you not know my name? It is 'You are so clever!' ". When the lion approached the sheepfold again (to demand the ewe as his reward), he called out : "I released you!" But goat, from the safe side of the fence, replied: "You released me; see how clever you are? Instead of all these sheep here you could not even hold me!" It is a pity that the pun is essentially untranslatable.

54 This is, of course, eerily reminiscent of the present-day 'moral majority'.

the fusion between the two formats is not perfect, for the narration remains somehow external to the debate and vice versa. The text remains a debate, albeit of an uncommon type. It is surmised that what has happened here came about almost spontaneously, and relates to the one thing fables and debates have in common: anthropoid, or at any rate talking animals.

2.2.3. Yet the combination of the fable format with the debate format, however slightly and haltingly done in this case, obviously opens the gates to a consciously intended fusion of formal features of existing types into something completely new. *Explicit and intended invention* is a third way in which a generic system may be changed by creating new types or genres. *The Tale of the Fox*[55] is the best example of such an invention. Fragmentary though it is, the material we have points out clearly that the composition makes conscious use of no less than five established types of literature. Obviously, the *Fable* has contributed the type of situation and the series of narrative episodes which oppose fox to wolf and dog – with also a lion and the supreme god Enlil as narratively speaking secondary personages. From the *Debate* stems the interlinked series of confrontational speeches, or dialogues, tending towards a verdict by a third person. *Court-of-Law fiction*[56] has provided the central theme. Wolf and Dog attempt to convict Fox, but at court he cleverly turns the tables and, although the text is not exactly clear on this point, the most reasonable reading is that Fox succeeds in securing punishment for his two erstwhile companions-in-crime who have turned against him. Incidentally, at the end Fox promises to mend his ways; as proof of his conversion to a virtuous life he promises to undertake a pilgrimage, with wife and children, to Enlil's sanctuary in Nippur.[57] The high-flown *epics* about the heroic deeds (and speeches!) of kings or gods are imitated expertly in the boastful speeches of Dog and Lion. Finally, much of Fox's grovelling pleading for mercy seems to come straight from *prayers*, *supplications* and *reflective poems* treating the abject fate of man in the awesome presence of the powers-that-be. All these links are to be taken seriously: there are even some direct quotations. This literal 'borrowing' confirms both the novelty of the genre, which we may well call a *satirical animal epic*, and the consciousness with which it was composed.

3. Our material also allows us to trace the life-cycle of certain genres. This life-cycle illustrates the force and the explicitness of the notion of genre. A splendid case is the group of poems referred to as 'historical laments'. These long and beautiful lyrical compositions commemorate the destruction of a city or the country, but they also express the fervent hope for a better future. We possess five major poems,[58] all to be situated near the beginning of the Old Babylonian period, so that it is highly probable that as a group they commemorate poetically the catastrophic destruction at the end of the Ur III period (about 2000 BCE). All these poems use the same mixed style and mode: an alternation of litanies, elegiac recollections of former happiness, sad descriptions of

---

55 See Vanstiphout 1988a and 1988b.

56 There are a few more stories about court cases. This type should be studied in depth. See provisionally Roth 1983.

57 Those familiar with our mediaeval Reynard may find this of somewhat more than passing interest.

58 See Green 1978 and 1984, Kramer 1940, Michalowski 1989 and Tinney 1996.

present misery, fierce denunciations of the perfidy and cruelty of the gods, and prayers for a better future. The poems are all divided into 'songs', indicated by a technical term[59] followed by a (short) antiphon,[60] which format may or may not imply a communal or public performance. The number of these songs varies, but among them they treat five main themes, to wit:

i A litany, summarising the destroyed cities or buildings in the city;
ii a monologue by the city divinity expressing his/her grief over the abandoned city;
iii contrasting descriptions of former happiness[61] and present misery;
iv reproaches to the unfeeling gods who have caused this unhappiness;
v hope for the future/ prayers for the future.

Close reading of the five major pieces reveals an interesting distribution of these types. The *Lamentation over Sumer and Ur* (LSU)[62] is structurally the 'oldest' text, since it uses the five themes as it were indiscriminately over its five songs. In the *Lamentation over Ur* (LU)[63] the classical form is laid down. It has eleven songs, which neatly arrange the themes:

Themes	Songs
i	1,2
ii	3,4
iii	5,6
iv	7,8
v	9,10,11

As far as we can judge the *Lament over Eridu* and the *Lament over Uruk* (LE; LW)[64] followed the classical model, although there seems to be some variation in the respective placing of the central themes (ii, iii and iv). Finally, the *Lamentation over Nippur* (LN)[65] shows that even the classical model, which appears to have become more or less normative, can be used in a highly original way – so original that the generic nature is altered! For the latter part of the text is no longer a Lamentation; it is the hymnal expression of the reconstruction of the city and its temple under king Ishme-Dagan (1953–1935 BCE),[66] Still, this is done in a very sophisticated way. Duly following the

59 Sumerian ki-ru-gu$_2$ 'place of countering' or 'place of kneeling'. Probably to be understood as 'place for changing turn (of speaker or singer)'.

60 Indicated by the technical term giš-gi-gal$_2$, the precise meaning of which still escapes us.

61 Very much in the style of the *ubi sunt* ... literature from mediaeval times.

62 Michalowski 1989.

63 Kramer 1940. The most recent translation is Jacobsen 1987: 447–74 who called it the most beautiful piece of Mesopotamian poetry.

64 Green 1978 and 1984 respectively. LW stands for Lament over Warka, the modern name for the city of Uruk. Both are much more fragmentary than the three other pieces. It is highly probable that there was at least one more major composition belonging to the type. UM 29–16–549 (University Museum, Philadelphia) is a largeish fragment of a multi-column, preserving parts of two columns on the obverse and three on the reverse. It mentions king Ishme-Dagan; it is divided into kirugus with their gishgigal lines; it mentions temples and cities (a.o. Nippur); it mentions a ga-ša-an-X. At present it has not been possible to place it in one of the known Lamentations. I hope to publish this text in the near future. See already Vanstiphout 1978: 47 note 13, Ludwig 1990: 25 and Tinney 1995: 23.

65 Tinney 1996.

66 See Tinney 1996: 44–46.

classical model, the division of the themes is:

i	1,2
ii	3,4
iii	5,6
v	7–16!

It is not strange that theme iv is omitted: after all, the rest of the poem is about the restoration, which is as a matter of course ascribed partly to the help of the gods. But songs 7 to 16 repeat the classical division scheme in the positive vein:

i	7,9
ii	8,11
iii	12,14
v	13,15,16

And in this arrangement the subtle alternation of themes to songs is remarkable.

Thus we perceive a line of development, from the formative stage in LSU, to the classical stage in LU, LE and LW, to the developed stage in LN, where the poet already is experimenting with the now classical format. This development, based upon actual, historical texts, is thus quite in accordance with Fowler's theoretical scheme of the life of genres.[67]

4. On the other hand, functional relations between empirically observed types of texts can also reveal much that is of interest in the present context. My example here comes from an apparently very diverse assemblage of texts which all pretend to hand down a form of knowledge or wisdom. As has been mentioned above, the texts used in school can be put in a kind of curricular order. We can put those types which are most central to a scribe's education, as indicated by their material remains, in a kind of grid according to the criteria of I : apparent intention (what is being taught?), II: manner of discourse (which discourse is chosen?), III: internal structure of the text (how is the piece of 'knowledge' organised?), and IV: external format of the text carrier (what types of tablets are typical?).

	I	II	III	IV
Lexical lists	conformal[68] practical direct	none	hierarchical open[70]	(model +)[69] exercises
proverbs	didactic	denotative	artificial[71]	collection +

[67] See Fowler 1970. When this scheme for the evolution of the Sumerian city laments was originally proposed (Vanstiphout 1986: 7–9) it was not known that it is actually borne out by historical information culled from the texts (Michalowski 1989: 5–6)!

[68] The sign is only a sign.

[69] The model may never be written down as such; this does not mean that it did not exist. See Veldhuis 1996 and Vanstiphout 1996: 7.

[70] The lists can be expanded, albeit in hierarchical ways, almost at will. See Veldhuis 1997.

[71] The grouping of proverbs happens on external grounds, not on the 'knowledge' contained in them.

	arbitrary direct polyvalent[72]	symbolic		units
instructions	practical purposive[73] direct polyvalent	conative	systematic closed[74]	master text + extracts
school texts	didactic indirect polyvalent	poetical	composed as a unit	master text + extracts

It is important to keep in mind that these textual groups were used in the school curriculum as an integrated continuum, so that in school practice they overlap to a high degree. Therefore it is relevant that this very rough sketch shows that there is an ascending line of development in these types. The *intention* gradually evolves from mere practical instruction to the inculcation of a poetical mode of language use; the *instruction* proper ranges from directness and single purpose to indirect presentation of the polyvalent material; the structure goes from the simple (though always hierarchical) open list over secondary systematics to an autonomous (and poetical) form principle; and all these evolutions or adaptations are reflected in the distribution of the material formats used. In short, one might well say that the whole evolution is one from direct and monovalent instruction to indirect, poetical and polyvalent teaching. This observation becomes even more relevant where we notice that in doing so the matter of formal poetical organisation becomes as important as, if not more important than, the representation of merely referential 'contents'. In other words, and in orthodox structuralist parlance, the texts used in school evolve to a point where *how* the 'text' means is in a way more important than *what* it means.[75] The important point in context is that there are clearly distinctive textual types for each of these stages, even on the purely material level.

5. The preceding section introduced the vexing problems of *function* and *intention*, in that it is possible in the assemblage as presented there to see a correlation between immanent structure and didactic purpose. It would make sense, and is in a way a necessary task, to try and expand this correlation also over other text groups, but as yet we are not in a position to do so.

Also a few remarks can be made on those texts that show an overt indication of a *performance*. We met this already in connection with the Lamentation texts.[76] The indication we use for dividing them up into 'songs' – and which we often simply translate

72 In that not only the substance of 'knowledge' contained in the proverb (if any) is taught, but also the language use.

73 The best known texts are indeed manuals.

74 The text stops when the instruction is thought to be complete.

75 Or even more radically: what a text means is largely how it means.

76 See above section 3.

as 'song' – is in fact someting else. The terms ki-ru-gu$_2$ and giš-gi$_4$-gal$_2$ are separated by a few lines, usually two to four, which in a way summarise or react to or reply to the preceding song. As far as we can tell they are also usually in another 'speaking voice' than the song itself; maybe they were a kind of choral reaction to the songs themselves. The first point is that in the Lamentations these indications combined with other formal features of the text point strongly at a communal[77] or perhaps even dramatic performance, possibly with interventions from the audience. One can imagine that the 'turning' was done by the narrator or chorus leader, who at this point turned towards the audience, exhorting them to sing or speak their 'antiphon'.[78] The least we can say is that in this way the formal format is in a not unimportant way related to the performance. The second point is, however, that the ki-ru-gu$_2$ + giš-gi$_4$-gal$_2$ system is also found in other and, as to contents, totally unrelated texts, such as a composition which may well have served as the libretto for a sacred marriage, or an unfortunately fragmentary text of which the preserved parts look like the celebration of a military victory. Does this mean that all these compositions were perceived by the Mesopotamians to form a single group – or a genre? I think not. It seems much more plausible that some types or individual compositions of different kinds received such a specific form of acceptance that they were singled out for *public* performance instead of the obligatory recitations in the Academy or at the court. We should try to find out which groups, or which individual pieces contain clear traces pointing to one or the other direction.[80]

6. Furthermore, the long (almost three millennia) history of the Mesopotamian literatures shows unmistakable shifts within the generic system. Jacobsen has noted one in the context of what he calls religious drama: while these performative genres in the early periods are almost exclusively about the fertility/sacred marriage complex (to be sure with a number of subtypes within the group), in the late period a second group comes into being, almost but not quite obliterating the first group. These are the Battle dramas dealing basically with the military deeds and prowesses of the gods.[81] And there are many more examples. While a spontaneous evolution is, of course, possible in any system, and no cultural system can be considered a closed system, in this case we know that these shifts were at least partially caused by external, or extra-literary factors. The most important of these extra-literary factors was undoubtedly the changed function of the scribal school. Whereas in the older period, specifically the Old Babylonian period, intellectual and literary life was to some extent independent or free,[82] the first millennium shows a different picture. At the royal courts of the Neo-Assyrian state the

77 For the Lamentations as a communal (and therefore publicly performed) genre in the Near East see in general Ferris 1992.

78 See Rosengarten 1968 for an intelligent but perhaps overargued interpretation of LU in this vein.

79 For the first, see Jacobsen 1975: 66–7 and 1987: 112–24. For the second, see Vanstiphout 1991a.

80 We should keep in mind (a) that the first and most immediate social context of almost all literary texts was the Academy, and that thus the acceptance was restricted to the academicians and/or the court; (b) that there is a fair number of 'unica': texts of which we have only one exemplar; that these are all flukes is improbable; that they somehow belong to a different social context than the school is impossible: they are found among the academical texts. They remain a fascinating problem.

81 Jacobsen 1975: 71–5.

82 In itself this is somewhat strange: the alumni of the scribal centres would end up in one or the other form of civil service anyway. See Veldhuis 1997: 142–6 on this point.

scribal craft was, as far as we can tell, simply that: a craft. Its performers were mere servants of officialdom, and the education of these clerks and scriveners was utilitarian and 'socially relevant' before it was anything else. They learn and perform only what they are ordered to by the powers that be. At least this is the picture arising from the plentiful correspondence we have from their circles. And Parpola, our best specialist in this field, has reconstructed the forms of this officialdom in great detail.[83] Though not explicitly saying so, Parpola seems to assume that this then was the intellectual or scribal community. The problem is that we have in this same period, or at least since 1150 BCE, a new and unexpectedly great flowering of literature, this time in the Semitic Akkadian (and in the Babylonian dialect, even in Assyria). One of the features of this *dolce stil nuovo*[84] is a much greater insistence on individual problems and, indeed, on soul-searching, than in the relatively carefree Old Babylonian period. Be that as it may, the new style has led to some of the best work to come out of Mesopotamia; it is often of very high poetic quality, reflective depth and earnestness. But who wrote these poems? Under what circumstances, and in which environment did they come into being? Who read them? There is not a shred of evidence that these authors belonged to Parpola's class of officials: the evidence we have of them is so overwhelmingly rich that we ought to have found one or two links to the great literature by now.[85] My surmise is that the intellectual and artistic community did survive somehow apart from officialdom as such; and I would suggest to look for them among the teaching staff of the scribal schools, who for a reason as yet unknown are hardly mentioned in the vast official correspondence.

But it is perhaps more important to note that the Old Babylonian generic system did not survive unscathed from the almost complete switch to Akkadian after 1500 BCE. A number of genres disappears; but another number is created anew. We note a shift in the balance between belles-lettres and applied scribal crafts – to the benefit of the latter. The literature which is meant to praise, comfort and enhance the powers of the king and the state assumes a much larger proportion than before. This means that also in its generic structure the literary system is made much more dependent upon the cultural policies the authorities wish to pursue.[86]

7. Finally, I would like to state my conviction that a close reading of the material shows that a rethinking of the relationship between theoretical and historical genres seems to be indicated, especially for these ancient literary systems: this relationship itself is not a stable factor. As an example allow me to return to my beloved Lamentations once more: here we can see that a historical genre *becomes* a theoretical genre. In any case, I think that generic distinctions and generic systems can only be found in demonstrable and sometimes very material relations between the texts themselves. And in our case, the case of Mesopotamia, we need to remind ourselves that we have a special situation.

---

83 Parpola 1993, Introduction.

84 The term is Oppenheim's: Oppenheim 1977: 268.

85 In fact, the problem is even more difficult than stated here. Livingstone, in two works, has edited a great number of literary and semi-literary works from the same state archives or closely related to them. Even here no clear relation can be found to the great literature (which, judging from the number of copies, was popular enough); but also the relations between Livingstone's material and the civil service as known from the wealth of bureaucratic documents is very tenuous at best. See Livingstone 1986 and 1989.

86 I gladly leave it to the reader to draw any parallels with present times.

The generic system is linked to writing much more closely than to language; one of the reasons for this is that the writing system remains basically and potentially bilingual till the very end. And it follows that the generic system also remains within the domain of the scribal education: the Academy.

Are we ready for a global reconstruction of these large systems?[87] I think not. Too many details have to be filled in before such an undertaking can be contemplated. Yet I presume to know *how* it should be done. Instead of trying to force our generic system, which despite all the lip service to Aristotle was first conceived in the classicist, not the classic, period, already subverted during the Romantic period, and made largely irrelevant during the late nineteenth century, upon these ancient literatures, we should approach the texts as such, and try to construct a system upon these texts themselves by using textual analyses, context features and intertextual phenomena. I also think that we should use criteria such as (1) discourse modality; (2) thematics and content selection; (3) spread and distribution; (4) evolution within groups and across groups. Only in the last instance should we try to construct more theoretical schemes based upon information from modern literary criticism. Still, I remain convinced that working towards such a reconstruction, however falteringly, can become a useful contribution to generic theory as such. For these literatures are not only the oldest ones we have. They are also preserved in such a way that it is still now possible to analyse them systematically with regard to a number of features (such as distribution, intertextuality, social function, mode of publication), which is a more fortunate circumstance than we find in many later literary traditions. And for this we must be grateful to a cultural factor – the Mesopotamian school – as well as to two natural ones: clay and reed.

[87] Lest I be accused of unwarranted bias by my *collegae proximi*, it is important to note that I am well aware that there are at least four large distinct generic systems: the early phase, comprising roughly the second half of the third millennium; the Old Babylonian system, covering the first third of the second millennium (and which proved to be the most vibrantly vital one); the middle and third quarter of the second millennium, in which the system was exported to neighbouring countries, mainly in the West and North; and finally the late system, which started about 1200 BCE and lived on well into our era.

REFERENCES

Alster, Bendt

1974 — *The Instructions of Suruppak. A Sumerian Proverb Collection.* Copenhagen: Akademisk Forlag.

1990 — "Sumerian Literary Dialogues and Debates and their Place in Ancient Near Eastern Literature," pp. 1–16 in E. Keck *et.al.* (eds.), *Living Waters. Scandinavian Orientalistic Studies Presented to Professor Dr. Frede Løkkegaard.* Copenhagen.

1997 — *Proverbs of Ancient Sumer. The World's Earliest Proverb Collections.* Bethesda, MD: CDL Press

Alster, Bendt & H. Vanstiphout

1987 — "Lahar and Ashnan. Presentation and Analysis of a Sumerian Disputation," in *Acta Sumerologica* 9: 1–43.

Borges, Jorge Luis

1974 — "El idioma analítico de John Wilkins," pp. 706–09 in *Obras completas.* Buenos Aires: Emecé editores.

Civil, Miguel

1993 — *The Farmer's Instructions. A Sumerian Agricultural Manual* (Aula Orientalis, Supplement 5). Sabadell: Editorial AUSA .

Cooper, Jerrold S.

1983 — *The Curse of Agade.* Baltimore: Johns Hopkins University Press.

Cooper, Jerrold S. & Wolfgang Heimpel

1983 — "The Sumerian Sargon Legend," pp. 67–82 in J.M. Sasson (ed.), *Studies in Literature from the Ancient Near East by Members of the American Oriental Society, dedicated to Samuel Noah Kramer* (*Journal of the American Oriental Society* 103/1).

Dijkstra, Klaas

1992 — *Life and Loyalty. A Study of the Socio-religious Cultures of Syria and Mesopotamia in the Greco-Roman Period.* University of Groningen Dissertation.

Dobbs-Allsopp, F.W.

1993 — *Weep, O Daughter of Zion: A Study of the City-Lament Genre in the Hebrew Bible* (Biblica et Orientalia 44). Roma: Editrice pontificio istituto biblico.

Edzard, Dietz O.

1994a — "Sumerian Epic: Epic or Fairy Tale?" in *Canadian Society for Mesopotamian Studies, Bulletin* 27: 7–14.

1994b — "Sumerische und Akkadische Hymnen," pp. 19–31 in W. Burkert & F. Stolz (eds.), *Hymnen der Alten Welt im Kulturvergleich* (Orbis Biblicus et Orientalis 131). Göttingen: Vandenhoeck & Ruprecht.

Falkowitz , Robert S.

1984 "Discrimination and Condensation of Sacred Categories : The-Fable in Early Mesopotamian Literature," pp. 1–32 in F. R. Adrados (ed.) *La Fable* (Entretiens sur l'antiquité classique 30). Genève: Vendœuvres.

Ferris, Paul W.

1992 *The Genre of Communal Lament in the Bible and the Ancient Near East.* Atlanta: Scholars' Press.

Frye, Northrop

1951 "The Archetypes of Literature," in *Kenyon Review* 13: 92–110.

1957 *Anatomy of Criticism.* Yale University Press.

Genette, Gérard

1977 "Genres, ≪types≫, modes," in *Poétique* 7: 389–421.

Hallo, William W.

1982 "Notes from the Babylonian Collection, II," in *Journal of Cuneiform Studies* 34: 81–93.

Heimpel, Wolfgang

1981 "The Nanshe Hymn," in *Journal of Cuneiform Studies* 33: 65–139

Jacobsen, Thorkild

1975 "Religious Drama in Ancient Mesopotamia,;" pp. 65–97 in H. Goedicke and J.J.M. Roberts (eds.), *Unity and Diversity. Essays in the History, Literature, and Religion of the Ancient Near East.* Baltimore: Johns Hopkins University Press.

1987 *The Harps That Once ... Sumerian Poetry in Translation.* Yale University Press.

Klein, Jacob

1997 "The God Martu in Sumerian Literature," pp. 99–116 in I.L. Finkel & M.A. Geller (eds.), *Sumerian Gods and their Representations.* Groningen: Styx.

Kramer, Samuel Noah

1942 "The Oldest Literary Catalogue. A Sumerian List of Literary Compositions Compiled about 2000 BC," in *Bulletin of the American Schools of Oriental Research* 88: 10–19.

1943 "The Oldest Book Catalogue," in *University of Pennsylvania General Magazine and Historical Chronicle* 46: 164–70.

1961 "A New Literary Catalogue from Ur," in *Revue d'Assyriologie* 55: 169–76.

1980 "Book Lists : The First Library Catalogue," pp. 250–54 in id., *History Begins at Sumer* (Third Revised Edition). Philadelphia:University of Pennsylvania Press.

Krispijn, Th.J.H.

1993 "Dierenfabels in het oude Mesopotamië," pp. 131–48 in W.L. Idema *et.al.* (eds.), *Mijn Naam is Haas. Dierenverhalen in verschillende Culturen.* Baarn: AMBO.

Lambert, Wilfred G.
1960 *Babylonian Wisdom Literature*. Oxford: Clarendon Press.

Livingstone, Alasdair
1986 *Mystical and Mythological Explanatory Works of Assyrian and Babylonian Scholars*. Oxford: Clarendon Press.
1989 *Court Poetry and Literary Miscellanea* (State Archives of Assyria vol. 3). Helsinki University Press.

Longman III, Tremper
1991 *Fictional Akkadian Autobiography. A Generic and Comparative Study*. Winona Lake: Eisenbrauns.

Ludwig, Marie-Christine
1990 *Untersuchungen zu den Hymnen des Išme-Dagan von Isin*. Wiesbaden: Harrassowitz.

Michalowski, Piotr
1989 *The Lamentation over the Destruction of Sumer and Ur* (Mesopotamian Civilizations 1). Winona Lake: Eisenbrauns.

Molina Martos, Manuel
1996 "Lexicografía y tradición literaria en la Antigua Mesopotamia," pp. 49–76 in E. Martínez Borobio (ed.), *Literatura e historia en el Próximo Oriente Antiguo*. Toledo: Museo Sefardi.

Oppenheim, A. Leo
1977 *Ancient Mesopotamia. Portrait of a Dead Civilization* (Revised edition by E. Reiner). Chicago University Press.

Parpola, Simo
1993 *Letters from Assyrian and Babylonian Scholars* (State Archives of Assyria 10). Helsinki University Press.

Ponchia, Simonetta
1996 *La palma e il tamarisco e altri dialoghi mesopotamici.*Venezia: Marsilio.

Reinink, Gerrit & H. Vanstiphout (eds.)
1991 *Dispute Poems and Dialogues in the Ancient and Mediaeval Near East* (Orientalia Lovaniensia Analecta 42). Leuven: Peeters.

Rosengarten, Yvonne
1968 "Au sujet d'un théâtre religieux sumérien," in *Revue de l'histoire des réligions* 145: 117–60.

Rosenmeyer, Thomas G.
1985 "Ancient Literary Genres: A Mirage?" in *Yearbook of Comparative and General Literature* 34: 74–84.

Sjöberg, Å.W.
1969 *The Collection of the Sumerian Temple Hymns* (Texts from Cuneiform Sources 3). Locust Valley: J.J. Augustin.
1975 "The Old Babylonian Eduba," pp. 159–79 in S. Lieberman (ed.), *Sumerological Studies in Honor of Thorkild Jacobsen on his Seventieth Birthday* (Assyriological Studies 20). University of Chicago Press.

Sollberger, Edmond & J.R. Kupper
1971 *Inscriptions royales sumériennes et akkadiennes* (Littératures anciennes du Proche-Orient 2). Paris: Les éditions du Cerf.

Sperber, Dan & Deirdre Wilson
1995 *Relevance. Communication and Cognition*, Oxford : Blackwells [Revised edition].

Tinney, Steve
1995 "On the Poetry for King Išme-Dagan," in *Orientalistische Literaturzeitung* 90: 5–24.
1996 *The Nippur Lament. Royal Rhetoric and Divine Legitimation in the Reign of Išme-Dagan of Isin* (1953–1935 B.C.) (Occasional Publications of the Samuel Noah Kramer Fund 16). Philadelphia: University of Pennsylvania Museum.

Todorov, Tzvetan
1976 "The Origin of Genres," in *New Literary History* 8: 159–70.

Vanstiphout, H.L.J.
1978 "Lipit-Eštar's Praise in the Edubba," in *Journal of Cuneiform Studies* 30: 33–61.
1979 "How Did They Learn Sumerian?" in *Journal of Cuneiform Studies* 31: 118–26.
1980 "Over het Vak 'Sumerisch' aan de Oudbabylonische Scholen," pp. 29–42 in A. Théodorides *et.al.* (eds.), *Het Kind in de Oosterse Beschavingen*. Leuven: Peeters.
1984 "On the Sumerian Disputation between the Hoe and the Plough," in *Aula Orientalis* 2: 239–51.
1986a "Some Remarks on Cuneiform *écritures*," pp. 217–34 in id. *et.al.* (eds.), *Scripta signa vocis. Studies about Scripts, Scriptures, Scribes and Languages in the Near East, presented to J.H. Hospers by his Pupils, Colleagues and Friends*. Groningen: Forsten.
1986b "Some Thoughts on Genre in Mesopotamian Literature," pp. 1–11 in K. Hecker & W. Sommerfeld (eds.), *Keilschriftliche Literaturen. Ausgewählte Vorträge der XXXII. Rencontre Assyriologique Internationale, Münster 8.–12.7.1985*. Berlin: Dietrich Reimer.
1987 "Towards a Reading of 'Gilgamesh and Agga'. Part I : The Text," in *Aula Orientalis* 5: 129–41.
1988a "The Importance of the Tale of the Fox," in *Acta Sumerologica* 10: 191–227.
1988b "Een (k)oud spoor in de vossejacht," in *Belgisch Tijdschrift voor Filologie en Geschiedenis* 66: 5–31.
1989 "Fabels uit Mesopotamië," in *Phoenix* 34/2: 15–28.
1990 "The Mesopotamian Debate Poems. A General Presentation. (Part I)," in *Acta Sumerologica* 12: 271–318.
1991 "Lore, Learning and Levity in the Sumerian Disputations. A Matter of Form, or Substance?" pp. 23–46 in G. Reinink & H.

Vanstiphout (eds.), *Dispute Poems and Dialogues in the Ancient and Mediaeval Near East* (Orientalia Lovaniensia Analecta 42). Leuven: Peeters.

1991a "The Man from Elam. A Reconsideration of Ishbi-Erra 'Hymn B'," in *Jaarbericht van het Vooraziatisch-EgyptischGenootschap Ex Oriente Lux* 31: 53–62.

1992a "The Mesopotamian Debate Poems. A General Presentation. Part II : The Subject," in *Acta Sumerologica* 14: 339–67.

1992b "The Banquet Scene in the Mesopotamian Debate Poems," in *Res Orientales* 4: 9–22.

1996 "Introduction," in H. Vanstiphout (ed.), *Aspects of Texts in the Ancient Near East* (Dutch Studies published by the Near Eastern Languages and Literatures Foundation 2/1): 5–10.

1997a "School Dialogues," pp. 586–91 in W.W. Hallo (ed.), *The Context of Scripture I*. Leiden: Brill.

1997b "The Disputation between Ewe and Wheat," pp. 573–76 in: W.W. Hallo (ed.), *The Context of Scripture I*. Leiden: Brill.

1997c "The Disputation between Bird and Fish," pp. 579–82 in: W.W. Hallo (ed.), *The Context of Scripture I*. Leiden: Brill.

Veldhuis, Niek

1996 "The Cuneiform Tablet as an Educational Tool," in H. Vanstiphout (ed.), *Aspects of Texts in the Ancient Near East* (Dutch Studies published by the Near Eastern Languages andLiteratures Foundation 2/1): 11–26.

1997 *Elementary Education at Nippur. The List of Trees and Wooden Objects*. (University of Groningen Dissertation).

CONTINUITY AND CHANGE IN THE MESOPOTAMIAN LEXICAL TRADITION

Niek Veldhuis

0. The opening story of Woody Allen's *Getting Even* (1966) pretends to be a scholarly discussion of the recently published laundry lists of the novelist Hans Metterling. The interpretation of such lists as:

6 handkerchiefs
5 undershirts
8 prs. socks
3 bedsheets
2 pillowcases

involves a discussion of Metterling's habits and psychology in their relation to his creative work. Allen's message seems to be that nothing can be too silly to prevent scholars from inventing foolish interpretations.[1]

The learned energy devoted to Mesopotamian lexical lists may seem to be a case in point. These lists often consist of nothing more than long strings of words or signs. Yet, the anthropologist Jack Goody gave pride of place to the Mesopotamian lexical list in the evolution of human cognition. He argued that a written list invokes aspects of classification not prompted by oral lists.[2] The prominent Assyriologist W. von Soden used these same lists as material for an interpretation of the 'nature' of the Sumerian people and their culture, where he perceived 'Ordnungswille' as a defining characteristic.[3]

1. At first sight the Mesopotamian lexical lists indeed are among the simplest and most boring types of text that mankind has ever produced. Yet the lexical list is one of the most characteristic features of Mesopotamian literacy. Throughout the three millennia of the history of cuneiform writing the lexical list has been more persistent than any other type of text. Notwithstanding their simple format, cuneiform lists exist in a large variety of types, and they have been put to use in several different ways.

The earliest examples in Mesopotamia are thematically organised enumerations of Sumerian words without any further explanation. They include for instance lists of trees, of birds, of fish, and of metal objects. These lists were rigidly standardised, and are attested from about 3100 BCE to about 1700 BCE. Archaic exemplars from Uruk[4] are approximately contemporary with the very first examples of writing that have come

1 [Editor's note. If I am not mistaken this 'motif' was first used by Kingsley Amis, by then an angry old man, in an interview where he stated that the only 'new' thing a specialist in English Romantic poetry could hope to discover would be Shelley's laundry lists.]
2 Goody 1977: 74–111 (= ch. 5: 'What's in a List?').
3 Soden 1936.
4 A city in southern Babylonia; modern *Warka*.

to light. In a time span of over a millennium the lists remained virtually unchanged. This is remarkable, since a good portion of the words contained in them had become obsolete over time, and probably already early in this period – or so we think, since those obsolete words are never found outside the lists themselves. An illuminating example is the list of professions, which is a hierarchically organised inventory of functionaries of Uruk in the late fourth millennium. The earliest copies from Uruk are usually extracts written by pupils. The list was used as an exercise in writing. A few centuries later the same list of professions was still being copied, even though many of the titles and names of professions had gone out of use. At the same time, important new titles, which are widely attested in the contemporaneous administrative texts were not added to the list. The copies of the list of professions from Fara and Abu Salabikh, which are dated around the middle of the third millennium, are usually written by advanced scribes on large well-formed tablets. Over the centuries the lexical texts had acquired the status of monuments of tradition. Whoever copied these lists put himself in a long and venerable tradition that went back all the way to the very inception of cuneiform writing.

At the beginning of the second millennium the lists take on an entirely different function. The scribes of the Old Babylonian period (ca. 2000–1595 BCE) used the ancient tradition to create their own lexical corpus. In many respects this new corpus differs radically from what existed before. All the ancient thematic lists were reworked, and new ones were added. Among these new lists there are, for instance, a list of reeds and reed objects, and a list of wild animals. But more importantly the lists lose their rigidly fixed, almost fossilised character. Old Babylonian lists exist in a state of flux, with local 'recensions' at every centre of education. Moreover, the list format which hitherto had been used almost exclusively for thematic lists of words is now explored with a view to wider application, resulting in a number of entirely new text types. Before discussing some of these Old Babylonian lists it is useful to say a few words about their primary context: the school.

2. In ancient Mesopotamia scribes were educated at the *Eduba*. The literal translation of this Sumerian word is 'tablet house'. We are best informed about the Old Babylonian school in Nippur.[5] This school flourished in the eighteenth century BCE. Its organisation and day-to-day practice are known from a variety of sources. There are a number of literary compositions which describe life at school.[6] These texts show, among many other things, the diversity of topics treated in school: music, arithmetic, language and writing, literature, drawing up contracts etc. The data contained in these so-called 'Eduba texts' have been summarised in various publications.[7] Excavated remains of schools have led to the conclusion that education was basically a private enterprise. Architecturally the schools cannot be distinguished from common houses. A scribe who wanted to initiate his son in the art and science of writing did so at home. He may have accepted a few other children from the neighbourhood; but that was all there was to a school. Yet

5 Nippur, modern *Nuffar*, is a city in central Babylonia.

6 Recent translations of some of these texts are found in Civil 1985, von Soden and Römer 1990 and Vanstiphout 1997.

7 The *locus classicus* is Sjöberg 1975. See also Charpin 1986: 420–23; Waetzoldt 1989; Volk 1996. For a cautious view of the value of these texts, see Civil 1980.

the private nature of education does not mean that the teacher merely improvised his teaching. Scribal teaching was done on traditional lines, and it shows only a relatively narrow band of variation. We know quite a few details about the curriculum, because school tablets with teachers' models and pupils' exercises have been found in large quantities. The normal fate of an exercise tablet was a water basin, where it was to be returned to mere clay. Fortunately numerous tablets escaped this destiny: in Nippur several thousands of them have been found.

One type of school tablet combines two different exercises: one on the obverse and one on the reverse of the tablet. On the left side of the obverse the teacher wrote an extract from one of the lexical lists. This was a new exercise, treating something that had not been studied before. This extract was then copied several times on the right hand half of the obverse by a pupil. The reverse was used by the same pupil for repetition of an exercise studied earlier. By examining these obverse-reverse correlations it is possible to establish the curricular order of the exercises.

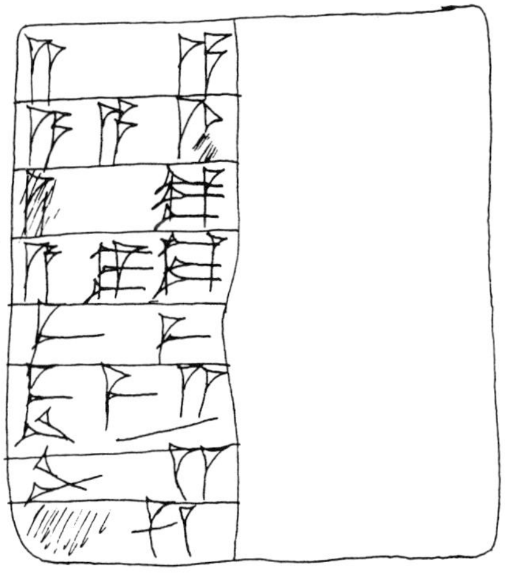

Fig. 1 N5147 (7.5x9cm). A-A A-A-A: easy signs.

3.1. The first list a pupil had to copy is called after its opening line *A-A A-A-A*.[8] The exact length of this list is not known. No complete exemplar has been found so far, but it probably had between 100 and 200 lines. In this list, basic signs were introduced one by one, and then practised in combinations with other signs. The exercise is intended to drill the design of the most common signs of the cuneiform repertory. The entries do

[8] In assyriological jargon the text is called 'Syllable Alphabet B'. It is edited and discussed in Çiğ, Kızılyay and Landsberger 1959. A related and contemporary elementary exercise is called ME-ME PAP-PAP, or Syllable Alphabet A; but this was used only outside Nippur.

not have a 'meaning' in any accepted sense of that term. Figure 1 shows the first eight lines of *A-A A-A-A* in cuneiform. In this opening passage the easiest signs, consisting of only a few strokes each, are repeated. In most exemplars the writing is executed in oversized format, so that the pupil could practise each and every detail of the sign.

3.2. In some Nippur schools *A-A A-A-A* was followed by *TU-TA-TI*[9] (Fig. 2). This exercise consists of sets of three syllables with permutation of the vowel in the order u-a-i. In its most common version the list has 116 lines, followed by the traditional subscript for school texts: "Nisaba (the goddess of writing) be praised![10]" In this list the focus is not so much on the design as on the phonemic value (or 'reading') of a number of common signs.

1	¶ tu	9	¶ bu
2	¶ ta	10	¶ ba
3	¶ ta	11	¶ bu
4	¶ tu-ta-ti	12	¶ bu-ba-bi
5	¶ nu	13	¶ zu
6	¶ na	14	¶ za
7	¶ ni	15	¶ zi
8	¶ nu-na-ni	16	¶ zu-za-zi

Fig. 2 TU-TA-TI, lines 1–16. Each entry is preceded by a single vertical, here indicated as ¶.

3.3. Shortly after *TU-TA-TI* the student started to copy thematic lists of Sumerian nouns. Modern Assyriology refers to these lists as Old Babylonian *ur*$_5$*-ra*[11] (Fig. 3). This label is somewhat anachronistic, because *ur*$_5$*-ra* 'loan' is actually the opening line of the post-Old Babylonian versions of this composition. The entry belongs to a section 'business terminology', which was added to the body of the list, and in first position, only in Middle Babylonian times.[12] Even without this later addition, Old Babylonian *ur*$_5$*-ra* is considerably longer than *A-A A-A-A* and *TU-TA-TI*. In Nippur *ur*$_5$*-ra* consisted of six chapters or 'tablets', with each between 500 and 700 lines. The division of the contents over the chapters is summarised in table 1. In scribal centres outside Nippur other divisions were in use, although the subjects treated were roughly identical.

In the Old Babylonian period Sumerian had died out as a spoken language, though it was retained for a variety of textual types. An apprentice scribe therefore had to learn Sumerian as a second language. Going through all the entries of *ur*$_5$*-ra* the pupil gradually built up a Sumerian vocabulary.

9 *TU-TA-TI* is edited in Çiğ, Kızılyay and Landsberger 1959.

10 The edition does not contain the end of the list; but this appears on a few unpublished texts in the University of Pennsylvania Museum, Philadelphia.

11 In earlier literature ḪAR-ra or ḪUR-ra.

12 I.e. the second half of the second millennium (after 1595 BCE). However, in order to avoid confusion and to acknowledge the historical continuity between the Old Babylonian text and its later descendants it is advisable to keep the conventional modern name – but always bearing in mind that the scribes in Old Babylonian times would not have recognised the composition under this name!

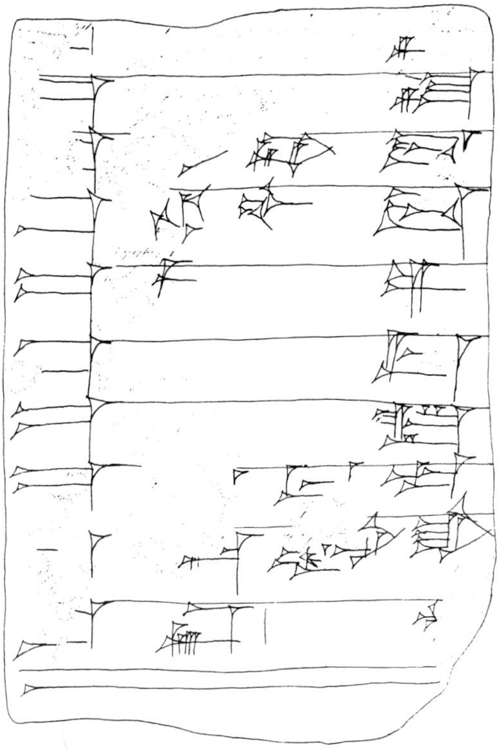

Fig. 3 UM 29–13–163 (7.5x7.8cm). Ur$_5$-ra exercise tablet: a list of wooden objects.

Chapter	Contents
1	trees and wooden objects
2	reed and reed objects; vessels and clay; hides and leather objects; metals and metals objects
3	domestic animals; wild animals; meat cuts.
4	stones and plants; fish and birds; clothing.
5	geographical names and terms; stars.
6	foodstuffs

Table 1: Nippur Old Babylonian ur$_5$-ra

To demonstrate the style of *ur$_5$-ra* the section 'chariot' is reproduced here in transliteration (Fig. 4). The numbers to the left represent the line numbers in the composite edition. Not every line is necessarily represented on every exercise tablet containing (part of) this section. Variants are not uncommon. Some exercises exhibit variants in the order of the entries as well; the significance of these will be discussed below. The list *ur$_5$-ra* contains many unusual and rare words. Accordingly the translation of some items in the example is uncertain.[13]

326 ${}^{\text{giš}}$gigir	chariot
327 ${}^{\text{giš}}$é-gigir	cabin of the chariot
328 ${}^{\text{giš}}$é-ùsan-gigir	box for whip of the chariot
329 ${}^{\text{giš}}$SUM-KA-A-gigir	(unidentified)
330 ${}^{\text{giš}}$kun-gigir	rear part of the chariot
331 ${}^{\text{giš}}$GUL-gigir	(part of) the yoke of the chariot?
332 ${}^{\text{giš}}$sahar-gi-gigir	'dustguard' of the chariot
333 ${}^{\text{giš}}$su-din-gigir	part of the pole of the chariot?
334 ${}^{\text{giš}}$su-lum-mar-gigir	tethering ropes of the chariot
335 ${}^{\text{giš}}$sag-kul-gigir	side poles$^{?}$ of the chariot
336 ${}^{\text{giš}}$sag-dúr-gigir	seat of a chariot
337 ${}^{\text{giš}}$gìr-gub-gigir	footboard of the chariot
338 ${}^{\text{giš}}$mud-gigir	handle of the chariot
339 ${}^{\text{giš}}$gag-mud-gigir	peg of the handle of the chariot
340 ${}^{\text{giš}}$šudul-gigir	yoke of the chariot
341 ${}^{\text{giš}}$gag-šudul-gigir	peg of the yoke of the chariot
342 ${}^{\text{giš}}$umbin-gigir	wheel of the chariot
343 ${}^{\text{giš}}$gag-umbin-gigir	peg of the wheel of the chariot
344 ${}^{\text{giš}}$si-gigir	horn of the chariot
345 ${}^{\text{giš}}$gaba-gigir	front guard of the chariot
346 ${}^{\text{giš}}$gaba-gál-gigir	front guard of the chariot

Fig. 4 Nippur Old Babylonian ur$_5$-ra 1, 326–346 (composite text).

3.4. The fourth example is a list of signs. This extract is from a composition called (Proto-)Ea, again anachronistically after the opening line of a later version.[14] Ea lists all possible phonemic values for each sign; it occasionally throws in a few impossible ones. In most cases a cuneiform sign can be used for different Sumerian words. Which word is meant can be derived from the context. In the example in Fig. 5 we see that /a/ and /duru/ are among the phonemic values of the sign A. When the sign is read /a/ it means 'water' or 'semen'; when read /duru/ it means 'wet'. The information collected in EA is absolutely necessary for writing and reading Sumerian. Without the realisation of the polyvalency of the cuneiform signs the writing system would have remained impenetrable.[15] It was long held that Ea belonged with *A-A A-A-A* and *TU-TA-TI* to the elementary stage of learning to write, since it was surmised that familiarity with Ea was indispensable for any further use of the writing system. However, incontrovertible evidence of the exercise tablets shows that pupils who studied Ea had already copied long extracts from the thematic lists. In these lists they necessarily encountered polyvalent signs. The very first entry in chapter one of *ur$_5$-ra* is GIŠ KU, to be read as ${}^{\text{giš}}$taškarin (a

[13] For the terminology of the chariot see Civil 1968 and Klein 1989.
[14] All versions of this list are edited in Civil 1979.
[15] Lists such as Ea have been particularly instrumental in deciphering Sumerian. Without it and related compositions the reading of many cuneiform signs would still be unknown to us.

tree).[16] Later in the same chapter the same combination is to be read ^{giš}dur$_2$ (a board), and ^{giš}tukul (a mace). We must assume that the teacher orally explained how the sign combination had to be pronounced in each case. Ea therefore did not introduce new material; it presented the student with the systematisation of an aspect of cuneiform with which he was already familiar from practice.

gloss	sign	gloss	sign
1 ¶ á	A	10 ¶ ku-ù	KU
2 ¶ ia	A	11 ¶ ku-ú	KU
3 ¶ du-ru	A	12 ¶ sú-uš	KU
4 ¶ e	A	13 ¶ tu-uš	KU
5 ¶ a	A	14 ¶ su-úh	KU
6 ¶	A.A	15 ¶ ši-i	KU
7 ¶ sa-ah	HA.A	16 ¶ bé-e	KU
8 ¶ am	A.AN	17 ¶ bi-id	KU
9 ¶ še-èm	A.AN	18 ¶ du-ru	KU

Fig. 5 Proto-EA 1–18

3.5. The fifth example is a passage from a list of standard phrases and expressions used in contracts Fig. 6. It is called Old Babylonian ki-ulutin-bi-še$_3$,[17] after its first entry. This is one of the few exercises with immediate relevance for the duties of a scribe. At Nippur it is relatively rare.[18]

18 in-sum	he gave
19 in-na-an-sum	he gave to him
20 in-na-an-sum-me-eš	they gave to him
21 in dab$_5$	he took
22 in-na-an-dab$_5$	he took for him
23 [in-na-an-dab$_5$-eš]	[they took for him]
24 in-la$_2$	he paid
25 in-na-an-la$_2$	he paid him
26 in-na-an-la$_2$-me-eš	they paid him

Fig. 6 Old Babylonian Ki-ulutin-bi-šè; 18–26

3.6. A final example is the so-called *mathematical list*. Such lists are in fact generally mere tables of multiplication or other forms of mathematical or conventional correlation. There are different formats, but the most common type runs:

16 In this case the sign GIŠ is not a phonological part of the word as such, but belongs exclusively to the *writing*. It indicates that the following word denotes a tree or a wooden object. Other so-called 'determinatives' denote birds, fish, geographical names, or copper objects. In modern transcription determinatives are represented in superscript.

17 In modern literature the bilingual first millennium version of this list is called *ana ittišu*, which is the Babylonian translation of the expression ki-ulutin-bi-še$_3$.

18 The passage has been reconstructed from unpublished sources. See provisionally Roth 1979: 291–301.

1	6
2	12
3	18
4	24 etc.

The table continues thus up to 20 times 6, and goes on with 30, 40 and 50 times 6. In the sexagesimal system used in ancient mesopotamia the table of six can equally be used for division by 10, which in fact happened.

These examples show that the list format was now employed in a variety of ways for a variety of educational purposes. Primary education in Nippur ended with copying collections of proverbs.[19] These *Proverb Collections* use literary Sumerian, and therefore provide a transition to the next educational phase, in which the pupils are confronted with literary texts. The organisation of the proverbs in a list-like format links them to the lists discussed above, so that we can say that proverbs straddle the two phases through which a Nippur schoolboy had to go.[20]

4. An important difference between the Old Babylonian lists and their third millennium predecessors is the flexibility of the former. The extreme conservatism of the early lists is alien to the nature of the Nippur school texts. A schoolmaster knew the lists by heart and transmitted this knowledge to his pupils. There are a number of features that demonstrate that the teacher did not use a master copy. The passage from *ur*$_5$*-ra* in figure 4 is known from several exercise tablets, none of which is the exact duplicate of any other. Every single exercise presents its own individual version, even though the deviations are usually small. Broadly speaking the text was standardised, but each realisation is unique on numerous points. The passage is organised by a few basically graphemic rules. Items beginning with the same sign are listed together. Lines 327–328 begin with ^{giš}e$_2$-; 333–334 with ^{giš}su-; 335–336 with ^{giš}sag-; and 345–346 with ^{giš}gaba-. Moreover, in the passage 338–343 we find those parts of the chariot which can have a 'peg' resulting in pairs of items such as 'handle of the chariot'; 'peg of the handle of the chariot' etc. The sign for 'peg' is KAK, an easily recognisable sign consisting of only a few (three) strokes. The visual effect is then a series of entries every second one of which begins with the sign KAK. Every exercise which preserves the chariot passage obeys these simple rules of organisation. Whatever variants the exercises may have, they do not separate ^{giš}sag-kul-gigir 'side bars' from ^{giš}sag-dur$_2$-gigir 'seat', even though the two items are hardly connected by any semantics. These variants cannot be explained in any meaningful way by arguing backwards to a single 'original text', nor by the assumption of 'errors' or 'corruptions' in the process of transmission. Instead of using such rather spineless alibis for our poor understanding, we will approach the phenomena described by trying to investigate the place where these 'texts' were primarily stored: memory.

[19] For which see now Alster 1997.

[20] For these phases see also H. Vanstiphout in this volume.

5. Recent cognitive-psychological studies have demonstrated that long-term memory, unlike a computer's hard disk, does not store a text as one long string.[21] Memory uses the redundancy inherent in every piece of language, or every text. Part of this redundancy is created by the rules and restrictions of the genre or textual type to which the piece to be stored belongs. In order to recall a nursery rhyme one uses the patterns of metre and rhyme that govern the genre and that restrict the number of possibilites for each word. In other genres, such as the oral epics sung by traditional singers in former Yugoslavia the genre restrictions will not so much fix every single word, but rather preserve the general outline and style of the story in question. In actual practice two performances of 'the same' epic may prove to be very different in wording and length. Still, singers and audience are likely to experience and accept these different 'versions' as identical, as long as each one fulfills the requirements for this specific epic tale.[22]

In the section 'chariot' of Old Babylonian *ur*$_5$*-ra* there are three basic rules. First, on the most general level, the style of *ur*$_5$*-ra* requires that it be a list of nouns. Second, the semantic range is given by the fact that the passage deals with chariots and parts of chariots. Third, the graphemic rules discussed above determine the organisation of the passage at its surface level. The first two requirements are so general as to be of little importance here. The third rule, however, as we have seen, leaves room for interpretation, or for variants. Memory does not function as a passive storage room where one can store and retreive at will anything one likes. Quite to the contrary, memory proves to be a formative element actively involved in the production of lexical lists.

In several respects the lexical text in the memory of the ancient teacher is not equivalent to any text found on clay tablets. In the first place the memory text is more abstract, and capable of producing all the variants found in the actual exercises. In the second place, and more importantly, Old Babylonian copies of *ur*$_5$*-ra* are always unilingual Sumerian. Bilingual, i.e. Sumerian-Babylonian versions only appear in post-Old Babylonian times. But there is evidence demonstrating that the text in the memory of the Old Babylonian teacher was bilingual. First, the pupils who used the text in their exercises had only just begun to learn Sumerian; without Babylonian translations the lists evidently made little sense to them. Second, the Babylonian translations occasionally leave traces in the Sumerian text: in some rare cases a Sumerian item is omitted and the Babylonian equivalent is found instead. Apparently the pupil confused the Sumerian with its translation – a confusion not difficult to understand since the Sumerian lists actually contained quite a lot of words borrowed from Babylonian. A less accidental, but rather structural way in which the covert Babylonian translation transpires through the Sumerian surface is found in those cases where an identical Sumerian term is repeated two, three or four times. We know from the later bilingual versions that these Sumerian words were traditionally provided with more than one Babylonian translation. The repetition makes sense only if these translations were somehow included in exercising the passage. Third, there is actually a list of human beings (another type of thematic list), which is cited in an Old Babylonian literary text by its bilingual opening line, even though all copies we have of this particular list are unilingual.[23]

---

21 See the fascinating study by Rubin 1995.

22 For this method of reproduction of a 'text', and some implications of performance see also Russo 1992; Kilmer forthc. and Kramer in this volume.

23 See Civil 1985: 74, commentary to l. 14.

Thus the text as written down preserves only half of the 'text' as it was memorised. This distinction between written text and memory text is not restricted to thematic lists. The sign list Proto-*Ea* (see fig. 5) is found in two formats: with glosses and without glosses. The exercises without glosses can be shown to have been written by more advanced pupils. Presumably they knew the glosses by heart, and did no longer need to *write* them down. After all, it is difficult to imagine what purpose Proto-*Ea* could have served in the total absence of glosses.

The exercise tablets we have are then the material products of the performance of the lexical compositions. This situation is almost diametrically opposed to the performance of dramatic texts. We have the *text* of Shakespeare's plays. But any historical *performance* of these texts, for instance in the famous Globe Theatre, must be reconstructed from whatever external evidence can be adduced.[24] The Old Babylonian lexical compositions as *texts* are lost forever, since they existed primarily in memory. But we can partly reconstruct them from the imperfect reflexion that we find in the remains of their *performance* on tablets.

6. Having acquired a bird's eye view of the body of Old Babylonian lexical texts and the ways in which they were transmitted and used in scribal education, we may justifiably ask: "What were they good for?". Obviously they were instrumental in learning how to read and write, but is that sufficient to explain their contents? We have seen that the thematic lists contain numerous obscure words. Proto-*Ea* lists nearly all the familiar signs, with all the values ('readings') a pupil needs to know; but in addition it also includes uncommon signs and values which have little if any relevance for someone who is struggling to master the writing system. For an administrative or commercial career the school curriculum contains much that is irrelevant. Moreover it has almost nothing on Babylonian writing; yet a number of highly important textual types, such as administrative and business letters, were conventionally composed in Babylonian only. Now generally speaking the lack of a direct relation between curriculum and scribal practice is not in need of explanation. Most formal schooling throughout the ages has hardly been 'practical' in the utilitarian sense of that term. But this observation does not absolve us from trying to explain the texts as they are. If they were not directed at practical utility, what did they aim at?

In earlier discussions of this problem the Mesopotamian lists were described as science ("Wissenschaft").[25] Somehow every list was as a remote ancestor of disciplines familiar to us. The multiplication tables are mathematics; Ea belongs to linguistics; and the thematic lists were assigned to the natural sciences: the list of stones to mineralogy, the list of trees to dendrology, the list of animals to zoology etc. This approach has two drawbacks. First, even though both zoology and the Mesopotamian list of animals name and classify numerous animals, this is about all they have in common. This 'ancient zoology' is disappointing and can hardly account for the energy invested in copying and transmitting these texts over the centuries. Second, a number of important lists needs

[24] On this point see also Kramer in this volume.

[25] The term "Listenwissenschaft" was introduced by von Soden 1936. Von Soden's argumentation is manifestly coloured and informed by the racist ideologies the author then embraced. This did not prevent the essay from becoming a 'classic' which was twice reprinted and is much quoted even today.

to be disregarded in this interpretation. This is true of the two most elementary (in the fullest sense) lists in the Old Babylonian curriculum: *A-A A-A-A* and *TU-TA-TI*. But also the list of wooden objects cannot easily be accomodated to any modern scientific discipline. Yet physically all these lists belong together; they are found on the same tablet types, under the same circumstances, and were used by the same people in the course of their scribal education.

Actually, what all lists have in common is their concern with *writing*. This is perhaps most obvious for the elementary lists (*A-A A-A-A* and *TU-TA-TI*) and the sign list *Ea*. But it is also true for the thematic lists. In a mixed logographic-syllabic writing system, such as cuneiform, the distinctions between orthography, spelling, and meaning are not as sharply defined as they are (or seem to be) in an alphabetic script. We have seen that the thematic lists do in fact include an element of graphemic organisation. And it seems fair to say that even the multiplication tables are at least as much about writing as they are about computing. Multiplication tables are most useful when they have been learned by heart. However, the sexagesimal system that was used in cuneiform mathematics was complicated enough to justify *copying* the tables on tablets in order to exercise number writing and computation *in writing*. Old Babylonian lexical lists are not about stones, birds, or language. They are about writing, and it is from their treatment of the writing system that the whole corpus acquires its unity. It is worth noting that this Old Babylonian attitude towards literacy and the writing system itself differs fundamentally from ours. For us the written text is a mere wrapping. It contains words combined into sentences, and connected to an argument. These words, sentences and arguments are what matters to us; not the writing as such. The writing only guarantees the preservation of the text. But to the Mesopotamians the writing system itself was a subject of inquiry. The lists not merely record the writing system as it is used. They analyse the system from various angles and in a theoretical way. The point of learning the lists is not simply to acquire the technique of writing. The pupil who had gone through this curriculum knew all the ins and outs of the highly complex cuneiform writing system. This 'science of writing'[26] was itself mainly preserved in memory. Indeed, the written documents, the exercise tablets, were not to be preserved at all. They were to be recycled to be inscribed over and over again – by other exercises.

7.1. Between the end of the Old Babylonian period and the first millennium, lexical lists from Mesopotamia proper are rare. The first millennium lists can be regarded as developments of their Old Babylonian counterparts. Most lists and types still exist, but they are expanded at great length. Thematic lists are now always *bilingual*: Sumerian and Babylonian. The six chapters of Old Babylonian Nippur *ur$_5$-ra* were expanded into a series of twenty-two tablets, and two tablets of a different nature and format were added in front.[27] The sign list *Ea* is also provided with a Babylonian column and has become several times as long as it was. All conceivable (and some inconceivable) Sumerian equivalences of one Babylonian word are collected in a newly created type of list. Notwithstanding these later additions the first millennium corpus is continuous to the Old Babylonian tradition. This fact has given rise to the concept of the 'forerunner'. The

[26] In Sumerian nam-dub-sar-ra; in Akkadian *ṭupšarrūtum*, both abstract formulations derived from the words for 'scribe'.

[27] See above, footnote 12.

unilingual Old Babylonian lexical lists are treated as forerunners to the first millennium bilingual composition. The implication of this concept is that the bilingual format is to be regarded as the authority, whereas the unilingual lists were so to speak in a less advanced stage of development.

It is important to note that, whatever their relationship to the Old Babylonian corpus, the first millennium lexical texts have an entirely different nature. The development from the Old Babylonian to the first millennium corpus cannot be understood in terms of textual tradition alone. This development has no internal necessity. It is explained by the different role assigned to lexical texts – and to texts in general – in the late period.

7.2. In addition to acquiring a bilingual format (or more precisely a Babylonian column) the most conspicuous change in the lexical tradition is its *standardisation*. We remarked above that there is not *one* Old Babylonian list of wooden objects. Each scribal centre had its own version, and even the extant copies from Nippur show important variation among themselves. By the end of the second millennium a *textus receptus* emerges.[28] This standard text remains in use during the whole first millennium and is attested over a large geographical area. The standardisation of the lexical lists is not an isolated phenomenon. Omen collections, medical texts, and literary texts all receive a standardised recension. This development is accompanied by the creation of a specialised technical vocabulary referring to faithful copying. A colophon may indicate that a text is complete, that it has been collated, and where the original came from. Some medical tablets contain the remark that they have been copied "hastily": tablet typology shows that these were extract tablets, which were not meant to be links in the chain of tradition, but were rather produced for or by a working physician for practical purposes. Another well-attested term is *ḫepi* 'broken'. This Babylonian term is not found in the colophon but within the text, and it indicates that the original was damaged at that point. Now standardised lexical lists tend to become obsolete rapidly, for the text can no longer be adapted as was regularly done in the earlier periods. Therefore three column texts were created, in which a Sumerian word was explained by two successive Babylonian ones. Columns i and ii are identical to the entries in the standard lexical text; column iii explains the obsolete Babylonian word of column ii by a current one. All these phenomena point to a growing respect for the *written* text. The memory of the teacher is no longer the place where knowledge is stored: reliable knowledge is now found on clay tablets, and stored in libraries or archives. Lexical lists are no longer used exclusively as exercises for pupils. They are upgraded to become crucial sources of a venerable tradition.

7.3. The standardisation of other textual types, such as omen collections, literary and medical texts, brought with it a new function for the lexical corpus. Traditional texts are constantly in need of interpretation and actualisation. Since this can no longer be done by updating the texts themselves, hermeneutical tools need to be created. And for this the lexical texts proved eminently useful. Learned commentary texts use the lexical tradition to explain difficult words or phrases. Some of these commentaries comply with

[28] For the standardisation process in Mesopotamia see Civil 1979: 168–69; Rochberg-Halton 1984; Lieberman 1990.

what we would call sound philology. But other commentaries use all the complexities of the cuneifrom system for their exegesis.[29] One of the more straightforward procedures is to analyse a *Babylonian* word into its component syllables, and then to explain each of these syllables as a *Sumerian* word.[30] . A comparison to the Old Babylonian material shows clearly that the lists were not originally created for this kind of pastime, but, at the same time, that they were perfectly suitable for their new function.[31]

7.4. In summary, we have described three closely connected aspects of changes affecting the place of the lists in the cultural system. First the lists have acquired a new status: from schoolboys' exercises they have evolved into a learned tradition. Second, their primary mode of existence has moved from the teacher's memory to clay tablets in a library. Third, they were given a hermeneutic function in the process of preserving other texts. Moreover, and this is the fourth and final change to be discussed here, first millennium lexical lists are found in a context that differs significantly from the Old Babylonian scribal school. The list format is as simple as can be, and was used from the inception of writing itself. The possibilities offered by the format are further exploited in the first millennium. In first millennium tablet collections ('libraries') the most important group of texts, both quantitatively and ideologically, is invariably the corpus of omen compendia. Each omen collection is specialised for the interpretation of a specific groups of 'signs'. An important example is *Enūma Anu Enlil*,[32] so called after the opening line of its introduction. This is a huge collection of astronomical and meteorological omens. Its main focus is on the heavenly bodies: movements, risings, conjunctions, eclipses, and such phenomena as haloes or colour variations. Other topics are rains, storms, and earthquakes. Another such collection is *Šumma ālu* 'If a city ...' (again its opening line); this series contains 'chance encounters' omens. It interprets observations of cities, houses, doors, animal behaviour, human sexual practice, the digging of a well, etc.[33] Other omen series may be labeled 'physiognomic' (describing and interpreting the bodily appearance of humans), 'diagnostic' (describing and interpreting the symptoms of diseased people), and 'teratological' (describing and interpreting monstrous births, both human and animal).[34] Assurbanipal's famous library consisted for the greater part of copies of these and other series of divinatory handbooks. In all the corpus of omen texts comprises several hundreds of chapters (corresponding to tablets), with tens of thousands of individual omens. A short example is taken from the collection of terrestrial omens (*Šumma ālu*) from the chapter on cats:

[29] For the various exegetical techniques used in bilinguals and commentaries see Maul 1997 and the literature mentioned there.

[30] The last tablet of the Epic of Creation is an illustration – on the grandest scale possible since it has cosmic meaning – of a procedure much like this. See Bottéro 1977.

[31] A concomitant reason for this development may well be that, after all, already in Old Babylonian times the lexical lists, or at least lexical procedures, were sometimes used as material for poetic invention, as Civil 1987 has brilliantly shown.

[32] For the history and function of the series see Koch-Westenholz 1995. See also Baigent 1994 and Reiner 1995: 15–24. Van Soldt 1995 is an edition of the solar omens. The series, or at any rate its methods and techniques, had an enormous influence on classical astronomy and astrology, for which see Barton 1994 and especially Pingree 1998.

[33] For a brief description see Cryer 1994: 161–67 with references to earlier literature.

[34] All these series are briefly described in Cryer 1994. See also Kraus 1939 and Bottéro 1985: 65–112 (on physiognomy); Labat 1951 (on diagnostics); Bottéro 1985: 1–28 (on teratology).

If a white cat is seen in the house of a man the country will suffer hardship.
If a black cat is seen in the house of a man the country will prosper.
If a red cat is seen in the house of a man the country will be rich
If a spotted cat is seen in the house of a man the country will not thrive.
If a yellow[35] cat is seen in the house of a man the country will have a good reputation.

Omen texts are generically related to lexical lists in at least two ways. Firstly, in an omen an observation is related to an explanation or interpretation. This is formally equivalent to an entry in most types of lists, where a sign is linked to a gloss, or a Sumerian word to a Babylonian one. Secondly, omens are found in systematic collections. Omens and lexical lists both have a horizontal and a vertical reading. The vertical reading uncovers the system behind the individual items. In both lexical lists and omen collections the system produces unlikely or utterly impossible items. The short passage from the cat omens cited above is a case in point. Whether cats in all these colours actually existed in ancient Mesopotamia is not relevant. The set of colours is a standard set, recurring everywhere in Mesopotamian tradition, and found also *passim* in the omen collections. In the lexical tradition this same set of colours is used for unripe dates. I cannot imagine what a white or red unripe date may be like, but they are listed anyway. And they are faithfully translated into Babylonian.

7.5. From the outset lexical lists have been the prime medium for bearing and transmitting knowledge. It is not by chance that the omen tradition more or less mimicked their format. Omen specialists were undoubtedly among the intellectuals of their times, in that they were highly trained in a specialised technique based on writing and reading. The interpretation of terrestrial and celestial signs is a hermeneutic procedure not unlike reading and understanding cuneiform. This similarity actually transpires through the technical vocabulary of the time. The two most important divinatory techniques were extispicy and astronomical divination. Extispicy is the interpretation of the entrails, almost always the liver, although other organs are also used, of a sacrificial animal, generally a sheep. In the ritual preceding the slaughter the gods are asked to "write a reliable message" on the liver.[36] The message transmitted by heavenly bodies was sometimes called *Šiṭir Šamê* 'celestial writing'[37] The formal similarity between omen compendia and lexical lists has its pendant in this terminology. Extispicy and astronomical divination are forms of *reading*.[38]

8. Using the concept 'genre' in the traditional manner, that is to say solely as a means for categorising texts and textual types is hardly a fruitful undertaking. It is bound to be frustrating, because there will always be texts defying such classification. It is also misleading, because it tends to obscure the fact that textual types are related to each

35 Or 'green'. As in most Semitic languages the Babylonian word for 'green' and 'yellow' is the same.
36 Some 350 reports of such divinatory procedures intended to ascertain divine advice about political and military matters, together with an introduction on the technique and terminology, are found in Starr 1990.
37 As in extispicy, the celestial omen collections were also used to interpret reported sightings of the phenomena. Some 560 reports are found in Hunger 1992.
38 For the perceived near identity between divinatory signs and writing, see also Bottéro 1974 and Vanstiphout & Veldhuis 1996. For divination as such see e.g. Oppenheim 1977: 206–27 and Reiner 1995: 61–79.

other in a dynamic way. Lexical texts from the various periods discussed here are so different in use, status, and mode of existence that they can hardly be put under a single heading. Yet it would be foolish to deny that they represent one and the same textual type, albeit used in very different ways. Also, it makes little sense to say that omen compendia are in reality, or by their deepest nature, lexical texts. Omens are a category of their own, and there is no danger of confusing the two textual types. It does make sense, however, to state that omen compendia by adapting themselves to the format of the lexical lists, appropriate part of the phenomenal prestige of the lexical tradition and of its significance in Mesopotamian intellectual history.

REFERENCES

Alster, Bendt
1997 *Proverbs of Ancient Sumer. The World's Earliest Proverb Collections*. Bethesda, MD.

Baigent, Michael
1994 *From the Omens of Babylon. Astrology and Ancient Mesopotamia*. London.

Barton, Tamsyn
1994 *Ancient Astrology*. London.

Bottéro, Jean
1974 "Symptômes, signes, écritures," pp. 70–197 in J.P. Vernant (ed.), *Divination et rationalité*. Paris.
1977 "Les noms de Marduk; l'écriture et la 'logique' en Mésopotamie ancienne," pp. 5–28 in M.dej. Ellis (ed.), *Essays on the Ancient Near East in Memory of J.J. Finkelstein*. Hamden, CT.
1985 *Mythes et rites de Babylone*. Paris.

Charpin, Dominique
1986 *Le clergé d'Ur au siècle d'Hammurabi (XIXe-XVIIIe siècles av. J.-C.)* (Hautes Études Orientales 22). Paris.

Çiğ, Muazzez, H. Kızılyay & B. Landsberger
1959 *Zwei altbabylonische Schulbücher aus Nippur*. Ankara.

Civil, Miguel
1968 "Išme-Dagan and Enlil's Chariot," in *Journal of the American Oriental Society* 88: 3–14.
1979 *Materials for the Sumerian Lexicon* vol. 14. Rome.
1980 "Les limites de l'information textuelle," pp. 225–32 in Th. Barrelet (ed.), *L'archéologie de l'Iraq du début de l'époque néolithique à 333 avant notre ère. Perspectives et limites de l'interprétation anthropologique des documents. Paris, 13–15 juin 1978* (Colloques internationaux du Centre nationale de la Recherche Scientifique 580). Paris.
1985 "Sur les 'livres d'écolier' à l'époque paléo-babylonienne," pp. 67–78 in J.-M. Durand & J.R. Kupper (eds.), *Miscellanea Babylonica. Mélanges offerts à Maurice Birot*. Paris.
1987 "Feeding Dumuzi's Sheep: The Lexicon as a Source of Literary Inspiration," pp. 37–55 in F. Rochberg-Halton (ed.), *Language, Literature, and History: Philological and Historical Studies Presented to Erica Reiner*. New Haven, CT.

Cryer, F.H.
1994 *Divination in Ancient Israel and its Near Eastern Environment. A Socio-Historical Investigation* (*Journal for the Study of the Old Testament* Supplement Series 142). Sheffield.

Goody, Jack
1977 *The Domestication of the Savage Mind*. Cambridge.

Hunger, Hermann
1992 *Astrological Reports to Assyrian Kings* (State Archives of Assyria vol. VIII). Helsinki.

Kilmer, Ann D.
forthc. " '*Ea balaṭka liqbi*!' Repertories and Genres of Vocal Musical Compositions," in H. Vanstiphout (ed.), *Genre and Type in the Mesopotamian Literatures*. Groningen.

Klein, Jacob
1989 "Building and Dedication Hymns in Sumerian Literature," in *Acta Sumerologica* 11: 27–67.

Koch-Westenholz, U.
1995 *Mesopotamian Astrology. An Introduction to Babylonian and Assyrian Celestial Divination* (Carsten Niebuhr Institute Publications 19). Copenhagen.

Kraus, F. R.
1939 *Texte zur babylonischen Physiognomatik*. Berlin.

Labat, René
1951 *Traité akkadien de diagnostics et pronostics médicaux*. Paris.

Lieberman, S.J.
1990 "Canonical and Official Cuneiform Texts: Towards an Understanding of Assurbanipal's Personal tablet Collection," pp. 305–36 in T. Abusch, J. Huehnergard & P. Steinkeller (eds.), *Lingering over Words. Studies in Ancient Near Eastern Literature in Honor of William L. Moran* (Harvard Semitic Studies 37). Atlanta.

Maul, Stefan M.
1997 "Küchensumerisch oder hohe Kunst der Exegese? Überlegungen zur Bewertung akkadische Interlinearübersetzungen von Emesal-Texten," pp. 253–67 in B. Pongratz-Leisten, H. Kühne & P. Xella (eds.), *Ana šadî Labnāni lū allik. Beiträge zu altorientalischen und mittelmeerischen Kulturen. Festschrift fürWolfgang Röllig*. Neukirchen.

Oppenheim, A. Leo
1977 *Ancient Mesopotamia. Portrait of a Dead Civilization* (Revised Edition by Erica Reiner). Chicago.

Pingree, David
1998 "Legacies in Astronomy and Celestial Omens," pp. 125–37 in S. Dalley (ed.), *The Legacy of Mesopotamia*. Oxford.

Reiner, Erica
1995 *Astral Magic in Babylonia*. Philadelphia.

Rochberg-Halton, Francesca
1984 "Canonicity in Cuneiform Texts," in *Journal of Cuneiform Studies* 36: 127–44.

Roth, Martha
1979 *Scholastic Tradition and Mesopotamian Law: A Study of FLP*

1287, a Prism in the Collection of the Free Library of Philadelphia. University of Pennsylvania Dissertation.

Rubin, D.
1995 *Memory in Oral Traditions. The Cognitive Psychology of Epic, Ballads, and Counting-Out Rhymes.* Oxford.

Russo, Joseph
1992 "Oral Theory: Its development in Homeric Studies and Applicability to Other Literatures," pp. 7–29 in M. Vogelzang & H. Vanstiphout (eds.), *Mesopotamian Epic Literature: Oral or Aural?* Lewiston.

Sjöberg, Åke W.
1975 "The Old Babylonian Edubba," in *Assyriological Studies* 20: 159–79.

von Soden, Wolfram
1936 "Leistung und Grenze sumerischer und babylonischer Wissenschaft," in *Die Welt als Geschichte* 2: 411–64 & 509–57.[Reprinted with addenda and corrigenda in B. Landsberger & W. von Soden, *Die Eigenbegrifflichkeit der babylonischen Welt. Leistung und Grenze sumerischer und babylonischer Wissenschaft.* Darmstadt 1965 and 1974].

von Soden, W. & W. Ph. Römer
1990 *Weisheitstexte* (Texte aus dem Umwelt des alten Testaments III/1). Gütersloh.

van Soldt, Wilfred H.
1995 *Solar Omens of Enūma Anu Enlil: Tablets 23(24) – 29(30).* Leiden.

Starr, Ivan
1990 *Queries to the Sun God. Divination and Politics in Sargonid Assyria* (State Archives of Assyria vol. IV). Helsinki.

Vanstiphout, H.L.J.
1997 "School Dialogues," pp. 588–93 in W.W. Hallo *et.al.* (eds.), *The Context of Scripture, Volume I: Canonical Compositions from the Biblical World.* Leiden.

Vanstiphout, H.L.J. & N. Veldhuis
1996 "*Ṭuppi ilāni takaltu pirišti šamê u erṣetim,*" in *Annali dell' istituto universitario orientale* 55: 30–32.

Volk, Konrad
1996 "Methoden altmesopotamischer Erziehung nach Quellen der altbabylonischen Zeit," in *Saeculum* 47: 178–216.

Waetzoldt, Hartmut
1989 "Der Schreiber als Lehrer in Mesopotamien," pp. 33–50 in J.G. Prinz von Hohenzollern & M. Liedtke (eds.), *Schreiber, Magister, Lehrer. Zur Geschichte und Funktion eines Berufsstandes* (Schriftenreihe zum Bayerischen Schulmuseum Ichenhausen, Bd. 8). Bad Heilbrunn.

When Phaedra left the tragic stage: GENERIC SWITCHES IN APULEIUS' METAMORPHOSES.

Maaike Zimmerman

0. Throughout the eleven books of the Latin novel *Metamorphoses*,[1] written in the second century of our era by Apuleius of Madaura, the reader occasionally meets with metanarrative[2] statements by the narrator (or by the author behind the narrator), which point to an awareness of genre, of generic boundaries, or reveal a self-conscious concern with crossing such boundaries. To quote some examples:

Already in the programmatic prologue to the novel phrases like "in that Milesian style" and "we are about to begin a greekish story"[3] are clearly meant to make the reader think about the work's relationship to various literary forms, and parts of the prologue bear, as has often been acknowledged, a close relationship with the prologues of Plautine comedy.[4] At many other places in the novel one encounters extensive allusions to the dramatic genres of Greece and Rome: from tragedy and comedy to the more subliterary genres of mime and pantomime.

The Ancient Novel's most generally accepted 'generic precursor' is the Homeric Epic, and especially the Odyssey, with its wealth of wonder tales, travel adventures, embedded tales, and even a long episode told in the first person. And, indeed, numerous are the allusions to epic: the narrating 'I' often compares himself to that outstanding epic hero, Odysseus. As recently stated by Selden,

> Greek and Roman classical writers worked within a highly elaborated field of generic classifications. Difference was recognized at every level of the discourse: pragmatic (epic, lyric, drama), syntactic (ode, elegy, epigram), and semantic ('komos', 'propemptikon', 'soteria'). All ancient genres originated in important and recurrent real-life situations. However, long after the different genres ceased to be occasional and to fulfill specific social functions, they continued to bear the marks of status,

---

1 *Metamorphoses* is the title of the work in the oldest extant manuscripts; to Augustinus (*De civ. dei* 18,18) it apparently was known under the title *The Golden Ass*; the original text may well have had a double title: 'The Golden Ass, on Metamorphoses' (*Asinus Aureus*, περὶ μεταμορφώσεων); see Winkler 1985: 292 ff.

2 'Metanarrative' statements are those parts of the narrator's discourse in which s/he refers to or comments upon her/his narrative activity.

3 Apuleius, *Met.* 1,1 (1,1–2.4 Helm): *At ego tibi sermone isto Milesio varias fabulas conseram, auresque tuas benivolas lepido susurro permulceam ... Fabulam graecanicam incipimus. Lector intende: laetaberis*: "But I would like to tie together different sorts of tales for you in that Milesian style, and to caress your ears into approval with a pretty whisper ... We are about to begin a greekish story. Pay attention, reader, and you will find delight." Throughout this contribution the English translation by Hanson (1989) has been used, albeit sometimes slightly modified in order to arrive at a more literal translation. We do not know the 'Milesian tales' themselves, but from remarks by other ancient authors we may conclude that in the period in which the *Metamorphoses* were written, these Milesian tales were an extremely popular genre: frivolous, diverting, often licentious short stories, possibly strung together in a kind of 'Sheherazade'-type frame. See Mason 1978: 7ff.

4 Smith 1968: 105 f.; Winkler 1985: 200 f.

class, ethnicity and gender, and for writers to uphold the propriety of these distinctions was felt implicitly to validate a social order. But, however strongly critics reinforced the notion of generic purity, the hallmark of Hellenistic letters became the crossing of literary kinds. Authors started to conflate genres, and in later imperial writers of prose fiction disparate generic forms are brought together piecemeal and collocated side by side.[5]

1. A special case of juxtaposition of genres, and of generic boundary crossing, occurs in two tales embedded in the tenth book of Apuleius' *Metamorphoses*. This contribution aims at tracing the generic tension in these tales. It will be argued that the reader, provided s/he becomes intensely aware of the conflations of genres presented in these tales, will be able to detect how these tales in this way have a foreshadowing function in the main narrative of the *Metamorphoses*.

It is necessary first to say a few words about the contents of the *Metamorphoses*, and about the vexed problem of this Latin novel's relationship to some Greek ass tales.

1.1. In the period in which it was composed, Apuleius' *Metamorphoses* must have been part of a larger intertext[6] of 'Ass Tales'. The ninth century Byzantine patriarch Photius reports in his *Bibliotheca* that he has read a long Greek work called 'Metamorphóseis'. This work has not been transmitted to us. However, Photius compares the Greek 'Metamorphóseis' to a shorter Greek text which we do still have: the 'Loukios è Onos' ('Loukios or the ass'; henceforth referred to as 'the *Onos*'). This text has been transmitted among the works of Lucian of Samosata. There is now general agreement that the *Onos* is not by Lucian, whereas there are strong arguments for assuming that the longer Greek 'Metamorphóseis', now lost, of which the *Onos* appears to be an abridged version, *may* have been by him.[7] Apuleius' *Metamorphoses* is clearly connected to the intertext just outlined: it displays in many passages a literal Latin 'translation' of the *Onos*. It is therefore now commonly believed that Apuleius has adapted the lost Greek 'Metamorphóseis' to the purposes of his Latin novel. So we may assume that at those places where the Latin *Metamorphoses* is close to the *Onos*, Apuleius' work is following the lost Greek 'Metamorphóseis'.

1.2. The first ten books of Apuleius' novel and the *Onos* share a whole lot of intertextemes:[8] both are told in the first person, in both the theme of 'man-in-ass, observer of human (dis)behaviour' is employed, in both texts we find travel and adventures, close escapes from death, ribald tales, robber episodes, and in both the protagonist observes, or is himself involved in, amorous and erotic situations. As an ass he is frequently exposed to beatings or other tortures by various and often cruel masters. Both texts display lightness of tone.

Near the end, however, the Latin *Metamorphoses* rather suddenly veers off into a

[5] Selden 1994: 39 f.

[6] By 'intertext' is meant: a group of texts, connected by one or more elements; these shared elements are called the 'intertextemes' of that intertext.

[7] See Holzberg 1984.

[8] See note 6.

tale of religious conversion, irrevocably leaving behind the intertext it shared with the *Onos*. This happens towards the closure of the tenth book: up to and way into the tenth book one has been able to observe that the Latin *Metamorphoses* has been following the framework of the *Onos*. Apart from more or less considerable additions (added episodes in the life of the ass, embedded tales not in the *Onos*; some changes in geographical environment, and some 'Romanising' adaptations), it has been possible to recognise the basic pattern of the *Onos*, and regularly the reader has even met with literal 'translations' from the Greek of the *Onos*. In book 10 the ass (Lucius) is taken by a soldier to a small provincial town, where the soldier leaves him at the house of a member of the local council. Just there a wicked crime has been revealed and the narrator relates this story of a wicked stepmother. After this, the ass is sold to two cooks, servants of a rich master. Lucius, the ass, who has never become accustomed to asinine fodder, steals freely from the delicacies which the cooks bring home as left-overs from their master's table. His taste for human food is thus discovered by the cooks, and they inform their master who thereupon buys the ass. From then onwards Lucius leads a life of luxury and is 'trained' in all kinds of human-like behaviour. His master takes him to Corinth where he turns into a public attraction. A wealthy Corinthian matron falls in love with the ass, and bribes his trainer into granting her a series of love-encounters with the animal. When the owner of the ass is informed about this, he decides to organise a spectacle in the theatre displaying the ass having sexual intercourse with a condemned woman. Follows the tale of this condemned woman. On the appointed day of the public spectacle Lucius, the ass, is led to the theatre, and is able to watch the preludes to his own dreaded performance. The narrator treats the readers to the titillating description of an elaborate ballet, and a sensually performed pantomime of the 'Judgment of Paris'. During the immediate preparations for his love-act with the condemned woman, the ass, full of shame, and fearing for his life because of the wild animals in the arena, manages to escape through the gates of the theatre to the beach of Cenchreai, Corinth's harbour. Night comes, and Lucius falls asleep. Thus ends book 10. Book 11 relates how Lucius regains his human form by the grace of Isis, and becomes a fervent adherent of the Isis cult. A series of initiations into the Isis and Osiris mysteries is described, and Lucius ends up as a devoted bald-headed priest.

1.3. Recent studies have convincingly shown that in this final book humorous and satirical elements are abundant, and that the religious fervour of the protagonist can be explained convincingly as another instance of his naive and gullible character.[9] The fact remains, however, that this book is altogether different in tone from the previous ten books: here one no longer finds embedded tales. Moreover, the *Metamorphoses* of Apuleius in this final conclusion has no counterpart in the *Onos* whatsoever.

In the *Onos*, too, the ass has become a celebrated member of the household of the rich master, and spends nights of love-making with the rich lady, which leads to the project of having the ass make love in the theatre with a condemned woman. However, in the *Onos* Loukios, just before his performance, manages to eat some roses and by this antidote he regains his human form. In the final chapters of the *Onos* Loukios in his newly regained human form revisits the lady who loved him when he was still an

[9] See Harrison 1995: 508 ff.; van Mal-Maeder 1997: 91 with further references in n.13, and 100 ff.

ass. But, instead of being allowed to make love with her again, the lady contemptuously throws him out of the house, since his human body lacks the one feature which had attracted her to him: the size of his genitals. In this way, the *Onos* concludes in the same vein of frivolity and burlesque which it had shown from the outset.

One cannot but conclude that the escape of the ass from the Corinthian theatre is the precise point where the Latin *Metamorphoses* irrevocably has left the intertext which it had shared hitherto with the *Onos*. The religious setting of the conclusion of the Latin novel comes as a complete surprise. This legitimises the question as to whether there are any forebodings of this generic shift already in the tenth book. It is only natural to look for such prefigurations in the two embedded tales, for throughout the *Metamorphoses* the many embedded tales have been the most conspicuous feature of 'deviation' from the *Onos*. It has been shown before that many of the embedded tales of the earlier books of the *Metamorphoses*, besides their intention of offering pure narrative entertainment, also have a function in the (re)construction of the framing tale, in that they foreshadow, or mirror, aspects of that framing tale, or in other ways have symbolic meaning referring to that frame.[10] Less attention has been paid to the two embedded tales of the tenth book; and to those we will now turn.

2.1. The *Story of the Stepmother* is told in chapters 2 to 12 of the tenth book. It runs as follows:

> The second wife of a 'paterfamilias' falls desperately in love with this man's son by a former wife. She declares her love to her stepson and tries to seduce him. When his unceasing pretexts make her realise that he has no intention at all to meet her wishes, her love turns into hatred. Assisted by her slave and confidant she plots to poison him. However, purely by chance it is her own son who drinks the cup of poison. She thereupon accuses her stepson of murdering his younger brother as well as of threatening her chastity. After the burial of his younger son the father asks the local magistrates to punish the elder son. A trial is held, and the false evidence by the stepmother's slave convinces everyone that the older son is guilty. Then, suddenly, a respectable old physician comes forward and declares that the slave had come to him to buy poison; suspecting a crime in the making, he sold him a strong sleeping potion instead. Everybody hurries to the grave, and indeed, the boy is alive and just awakening from a heavy drug-induced sleep. The criminals are punished.

2.1.1. In the introduction to this tale the narrator makes the following metanarrative statement:

> A few days later, I recall, an outrageous and abominable crime was revealed there, which I present in my book so that you can read it too.[11]

Note the stress on the 'book' as the intermediary between the fictional narrator and his public. Elsewhere in the *Metamorphoses*, when embedded tales are being introduced,

[10] Tatum 1969.

[11] Apuleius, *Met.* 10,2 (237, 1–3 Helm): *Post dies plusculos ibidem dissignatum scelestum ac nefarium facinus memini, sed ut vos etiam legatis, ad librum profero.*

the illusion of oral story-telling is always maintained. By this way of introduction the implied reader is being warned in advance that there is a literary feature to the tale, and that s/he is being invited to a critical reading of what the narrator "presents in his book".

After the necessary background information about the family relations has been given, and the illicit love of the stepmother has been mentioned, there is again an address to the 'reader':

> So now, excellent reader, know that you are reading a tragedy, and no light tale, and that you are rising from the lowly slipper to the lofty buskin.[12]

Note, again, the stress on reading, and the references to generic theory: The 'lowly slipper' (*soccus*), and the 'lofty buskin' (*cothurnus*), are terms which refer to comedy, respectively tragedy. In ancient comedy the actors were wearing a kind of slipper; in tragedy they walked on high-heeled buskins. The terms *soccus* and *cothurnus* were regularly used to refer to the genres of comedy, resp. tragedy.[13]

This address to the reader, announcing as 'tragedy' a tale which can be labelled as anything but 'tragic', has met with numerous and often irritated reactions of actual, real readers of the *Metamorphoses*, who accused Apuleius of giving "misleading clues", and of careless composition:

> Our author seems hardly to have known how his story was going to end when he launched it... .[14]

2.1.2. I propose a different approach. One may interpret the address "excellent reader" (*lector optime*) in two ways, either taking it at its face-value as "my dear reader" (a polite and meaningless invocation), or as an adhortation to be indeed a "super-reader" of the following tale, which means to become intensely aware – by the pointers to generic theory in this introduction to the tale – of the fact that this story is being launched as a tragedy, but gradually evolves into something completely different. Reading the tale in this way one soon finds out that the actors of this 'tragedy' either are not capable of living up to their 'tragic' role, or even appear to consciously resist that role, and so to step 'out of character'.[15] Some telling passages may illustrate this.

2.1.3. Right at the beginning of the tale the stepson is being introduced as "a young man well versed in literature, and consequently a model of filial devotion and modesty".[16] When soon afterwards it is revealed that he will play the Hippolytus part in the announced 'tragedy' we are already, by the given characterisation, in a position to realise that this "bookish" young man will never be able to act like the Hippolytus of tragedy, who certainly could not count modesty among his virtues, but prided himself for having his wisdom and chastity (Greek 'sophrosúnè') from nature itself and not from books.[17] And,

---

12 Apuleius, *Met.* 10,2 (237,12–14 Helm): *Iam ergo, lector optime, scito te tragoediam, non fabulam legere et a socco ad coturnum ascendere.*

13 See e.g. Horace, *Ars Poetica* 80, with Brink's commentary.

14 Walsh 1970: 171.

15 Whence the point of *soccus* and *cothurnus*.

16 Apuleius *Met.* 10,2 (237,3–5 Helm): *iuvenem...probe litteratum atque ob id consequenter pietate, modestia praecipuum.*

17 Euripides' *Hippol.* 75 ff.: (Hippolytus:) '...a virgin meadow, where no shepherd dares to graze his flock,

indeed, when this boy, well versed in literature, is confronted with the declaration of love by his stepmother his reaction is contrary to the primitively rude but honest abhorrence and downright refusal of the tragic Hippolytus: he takes his time to think things over and decides explicitly – after all he is versed in literature, and knows the Hippolytus tragedies by heart –

> that it was better not to worsen the crisis by the untimely harshness of a refusal, but rather to alleviate it by the delaying tactic of a guarded promise.[18]

This is exactly what Hippolytus did, with disastrous results. Shortly afterwards we find the boy in a lengthy deliberation with his old tutor about how to avoid disaster. This scene is very much reminiscent of the generic context of the 'book of jests',[19] in which professors (*scholastici*) often are the butts of jokes about their unpractical solutions to everyday problems.

It soon appears that the stepson's half-hearted promises and cowardly pretexts turn his stepmother's love into hatred. From this moment onward she ceases to be a tragic Phaedra, and emerges as the wicked and poisoning stepmother who is a stock character of rhetorical declamations.[20] Then the mistaken poisoning of the younger boy and the motif of apparent death and resurrection bring our tale into the context of Mimus and Romance. When the stepmother utters her false accusations she does this "playing her role with too much boldness".[21]

2.1.4. The father, precisely as Theseus did, believes his wife and asks for punishment of his son, without any investigation. Throughout literature the tragic Theseus figure who punished Hippolytus severely without investigating the matter has often been blamed for his credulity.[22] However, times have changed since this heroic period, and the father in our tale completely lacks the heroic stature of the tragic Theseus. This had already become apparent when his wife, in order to find an opportunity for seducing her stepson, dispatched her husband with a pretext to one of their remote country estates. In the Hippolytus tragedy Theseus had been away, too, when the disastrous encounter of Phaedra and Hippolytus occurred: he had been on a heroic journey to the Underworld! Also our bourgeois 'Theseus', returning from the country estate, has to request the local authorities to sentence his son. The authorities decide that a regular trial shall take place.

---

nor ever yet scythe swept, but bees thread the Spring air over the maiden meadow. There from the running stream Chastity waters the flowers; and those whose untaught natures Holiness claims entire may gather garlands there..' (transl. P. Vellacott 1953). A similar self-characterisation of Hippolytus can be found in Seneca's tragedy *Phaedra*, 483 f.

18 Apuleius, *Met.* 10,4 (239,2–4 Helm): *...non tamen negationis intempestiva severitate putavit exasperandum, sed cautae promissionis dilatione leniendum.*

19 See Winkler 1985: 160 ff. on this genre.

20 The *declamationes*, originally school exercises in rhetorical education, developed in imperial times as a genre in their own right. They became highly polished set pieces, no longer meant as school exercises, but as model speeches for professional rhetors, to be recited in public and published afterwards. They were enjoyed by the public not only as examples of rhetorical skill, but also their highly fictional bizarre and often gruesome themes evidently responded to the public's sensationalism. Evil stepmothers figured as stock characters in many of them. See Steinmetz 1982: 167 ff.

21 Apuleius *Met.* 10,5 (240,15 f. Helm) *...personata nimia temeritate*; there is even one manuscript reading which has: *personata mima temeritate* "playing her role with the boldness of a mime actress".

22 See e.g. Ovidius, *Metamorphoses* 15,498 "well known is the love of Phaedra, well known the injustice of Theseus; in his credulity he cursed his own son." Bömer in his commentary cites many other instances.

To the informed and attentive reader, the sentence in which they give their reasons for doing so hints that they implicitly condemn the manner in which king Theseus punished Hippolytus: "They must not, like savage barbarians or uncontrolled tyrants, condemn a man unheard".[23] The trial which follows is reminiscent of the fictional lawsuits in the declamations.

2.2. Passing over more instances we may now turn to the *Second embedded tale*:

> A pregnant woman, already having a son, is told by her husband that she must kill the new child if it turns out to be a girl. When during her husband's absence she is delivered of a girl, she gives the child to neighbours to be brought up instead of obeying her husband's orders. When the girl has reached marrying age the mother reveals the secret to her son. He takes his sister into his household and arranges a good marriage for her. However, his wife, unaware that this girl is her husband's sister, starts suspecting her of being his lover and kills her cruelly. With poison bought from a ruthless and greedy physician she also poisons her husband, and forces the doctor to drink his own poison as well. Before dying the doctor instructs his wife to go and demand the money for the poison, but the murderess also poisons the doctor's wife as well as her own little daughter. At last the crimes of the murderess are revealed (by the dying doctor's wife), and the jealous wife is condemned to be thrown to the beasts in the arena. This is the woman with whom Lucius, the ass, will have to copulate on the stage in the arena.

3. The two tales are connected by several motifs: both are about family disasters; both have evil females as protagonists; both make use of poison. But while the stepmother in the first tale might have intended to strike a bargain with a physician such as the greedy, unscrupulous physician we meet in the second tale, this first doctor has deliberately refused to be that kind of doctor, and has saved the victim(s) by his foresight. The bad doctor in the second tale is his counterpart.

In the opening of the second tale the reader will immediately be reminded of a typical theme of Greek and Roman comedy: a child growing up in the home of people who are not its own parents. In comedy this situation invariably leads to comic confusion: a highborn young man falls in love with the girl, but cannot marry her because of her suspected low birth. In comedy things turn out well by the benign working of Fortune. Often a recognition scene takes place, where the parents recognise their offspring and all ends happily. Thus the reader confronting the introductory information in the second tale is attuned to expecting comic confusion, benign Fortune, and a happy ending set in motion by a recognition scene. However, the actors in this tale, again, resist their generically prescribed role, or "act out of character". A few examples:

3.1. The mother, in order to prevent precisely that which would make the comedy work, viz. love between the neigbour girl and her son who is in fact her brother, reveals the secret to her son:

[23] Apuleius *Met.* 10,6 (241,20–23 Helm) *...nec ad instar barbaricae feritatis uel tyrannicae impotentiae damnaretur aliquis inauditus...*

> She was... very afraid, you see, that by some accident, under the impulse of hot-blooded youth, he might slip and attack his own sister without either of them being aware of their relationship.[24]

3.2. Fortune, too, forsakes her generically prescribed role of benign power but acts instead as the evil Fate that haunts so many protagonists of the ancient novels; she thwarts the excellent arrangements of the honourable brother by making his wife morbidly jealous:

> But these excellent arrangements, made in a thoroughly responsible way, could not escape the fatal nod of Fortune, at whose instigation cruel Jealousy steered her course straightly for the young man's house.[25]

3.3. Also we find here a signet-ring, which in comedies usually turns up as the piece of evidence which leads to a happy recognition scene. In the hands of the murderous woman it becomes an instrument of deceit and murder:

> She secretly removed her husband's ring and, setting off to the country, sent a servant of hers...to tell the girl that the young man had gone to his country house and wanted to see her there, adding that she should come as soon as she could, alone and unaccompanied. So that she would feel no hesitation about coming, the wife gave the servant the ring which she had taken from her husband, which he could show her to guarantee the reliability of the message. The girl...inspected the proffered seal...[26]

4. From these examples it may be clear that 'actors failing to keep to their prescribed or expected role', thus changing the course of their tales and switching to different generic contexts must be considered a recurrent feature of the two embedded tales of this tenth book. Even in the main narrative the narrator-protagonist himself seems to display an increasing difficulty to keep to his 'role': after his description of the sensual pantomime he already once 'steps out of character' when he suddenly reacts sternly at the immorality of the Judgment of Paris. He then calls himself back to his role of narrator of lustful tales, and promises his public: "I will again, from where I stepped out, return to my *fabula*".[27] However, in the 35th chapter of this book, Lucius, the ass, escapes from the Corinthian theatre, incapable of playing, and refusing to do so, the role his master had planned for him as an actor in a titillating pantomime. By this action he changes the course and the generic context of his tale decisively. A foreshadowing of such a change in the framing tale may be seen, as I hope to have shown, in the

[24] Apuleius *Met.* 10,23 (255,7–9 Helm) *nam et oppido verebatur, ne quo casu, caloris iuvenalis impetu lapsus, nescius nesciam sororem incurreret.*

[25] Apuleius, *Met.* 10,24 (255,17–20 Helm) *Sed haec bene atque optime plenaque cum sanctimonia disposita feralem Fortunae nutum latere non potuerunt, cuius instinctu domum iuvenis protinus se direxit saeva Rivalitas.*

[26] Apuleius, *Met.* 10,24 (255,26–256,5 Helm) *Anulo mariti surrepto rus profecta mittit quendam servulum...., qui puellae nuntiaret, quod eam iuvenis profectus ad villulam vocaret ad sese....et ne qua forte nasceretur veniendi cunctatio, tradit anulum marito subtractum, qui monstratus fidem verbis adstipularetur. at illa...respecto etiam signo eius...*

[27] Apuleius, *Met.* 10,33 (264,23 f. Helm) *rursus, unde decessi, revertar ad fabulam.*

two previously embedded tales. However seriously or frivolously one wants to take the religious finale of the Latin *Metamorphoses*, the ass's escape from the theatre is at the same time undeniably the entrance of the *Golden Ass* into a new generic intertext of religious conversion and devotional literature. And this time the narrator does not call himself back to return to his *fabula*.

REFERENCES

Hanson, J.A.
1989 — *Apuleius, Metamorphoses*, edited and translated, 2 vols.. London.

Harrison, S.J.
1996 — "Apuleius' *Metamorphoses*," pp. 491–516 in: G. Schmeling (ed.), *The Novel in the Ancient World*. Leiden.

Helm R.,
1955 — *Apulei opera quae supersunt I: Metamorphoseon Libri XI*, Leipzig ^{3}1931 (repr. with addenda 1955)

Holzberg, N.
1984 — "Apuleius und der Verfasser des griechischen Eselsromans," in *WJA* 10: 350–64.

Mal - Maeder, D. van
1997 — "*Lector, intende: laetaberis*. The enigma of the last book of Apuleius' *Metamorphoses*," pp. 87–118 in H. Hofmann & M. Zimmerman (eds.), *Groningen Colloquia on the Novel* Vol. 8, Groningen.

Mason H.J.
1978 — "Fabula Graecanica: Apuleius and his Greek Source," pp. 1–15 in B.L. Hijmans & R. Th. van der Paardt (eds.), *Aspects of Apuleius's Golden Ass*. Groningen.

Selden, D.L.
1994 — "Genre of Genre," pp. 39–64 in J. Tatum (ed.), *The Search for the Ancient Novel*. Baltimore.

Smith, W.S.
1968 — *Lucius of Corinth and Apuleius of Madaura. A study of the narrative technique of the Metamorphoses of Apuleius*. Diss. Yale University.

Steinmetz, P.
1982 — *Untersuchungen zur römischen Literatur des zweiten Jahrhunderts nach Christi Geburt*. Wiesbaden.

Tatum, J.
1969 — *Thematic Aspects of the Tales in Apuleius' Metamorphoses*. Diss. Princeton University.

Walsh, P.G.
1970 — *The Roman Novel. The Satyricon of Petronius and the Metamorphoses of Apuleius*. Cambridge.

Winkler, J.J.
1985 — *Auctor and Actor. A narratological reading of Apuleius's 'The Golden Ass'*. Berkeley-Los Angeles-London.

POSTSCRIPTUM
Generic Studies in Pre-Modern Traditions: Why and How?

1. The concepts of genre and type confront specialists in the pre-modern cultures with an important and specific problem that is central to the demarcation of sources and their collections, to the identification of their subject matter, and even to a self-definition of their (sub)disciplines. Yet it can hardly be stated truthfully that hard-core methodological and theoretical issues concerning genre and typology are regularly and seriously reflected upon by pre-modernists. Generally, problems of genre are dealt with by literary theorists and critics in the context of modern literature. More often than not this subsumes only those kinds of modern writing which, to use a formalist distinction, show "literariness". By that token many kinds of writing and discursive practices are left out of purview, because they are thematic (and thence schematic), referential or communicative, and thus would seem to lack the density or richness of literature proper.

1.1. The dominant literary genre of the modern era, which therefore also has figured prominently in literary theory in the present century, is the novel.[1] This genre is widely regarded as a form of "realistic" literary writing, exploring the individual and his/her relationship to the outside (material, cultural, ideological) world. Novels, moreover, as their preferred mode of discourse make use of narrative prose, which for many centuries has been regarded as a mode connected with "truth" and verisimilitude (or "mimesis"), and which is therefore eagerly embraced as a transparent vehicle of meaning. This preference for narrative prose is so basic to the genre that it has led, and is still leading, to many experimental explorations of the boundaries of that mode, as can be clearly seen e.g. in Joyce's *Ulysses*, or in the French *nouveau roman*, but which actually started long ago at the beginning of what is generally regarded as the "modern" novel in the eighteenth century with Sterne's unbeatable *Tristram Shandy*. On the other hand, it has long been realised that the "transparency" of the vehicle in e.g. "realistic" or "naturalistic" novels is a poetical mode in its own right, and even in the first place.

Be that as it may, as long as the "literariness" or self-referentiality of the novel and of works of art in general was deemed to be central, the distinction between literature and other kinds of writing was to be maintained; or rather a threefold distinction was made: there were literary works, sub-literary (or "trivial") works,[2] and non-literary

---

[1] Although some of the finest work in modern literary criticism, with obvious generic overtones, was done on poetry; see e.g. William Empson's *Seven Types of Ambiguity*.

[2] It was, and to a great extent still is, accepted practice to put detective novels as well as historical novels in this category; in many cases, however, the tripartition falls down under its own weight. Is Dickens' *Bleak House* a work of "serious literature" as against the "trivial" *Mystery of Edwin Drood*? How to "classify" Wilkie Collins' *The Moonstone*, or Robert Graves' Claudius novels? What is more, in recent years we perceive a growing type of fiction, sometimes authored by theoretists, that make much use of the "trivial" modes of detective and historical fiction, often in combination. Of course Eco's *Il nome della rosa* and *Isola del giorno prima* spring to mind, but we might cite also works as diverse as e.g. Patrick Süskind's *Das Parfum*, Juan José Saer's *El entenado*, José Saramago's *Memorial do convento*, and particulary Arturo Pérez-Reverte's *El club Dumas* and *La tabla de Flandes* as cases in point (we can offer no explanation of the fact that this mode of fiction is so pronouncedly latin). To be quite fair, it should be noted that also criticism

works. One of the results of this tripartition was that discussions of genre among literary theorists more often than not have kept aloof from discussions of generic problems among scholars with other aims, and most importantly working with other kinds of writing, such as historians and philologists dealing with chronicles, administrative texts, academic commentaries, letters etc.[3]

1.2. However, with the rise of post-modernism[4] in the second half of the present century, the privileged status of literature has changed considerably, whereas, on the other hand, more interest is shown for the tropological strategies and rhetoric at work in non-literary, or sub-literary, kinds of writing. These days we also perceive a tendency to challenge the privileged place of the individual as the locus of meaning,[5] and as a meaningful entity as such in the novel. We also see the growing importance in critical discourse of some stereotypically encoded subgenres, which hitherto remained at the periphery (detective stories, romances etc.),[6] as well as a blurring of the distinction between literary and non-literary genres. The emergence of new subgenres, which are so to speak doubly encoded, in that they have a parodistic or metafictional character, yet can also be read as orthodox examples of the subgenres to which they in fact belong, allows for both a naive and an intertextual way of reading. In both ways they challenge the prominent place of the "conventional" novel. Moreover, much more than this conventional novel with its strong ideology of mimesis, they are deliberately constructed around or make play with set codes and patterns, the elements of which are supposed to be "read" in relation to the stereotyped structures connected with the subgenres in question, which leads to a generic rather than a mimetic frame of reference.[7]

1.3. Whatever the consequences of this development may turn out to have been for the present situation, or to be for the future, it has a corrollary – maybe as a by-product – in a deepened interest in generic questions as such, and that applied to a broader range of literary production. This in itself enhances the credibility of scholarship devoted to forms

---

is giving renewed attention to "mystery" as a theme and/or genre: see e.g. Grossvogel 1979.

3 In fact, the case of historical fiction is a truly sad one. It is not taken seriously as a contribution to "history", and it is not often taken as "serious" literature either – which seems harsh on Tolstoi. Nor can the heart of the matter be confined to historical fiction as such: in most if not all pre-modern literary cultures there was a broad range of "historical" discourse, by which we mean a discourse about a past perceived and presented as "real" one one or more levels. Many of these types of discourse are hard if not impossible to categorise if we are fettered by the simplistic triad mentioned above; and they are deliberately put aside as being irrelevant by many historians of the "So wie es gewesen" school. Yet both preconceptions (or prejudices) overlook the important fact that these types – and in many cases *only* these types – give us an insight in the conceptions of near-contemporaries (at any rate, nearer than we ourselves can ever hope to get) about the idea, structure, and meaning of their own historical past.

4 Since terminology far too often plays a much too preponderant role in generic discussions, it is perhaps ironic that in the context of this essay we are forced to use two terms that look deceptively as being complementary, but that are nothing of the kind. Among professional scholars "pre-modern" indicates only a certain period in time (even though it has an atavistic connotation in present-day culture) – which by the way is the longest by far in the recorded history of culture. Post-modernism, on the other hand, is a recent "school" in cultural analysis, and stands in opposition to modernism, not to pre-modern times.

5 See e.g. Foucault 1971.

6 To mention just a few, see Grossvogel 1979; Cawelti 1976; Todorov 1970 and 1978.

7 And this is only about the theoretical stance on "literary" versus "sub-literary" or "non-literary". Actually, a not unimportant type of "literary" novels in the present century used "non-literary" material as a part of its texture. Famous examples are John Dos Passos' trilogy, or Louis Paul Boon's *De Kleine Oorlog*. It is ironic that this happened in a period when post-modernism as a concept did not yet exist.

of (pre-modern) literature which seem to adhere to comparable stereotyped structures as some of the modern subgenres (like the fairy tale, the fable, epic songs etc.). By highlighting the generic frame of reference, seemingly established boundaries between "literature" and "other kinds of writing" once more become vague. The "palimpsest" character of many works belonging to succesful subgenres, such as the present-day historical novels, makes it difficult to clearly distinguish between, let us say, literature, history and some kinds of forensic discourse. For one thing, the modes of emplotment of the literary and the non-literary seem to coincide more and more.

2. Keeping all this in mind, it seems logical to draw attention to the generic issues pertaining to a broad range of pre-modern artefacts or types of texts, "literary" or not. Pre-modernists may not often be theoretically inclined; but these students of older and not seldom rather arcane materials generally show a pragmatic but at the same time sincere commitment to generic issues, even if they shun overtly theoretical discussions; and independently of the question whether or not they are working with "literature" in the accepted sense of the term.

There are, historically, two plausible reasons for this phenomenon. First, for all kinds of scholarly purposes, it has always seemed and still seems necessary to construct a pragmatically satisfactory grouping (or "classification") of sources, if only to identify a manageable corpus of texts that can be defended against reviewers. Second, the generic consciousness of past civilisations, as well as the generic systems by which literary and non-literary works were classified in the past, can be quite different. Therefore generic issues have to be taken into account in order to arrive at a "proper", non-anachronistic interpretation of surviving materials. And so for the pre-modernist scholar, generic issues are to some degree an indispensable element of the heuristics of his or her research. The rub is that scholars have long recognised that any "traditional" generic consciousness – where recoverable – uses criteria which in themselves are not compatible, or certainly not coherent from our point of view. Although many textbooks and source typologies tend to smooth over these problems by simply labelling sources, and presenting them in seemingly coherent groups, it remains a cause of great frustration, especially when scholars try to use historic generic labels to construct a theoretical genre, that is: a genre with clearly identifiable properties which can be neatly distinguished from other groups of texts. This problem is illustrated in several essays in this volume. The problem as such is effectively the problematic relation between "ethnic genre" and "critical genre" – a problem to which we shall return later.

3. In fact, it is difficult to combine such predominantly pragmatic concerns about genre with the theoretical discussions in the general field of literary theory and criticism, if only because the latter often do not address the same kind of material. Still, there are important points of contact, and even of exchange, where modern generic issues tie in with the world and the work of the pre-modernist, mostly through a shared inheritance of a range of often competing critical terminologies.

3.1. First of all, there is the overall legacy of the so-called classical conception of genre, which not only informs many modern discussions of genre, but also has been constitutive for many generic *prescriptions* throughout the centuries.[8] Even when and where literary traditions or systems developed in comparative autonomy, the legitimation of form and content is often based on a terminology borrowed from classical antiquity, since this was the terminology taught in school till very recently. The poetics of Aristotle in particular, and its popularisation in the treatises of Horace and Cicero, have taught us to differentiate genres by means of the medium used (rhythm, melody, verse or a combination of these), the way in which it represents its object of imitation (the basis for the distinction between tragedy and comedy), and the manner of imitation (direct or indirect speech).

On the basis of these criteria, the classification and interpretation of the different genres (tragedy, comedy, epic, satire etc.), was to have provided subsequent generations with the necessary and sufficient tools for literary analysis. The central assumptions are that each subject requires an appropriate form and style; that there is a perfect model for each type of art; and that therefore there is a hierarchy of genres – with tragedy at the top. Generic boundaries are seen as preconditions for literary production, and for understanding by the reader. Hence Horace's famous dictum "Descriptas servare vices operumque colores cur ego si nequeo ignoroque, poeta salutor?" These assumptions were guidelines for artistic craftmanship in many different genres, but even more importantly, they were guidelines for critical evaluation. The cult of the classics has been fundamental for our (mis)representation of the pre-modern and the archaic: everything deviating from the "classic ideal" is mediocre, primitive, mediaeval or in decline. In many ways our current struggles with generic issues must be seen as an emancipation from the classical – or rather classicist – bridle.[9]

3.2. Second, there is a common romantic inheritance, which in itself constitutes one of the first attempts to break free, theoretically, from this classicist bridle. From the eighteenth century onwards, beginning with the work of Giambattista Vico and culminating in the work of Croce, theorists began to claim the virtue of originality. This lead to concepts of creativity and authorship that are impatient with the seemingly formulaic and anonymous productions characteristic of the pre-modern era. Combined with the rise of evolutionist criticism in the nineteenth century, in which genres go through cycles of infancy, maturity and decline, it has in fact strengthened the negative verdict on the archaic and the pre-modern literatures,[10] whereas it also has been very influential for our views on the internal periodisation of pre-modern cultures: for the notion of renaissance and decline is firmly inscribed in the scholarly consciousness of almost all pre-modernists. However, though this biological metaphor is often called

---

[8] It would be a daring, but very relevant, venture to examine how and why the identical "prescriptions" gave rise to such completely different products thoughout the ages.

[9] In a way this situation is preposterous. For one thing, Aristotle actually treated only an extremely limited corpus of writings, and did this on purpose; he nowhere claims universal applicability. Second, the mediaeval followers of the classical prescriptions were able, in the grandest possible manner, to incorporate all and sundry kinds of literature into the classical framework, which shows the adaptability of any generic system. Third, the idea that Aristotle's system *as a system of literature* has universal value is very recent. Fourth, in a way the misrepresentation also applies to the classical material itself; for this reason the term "classicist", referring to the "modern", i.e. 17th- and 18th-century, re-interpretation of the classical stance seems more appropriate.

[10] See note 4.

evolutionist, it was first conceived in the early years of last century to be much more an illustration of the principle that the life-cycle of an individual is the model of all cultural as well as most natural phenomena. It is not sufficiently realised that this flies in the face of orthodox evolutionism. We will return to the point.

3.3. Third, we all have benefitted strongly from some basic tenets of formalist and structuralist criticism, which in their purest form ignored issues of "extrinsic criticism", to concentrate on phonic elements and plot structures. We have learned that texts and works are part of a literary system, identifiable on the basis of a range of formal textual properties on different levels. Thus a hierarchy of textual production can be perceived, in which different "genres" and "subgenres" can be identified. Whereas pure formalism concentrated on poetic language, and maintained a strong division between literary and non-literary language, structuralist criticism applied its principles to all kinds of texts and artefacts. In its focus on deep structures and pervasive elements, the formalist-structuralist revolution has in a sense redeemed the pre-modern and the "primitive" as worth-while objects of study. Moreover, it has given the pre-modernist an important toolkit to deal with his own source materials in a way recognisable for modern critics, in that it enables him or her to (re)create synchronically and diachronically complete generic systems, in which location, relative dominance and literary function of various genres can be charted.

4. Although far from unique in the field of pre-modernist studies, the most famous and influential practitioners of genre criticism in this vein are the romanists Zumthor and Jauss, who have combined such interest in the morphology of literary systems with mere straightforward historical approaches. Zumthor tried to arrive at a refined typology of mediaeval literary texts on different levels by distinguishing between registers, genres, types, and textual witnesses; but he was also much interested in reconsidering factors such as the power of poetic traditions and the influence of literary topoi in pre-modern culture. Zumthor and Jauss (who is somewhat more hermeneutical) have again convinced many scholars that genres should be seen as groups or historical families: "Sie können als solche nicht abgeleitet oder definiert, sondern nur historisch bestimmt, abgegrenzt und beschrieben werden." From this point of view it is not very fruitful to arrive at normative (*ante rem*), or classificatory (*post rem*) typologies. Instead, it should be tried to arrive at a historical (*in re*) typology. Examples of this too can be found in this volume.

Function and place of genres in the generic system therefore can be evaluated on the basis of several modalities such as author and text, *modus dicendi* (forms of representation), *Aufbau und Ebenen der Bedeutung* (*Einheiten des Dargestellten*), *Modus Recipiendi und gesellschaftliche Funktion* (Jauss). If done systematically – which often is difficult due to blank spots and missing links in the source materials – it might be possible to obtain a synchronic overview, in which can be highlighted the historical position (*Sitz-im-Leben*[10]) of both canonised and non-canonised genres. When this is

[10] The term is used here in its apparently widely accepted broad sense of "the external circumstances which govern the genesis and acceptation, and thereby the function, of a literary work". To be quite fair, it should be noted that the term as conceived originally in Biblical criticism was much more restricted, and meant roughly and in a somewhat mechanical way that different social and political circumstances shape and determine the

amplified over a longer period of time, the diachronical development could be charted of generic systems and the place of genres in it.

In the work of Zumthor and Jauss, therefore, there is no rise and decline, but "ein Prozeß fortgesetzter Horizontstiftung und Horizontveränderung" (without teleological connotations), by which genres evolve and change and hence switch places with other genres in the system, in that a genre can become less or more dominant, and in changing the function(s) it is manifestly seen to perform. This can lead to change and innovation, or to "fossilisation" in a neutral sense. This process is regulated or at the very least influenced by a mixture of intersecting factors, namely those of literary traditions, author and society, reader's expectation and literary objectives. It also illustrates the relevance of one of the central points in any consideration of generic problems, viz. is there such a thing as a theoretical genre; and if so, what is the relation between theoretical genre and historical genre?

5. The transcendence of the structuralist system brings us to yet another range of formative critical vocabularies with a significant influence on present-day scholarship, namely those known under the vague name of post-modernism. In the so-called post-modernist vocabularies both the structuralist system and the humanist author are challenged by a host of corrosive concepts, such as generic instability, generic overflow, use-value, pragmatics, and ideology. Often the emphasis is on all those cases in which the poetic text wittingly or unwittingly seems to transgress or to play around with the boundaries set by generic constraints.[11] This allows us to transcend the verdicts inherent in naive forms of so-called evolutionist generic criticism, and helps us to understand the phenomenon of unexptectedly fast and rich development in so-called "periods of transition", such as the Hellenistic period, and the "waning of the middle ages". Traditionally these periods and their literary products have been described as times of decline. The new critical vocabularies, however, make it possibe to emphasise the dynamics and power shifts at work.[12] More often than not this implies a return to history and to sophisticated forms of extrinsic criticism, as well as to an ongoing questioning of the factual-fictional distinction and its changing meaning within various textual contexts and communities.

6. At this point it is perhaps useful to discuss a few problem areas which seem to be particularly relevant for pre-modern texts.

---

genesis of different textual forms, and thereby are indicative of their "true meaning".

[11] But is should be noted that post-modern criticism of mainly structuralist work often seems to be based on a misunderstanding. The great structuralist studies invariably emphasise that the main interest in generic studies is in the body of a genre (or even specimen), and not in the boundaries between genres. This is, by the way, strict structuralist orthodoxy, since it is an illustration of the all-pervading concept of dominance. An interesting case in point – which is always consciously produced – is the parody, a form wherein precisely the formal border "characteristics" have become or are made dominant, and the conceptual centre or body is left empty, or at least bears no real relation to its parent genre.

[12] In this respect a term from real evolutionist biology is almost inescapable: according to a major school in evolutionist thinking (S. J. Gould), natural life and its forms evolve (not, of course, "progress") according to a scheme called "punctuated equilibrism" by which is meant the alternation of periods of fast and furious genesis of new forms and periods of relative stability or stasis. This seems to be a useful concept for understanding what is at hand in the periods mentioned.

6.1. First there is the matter of the different kinds of genre one can discern. Ben-Amos has recently introduced the concept "ethnic genre",[13] which he sets besides "critical genre", not to replace it, but to explore the native criteria, formal as well as sociological, for the assignment of "genres" in their own right. Writing about folklore, he understands ethnic genre as the native construct of genre, or as a "grammar of folklore, a cultural affirmation of the communication rules that govern the expression of complex messages within the cultural context", noting that "each genre is characterized by *a set of relations between* its formal features, thematic domains, and potential social usages."[14] Furthermore, ethnic genre systems in two closely related cultural communities can also differ greatly. Ben-Amos cites examples of the same texts whose generic distinctions vary between sub-groups of a society.[15] Finally, Ben-Amos ends his exploration of the possibilities of using the ethnic taxonomic labels with a caution which is worth quoting fully:

> The inquiry into the names for genres must extend beyond the limits of etymological interpretation. Historically and geographically the same names may mean different things in the same language in separate periods and in distinct regional dialects. Conversely, two different words may acquire the same meanings in different periods. Moreover, with usage, the names may develop a complex semantic structure, for which etymology alone would not account. hence the study of the ethnic system of genres must combine the cognitive, expressive and behavioral levels of genres in each culture.[16]

It is clear that the main difference on the theoretical level between ethnic and critical genre is that the latter is almost exclusively concerned with formal features and thematic domains, while the social usages are relegated to the *history* of a genre, not its essence. On the practical level, one often perceives a far greater chasm between the two: ethnic genre systems are often in stark contrast to our critical approach, and they seem to be more dependent on social usage.

But there is more; in cultural communities heavily influenced by writing there is usually a fourth factor influencing the native classification, besides the formal, thematic and social factors: the literary context.[17] Since it is not easy to conceive of any genre in total isolation, it follows that the context is very relevant, and the position of a certain genre may be defined partly by its relative propinquity or distance to other genres. In a way, it seems that formal, thematic and social/functional considerations would all enter

---

13 Most of this discussion of Ben-Amos' concept of "ethnic genre" comes from the second chapter of Steve Tinney's excellent edition and study of a Sumerian city lament: Tinney 1996: 11-25.

14 Ben-Amos 1976: 225; editors' italics. A few pages later he adds: "each society defines its genres by *any number or combination of terms*" (Ben-Amos 1976: 227; editors' italics).

15 The Yoruba generally distinguish between prose narratives that are "folktales" (*alo*) and those that are "histories" (*itan*); but the professional sub-group of the diviners (*Ifa*) do not accept this distinction: since all traditions have the same symbolic valency, they simply label all narratives as *itan* (Ben-Amos 1976: 231–35).

16 Ben-Amos 1976: 237. On the same point, or at any rate a related and important one, see Fowler 1982: 147; writing about the mediaeval period he states : "the confusing generic labels of the period are far from proving it a time innocent of genre".

17 For an example of the relevance of a (strictly defined) "literary context" on the interpretation and status of a particular text, see Tinney 1996: 27–53. Perhaps one should not insist too much on literariness as a condition for the influence of literary context. In illiterate societies with a highly developed and articulate oral poetic system is would be just as important. The most important factor would seem to be the degree of explicit articulation of the poetic system, oral *or* written.

into the matter of literary context.

Thus, in order to understand the generic systems of the pre-modern literatures one should ideally approach the matter from four directions: the *critical*, which obviously should be based mainly on incontrovertibly formal features on all levels of language; the *historical*, which should describe generic variation diachronically and thus may also be able to grasp the life-cycle of specific genres and/or a whole system; the *ethnic*, which informs us about the contemporary approaches and will be informative about the life of the genre in its own period; and the *contextual*, which will help to define the position of a genre synchronically. The need for such a fourfold approach, and also the possibilities for it, are well illustrated in several contributions to this volume.

6.2. Secondly, the nature of the concept genre itself remains problematic, despite the brilliant work by the structuralists in general and some practitioners in specific fields in particular. Thus there is still too much confusion and imprecision in somewhat naive treatments of pre-modern literary material. Too often the practical need for classification on any criterium leads students to present their purely practical scheme as a genre system; or, which in a way is worse, the so-called classical scheme is regarded as having universal and eternal value, so that a discussion of genre is deemed superfluous for the appreciation and evaluation for a text (it goes without saying that this implies that a comparison of any pre-modern text to the models which informed the so-called classical system will inevitably be to the detriment of that text); lastly, and which is the worst of all, one applies restrictive and prescriptive but nonetheless "universal" notions found in positivistic nineteenth-century handbooks (usually in German).[17] While literary criticism for more than fifty years has insisted upon the chronological variability and indeed the dynamic nature of genre, best illustrated by Fowler's famous dictum that genre is not a pigeon-hole, but a pigeon, this kind of "doctrinaire sluttishness"[18] remains hard to eradicate.

The dynamic nature of genre has everything to do with the difficult matter of a genre's life-cycle. This cycle was first formulated by Fowler; but this too can lead to misunderstanding. The terms as meant by Fowler are aggregation-maturity-decay; they remain somewhat biologically related, but the biological model is the evolution of (a) species, not the cycle of individual human (or animal) life. The critical term here is evolution, which is of course not "purpose" or – even worse – "progress". In this context the notion of "punctuated equilibrium" might turn out to be very useful.

6.3. Our pre-modern literatures also presents us with some specific difficulties which are less important in modern Western literature. Of course, there are the usual linguistic, textual and material uncertainties. But there are a few areas which show specific problems. We will indicate only a few instances.

First, there is the problem of submerged genres, by which we mean genres one can obliquely perceive to have existed in a certain literary tradition, but of which no or only

[17] Black 1988: 15 with fn. 44 gives a telling illustration: an authoritative study of imagery in Sumerian poetry, in defining metaphor, defers without question to the definition found in the Grosse Brockhaus (16th edition, 1952–8). The definition found in that edition ("völlig neubearbeitet") "is abbreviated from that in the 10th edition of 1851–5, and gives even some of the same examples".

[18] The term is William Empson's, not ours.

very few actual specimens have reached us.[19] Incidentally the search for such submerged genres can contribute in a meaningful way to the difficult matter of the structure of a genre's life-cycle.

Secondly, there is the matter of non-existent genres. This can be regarded as a problem of comparative literary history: why does classical Hebrew not know the epic as a format, while the surrounding literatures are rich in epics? But more interesting from the theoretical and methodological point of view is the opposite case, wherein a genre-label is forcibly and often artificially coined mostly after a venerable historical model or example. After that, one goes out into the literary field to sample the constituent members of this "genre".[20] One such example is "Wisdom Literature", a term widely used in presentations of Near Eastern literatures. Yet the types grouped under that heading may and generally do belong to totally different formats, and even treat of starkly contradictory themes in a completely unrelated manner. The conclusion in all cases must be that, apart from a small group of formally coherent texts ("Instructions"), there is no "wisdom genre", and it is not a good use of time to try and construct one. In a recent typology of wisdom[21] (not "wisdom texts"!) as a literary theme, three types of wisdom were characterised, or even emblematised as the wisdom of *Polonius*, being the traditional and often pedestrian and utilitarian "knowledge" beqeathed to us (or forced upon us) by our forefathers; the wisdom of *Prospero*, being the artifices of magic (and science?); the wisdom of *Jaques*, being the realistic, cynical, humanistic and intellectually honesty of a wise man surrounded and beset by foolishness.[22] Is the proposition that *Hamlet, The Tempest* and *As You Like It* belong to a genre called "wisdom literature" a reasonable one?

Thirdly, there is the problem of generic shift and drift. By *shift* we mean that in the course of literary history a kind of text can change its place in the sequence of prevailing systems as such. Here our problems are often of a material nature, in that in most cases our evidence is very often fragmentary, at least when compared to modern literatures. Also, in a number of cases the materials we possess have come to us through the filter of a long tradition, which more often than not locates types of text according to a system that is much later in time than that in which the type was originally produced.[22] Canonisation of earlier textual traditions regularly wreaks havoc with large parts of that tradition, not to mention that it practitcally always truncates it. This in itself, however, is at the same time an opportunity for us to investigate the generic system and the undoubtedly important

---

19 Thus a recent study (Dobbs-Allsopp 1993) argues that the OT book of lamentations is the single attestation in its own right of a genre which pervades some other parts of the OT, but was "written away" in the final redaction of those books.

20 A related problem is, of course, that of non-existent or irrelevant generic *distinctions*. A good example of this would be the case of "germanische Heldendichtung" as a genre distinct from "höfische Epik" in the 13th century, for the artificiality of which distinction see Rupp 1960.

21 Assmann 1991: Introduction.

22 The fourth kind of wisdom is of course the wisdom of *Salomo*, being the rule of honesty, equity and clemency in government and justice.

22 Both aspects (fragmentation and filtered tradition) are less important in some literatures than in others. The cuneiform literatures, fragmentary though they are to a high degree, are much less hindered by filtered tradition than many later literatures. Since the material is virtually indestructible, we are not forced to assume "forerunners" or "Urtexte" or such like constructions: we simply *have* the kinds of text that in many other disciplines necessarily remain hypothetical. And a thorough study of these existing fragments of a long (in some cases over 1800 years) literary tradition tends to show that terms like "forerunner" or "Urtext" or even "canonical version" are often misleading if not downright mistaken.

matter of the reception of types of texts along a diachronic axis. But there is so much that we miss. For the same reason, viz. fragmentation of the material, generic *drift* by which we mean not so much the chronological changes in a system but the observable behaviour of texts that in themselves, and synchronically, already indicate the (future or potential) evolution or development of their "type" and its locus within the system should also be investigated. This can sometimes be predicted from individual examples or groups that show the tendency to evolve in one or two specific directions — among a number of other possible ones. This virtual evolution can in cases be predicted from either a marked set of formal features which are in alliance with neighbouring types; or from the predilection for certain thematic concerns also shared with other types; or from the social locus of production and performance; or from all three aspects – and possibly more. In this respect the concepts of ethnic genre and literary context will probably play an important role. But much remains to be done.

7. It would be nonsensical to deny the extreme variety of the materials discussed, the differences between the approaches taken, or the interests pursued in this volume. Moreover, this volume is the product of specialists often hesitant to adopt the reigning critical vocabularies used in the present-day scholarly communities fully devoted to literary theory and criticism. Yet the attentive reader will perceive in these articles the ways in which pre-modernists have to cope with the legacies of critical vocabularies such as those mentioned above. Theirs is also the concern with generic labelling, generic prescriptions (old and modern), generic exclusion, and the *Sitz-im-Leben* of genres, both within the generic system and in the wider historical context. In many ways the materiality of the sources and the absence or incompleteness of source material complicate the work of the pre-modernist. (S)he seldom can pursue a fully coherent or fully systematic critical analysis, but is forced to apply different mixtures of internal and external criticism. For the pre-modernist generic criticism and typological strategies often are means to an end, namely a better understanding of a foreign past and its cultural products. This understanding necessarily starts from assumptions and categories which are "unzeitgemäß" with the subject under description. And it can only be beneficial for our critical enterprise to make this clear once again.

Bert Roest
Herman Vanstiphout

REFERENCES

Assmann, J. and A. (eds.)
1991 *Weisheit. Archäologie der literarischen Kommunikation, Bd. 3*. München.

Beebee, T.O.
1994 *The Ideology of Genre. A Comparative Study of Generic Instability*. Philadelphia.

Ben-Amos, D.
1976 "Analytical Categories and Ethnic Genres," pp. 215–42 in id. ed., *Folklore Genres*. Austin, TX

Bertens, Hans & d'Haen, Theo
1988 "Realisme, fabulisme en genreconventies," in idd. eds. *Het postmodernisme in de literatuur*. Amsterdam.

Black, Jeremy
1998 *Reading Sumerian Poetry*. London.

Collini, Stefan (ed.)
1992 Over interpretatie: Umberto Eco in debat met Richard Rorty, Jonathan Culler en Christine Brooke-Rose , Kampen.

Dobbs-Allsopp, F.W.
1993 *Weep, O Daughter of Zion: A Study of the City-Lament Genre in the Hebrew Bible*, Roma.

Dubrow, Heather
1982 *Genre* (The Critical Idiom 42). London.

Cawelti, John G.
1976 *Adventure, Mystery and Romance*. Chicago.

Culler, Jonathan
1975 *Structuralist Poetics*. London.

Foucault, M.
1971 *L'ordre du discours*. Paris.

Fowler, Alastair
1982 *Kinds of Literature*. Oxford.

Grossvogel, David I.
1979 *Mystery and Its Fictions: From Oedipus to Agatha Christie*. Baltimore, MD.

Jauss, H.-R.
1972 "Theorie der Gattungen und Literatur des Mittelalters," pp. 103–38 in M. Delbouille (ed.), *Grundriß der romanischen Literaturen des Mittelalters* I. Heidelberg.

Rupp, Heinz
1960 "Heldendichtung als Gattung der deutschen Literatur des 13. Jahrhunderts," pp. 9–25 in K. Bischoff et.al. (eds.), *Volk, Sprache, Dichtung. Festgabe für Kurt Wagner.* (*Beiträge zur deutschen Philologie* 28). Giessen.

Tinney, Steve
1996 The Nippur Lament. Royal Rhetoric and Divine Legitimation in the Reign of Išme-Dagan of Isin (1953–1935 B.C.). Philadelphia.

Todorov,Tzvetan
1970 *Introduction à la littérature fantastique*. Paris.
1976 "The origin of genres," in *New Literary History* 8: 159–70.
1978 *Les genres du discours*. Paris.

Zumthor, Paul
1972 *Essai de poétique médiévale*. Paris.